6-19-95

Happy Daddies Day

Love,
Eric & Leta

ROMMEL

IN HIS OWN WORDS

ROMMEL
IN HIS OWN WORDS

Editor: Dr John Pimlott

Greenhill Books, London
Stackpole Books, Pennsylvania

First published in 1994 by Greenhill Books, Lionel Leventhal Limited
Park House, 1 Russell Gardens, London NW11 9NN
and
Stackpole Books, 5067 Ritter Road, Mechanicsburg, PA 17055, USA

ISBN 1-85367-185-1

Editorial and design:
Brown Packaging Limited, 255-257 Liverpool Road, London N1 1LX

Printed in the U.S.A.

Picture credits

t= top, b= bottom, c= centre, r= right, l= left.

Hulton Deutsch Collection: 9, 10/11;
Robert Hunt Library: 2/3, 14, 18, 20(t), 24/25, 27, 30, 31, 34, 35, 36/37, 39, 41, 48/49, 60, 62, 63, 67, 68, 70, 71, 74, 75, 77, 78, 79, 80, 86, 88, 92, 94, 98, 99, 102, 108, 112, 114, 116/117, 118, 119, 120(both), 123, 125, 126, 127, 131, 133, 134, 135, 137, 139, 140, 142, 145, 146, 152, 155, 156, 158, 161, 166, 167, 168, 172, 174, 178, 184, 186, 187;
Imperial War Museum: Back cover, 7, 15, 19, 20(b), 23, 26, 28, 42, 44/45, 46, 50, 51, 53, 54/55, 56, 59, 65, 73, 84, 87, 90/91, 96, 101, 103, 104, 107, 111, 115, 122, 128, 136, 138, 150, 154, 162, 181, 185, 189;
Peter Newark's Pictures: 12;
Rommel Family Collection: 8, 16, 29, 32;
T.R.H. Pictures: 64, 66, 83, 164, 165, 170, 171, 176, 177, 182;
United States National Archives: Front cover, 180

PREVIOUS PAGES: Rommel and officers of the 7th Panzer Division at a briefing during the Battle of France, June 1940.

CONTENTS

Introduction

Opposite: A war hero with his family. The 'Desert Fox', wife and son photographed during one of their rare times together.

Field Marshal Erwin Rommel (1891-1944) is one of the few German generals of World War II who is still widely remembered. Whether directing a battle from the top of his command vehicle in the North African desert or sitting rather self-consciously in a studio, his weather-beaten face, with its calculating eyes and firm jaw, immediately conjures up images of the 'Desert Fox', capable of defeating superior forces with consummate ease.

In pictures he appears invincible, commanding all-powerful mobile units against rather plodding, unimaginative enemies who depend for their eventual success on superior equipment rather than operational skill. Even the manner of his death – taking poison rather than risk a public trial that would endanger his family as Adolf Hitler took revenge against any officer implicated in the July 1944 Bomb Plot – seems romantic, leaving an impression of military professionalism hopelessly compromised in the service of the Fuehrer.

Like all legends, it contains a measure of truth. Rommel was, first and foremost, a fighting soldier. He was undeniably brave – his Pour le Mérite, or 'Blue Max', was earned in the heat of battle and is, deservedly, regarded as the equivalent of the Victoria Cross or Medal of Honor – and his qualities of leadership were high. He cared about his men and was determined from the start of his fighting career to master the tactical skills that would enable them to survive and win, even amidst the horrors of trench warfare on the Western Front in 1914-15.

But there was much more to it than that, for it was obvious from the start that Rommel was a cut above the majority of his contemporaries. His transfer to a mountain battalion in October 1915 and his subsequent experiences in Romania and northern Italy gave him the opportunity to perfect techniques of mobile warfare that he would use to such devastating effect in later years. Leading small groups of fast-moving infantry, he surprised the Italians and drove deep into their rear areas. Such tactics demanded he be fit and inherently flexible to grasp the opportunities presented to him. He was undoubtedly helped by the prevailing German system of command known as 'Auftragstaktik', or 'mission command', whereby officers were expected to achieve objectives free from interference from above.

During the inter-war years he analysed the battles he had fought and passed his wisdom on to officer cadets. Despite his lack of experience in armoured warfare, his emphasis on flexibility and initiative in mobile operations enabled him to transfer his ideas easily.

He led from the front so that he could grasp every opportunity, he appreciated the value of all-arms cooperation – the tanks for 'punch' and mobility, mechanised infantry for protection, artillery for firepower, anti-aircraft and anti-tank tasks, the engineers for clearing a way across the battlefield – and was aware of the advantages of air power. His aim was to keep moving, to sever the links between the enemy command 'brain' and his front-line 'muscles'.

These were techniques that were to be refined and exploited in North Africa in 1941-42, with the added advantage that the battle area was ideal for manoeuvre operations. Rommel's wide right-flanking attacks, designed to cut behind British defensive positions and sever the command links, worked on a number of occasions, not least in the Battle of Gazala in May-June 1942.

However, in North Africa he came up against things he could not control: his unreliable supply chain and poorly equipped Italian allies. In addition, he took risks, which proved his undoing against the cautious but calculating Montgomery. And Montgomery got the measure of Rommel again in Normandy in 1944, denying the Germans the type of mobility Rommel was keen to use.

The overall impression of Rommel is of a quick-thinking and swift-moving commander, at his best in situations in which he could exploit his advantage. He was prepared to take risks – indeed, it was an integral part of his command style – and if they worked the rewards were often enormous. However, if they failed he was forced onto the defensive and became frustrated. The battlefield was his arena, but it was a battlefield that he preferred to control and shape. He was not always able to do so.

Chapter I

Young Rommel

Born into a strict, typically middle-class southern German family, the young Erwin Rommel showed no early signs of military genius. A pale and sometimes sickly child, he nonetheless enjoyed physical challenges, and had youthful ambitions of becoming an aeronautical engineer. However, his future was to be in another profession...

Erwin Johannes Eugen Rommel was born on Sunday 15th November 1891 at Heidenheim, near Ulm in Wuerttemberg. His father, after whom he was named, was a schoolmaster and a mathematician of some distinction; his mother, Helene, was the eldest daughter of Karl von Luz, President of the Government (Regierungs-Praesident) of Wuerttemberg. Erwin was therefore assured of a comfortable upbringing; as he was later to recall: 'my early years passed very pleasantly as I was able to romp around our yard and big garden all day long'. He had an elder sister, Helena, and two younger brothers, Karl and Gerhardt; an elder brother, Manfred, died while still an infant.

RIGHT: Officer Cadet Rommel photographed in 1911, an official portrait he gave to his mother at the beginning of his military career.

There was no indication in his early years that he would pursue a military career. As a child, Erwin was so pale and sickly that, according to Helene, he was known in the family as the 'white bear'. He also displayed little intellectual capacity. In 1898 his father was appointed headmaster of the secondary school (Realgymnasium) at Aalen, but as there was no primary school in the town, Erwin had to be educated by private tuition. Although this proved sufficient to gain him a place in his father's school in 1900, he had clearly not kept up with his contemporaries. Aware of this, he became even more pale and sickly, falling so far behind in his work that he gained a reputation for being lazy and inattentive.

But he did have potential. According to an anecdote recalled to Desmond Young when he was researching his book Rommel *(Collins, London, 1950), he was so careless that it became a standing joke, leading his teacher to declare that 'if Rommel ever shows up [with] a dictation without a mistake, we will hire a band and go off for a day in the country'. On hearing this, the youngster woke up and produced a perfect piece of work. When the day in the country did not materialise, however, he soon reverted to his former character. Erwin suddenly changed when he was in his teens, showing a flair for mathematics, taking an interest in sport and, with a friend, building a glider in the countryside near his home. Indeed, at this stage he seems to have wanted to be an engineer, with particular reference to the new and exciting field of aeronautics.*

He was stopped from doing this by his father, however, who had a reputation for being strict and insistent. Instead, the young Erwin changed his mind and declared that he wanted to join the Wuerttemberg Army. Erwin senior, who had served in the artillery as a young man, accepted this and did all he could to help his son, even though he would probably have preferred him to further his education. In March 1910, young Rommel was ordered to report to his local garrison for a medical; although he was found to be suffering from an inguinal hernia, this was rectified by a small operation and, on 19th July, he was told to report to the 124th Wuerttemberg Infantry Regiment as a lowly Fahnenjunker (officer candidate).

After rudimentary recruit training, he was posted to the Royal Officer Cadet School in Danzig. His career had begun. Just before he joined the school, he was asked to produce a short account of his early life.

Aalen, March 1910 – I was born on 15th November 1891 at Heidenheim on the Brenz as the second son of the schoolmaster Erwin Rommel and his wife Helene, née Luz, both of the Protestant faith...

I was supposed to start primary school in the autumn when I was seven; but as my father was promoted to headmaster at Aalen that year and there is no primary school there, I had to acquire the necessary knowledge by private tuition in order to be able to get into the elementary school at Aalen. Two years later I entered the Latin School, and stayed there five years...

BELOW: Kaiser Wilhelm II (smoking cigarette) and von Moltke peer suspiciously at the camera during a pre-war military ceremony. Moltke succeeded General von Schlieffen as Chief of the German General Staff, and also largely succeeded in dismantling Schlieffen's inspired plan for the rapid defeat of France.

In the autumn vacation of 1907 I had the misfortune to break my right ankle jumping over a stream. But the foot was well set and it has healed satisfactorily, so that despite even the most strenuous activities I have never noticed any after effects. In the autumn of 1908 I started the fifth grade of the Royal Secondary Modern school at Gmund and a year later the sixth grade, to which I still belong...

I have occupied my spare time with homework and reading, and apart from that with physical exercises like cycling, tennis, skating, rowing, skiing, etcetera. (From David Irving, *The Trail of the Fox: The Life of Field Marshal Erwin Rommel*, Weidenfeld and Nicolson, London, 1977.)

Cadet Rommel did well. According to a report by the commandant of the cadet school in March 1911, he was 'quite good' at rifle and drill work, 'adequate' at gymnastics, fencing and riding, and 'a useful soldier'. He was duly commissioned as a lieutenant in January 1912 and posted back to the 124th Infantry at Weingarten, spending the next two years learning his trade and training recruits. As a young officer, he was unusual in that he was virtually teetotal and a non-smoker, but he showed great interest in even the most mundane of military matters. He was also deeply in love with Lucie Mollin, whom he had met in Danzig where she was studying languages. They were to get married in 1916. Meanwhile, in March 1914, Rommel was attached to the 49th Field Artillery Regiment to gain experience, and he was with that unit in July when the war clouds began to gather. He described the atmosphere of the time in his book Infanterie Greift an (Infantry Attacks), *published in 1937:*

Ulm, 31st July 1914
The danger of war hung ominously over the German nation. Everywhere, serious, troubled faces! Unbelievable rumours which spread with the greatest of rapidity filled the air. Since dawn all public bulletin boards had been surrounded. One extra edition of the papers followed the other.

At an early hour the 4th Battery of the 49th Field Artillery Regiment hurried through the old imperial city. *Die Wacht am Rhein* ['Watch on the Rhine'] resounded in the narrow streets.

Below: German military manoeuvres towards the end of the nineteenth century. Serried ranks of riflemen waiting to fire and advance were a far cry from the reality of trench warfare and artillery barrage characterising the war when it finally came.

I rode as an infantry lieutenant and platoon commander in the smart Fuchs Battery to which I had been assigned since March. We trotted along in the bright morning sunshine, did our normal exercises, and then returned to our quarters accompanied by an enthusiastic crowd whose numbers ran into thousands.

During the afternoon, while horses were being purchased in the barrack yard, I obtained relief from my assignment. Since the situation appeared most serious, I longed for my own regiment, the Kaiser Wilhelm I, to be back with the men whose last two years of training I had supervised in the 7th Company, 124th Infantry (6th Wuerttemberger).

Along with Private Haenle [Rommel's orderly], I hurriedly packed my belongings; and late in the evening we reached Weingarten, our garrison town.

On 1st August 1914, there was much activity in the regimental barracks, the big old cloister building in Weingarten. Field equipment was being tried on! I reported back to headquarters and greeted the men of the 7th Company whom I was to accompany into the field. All the young faces radiated joy and anticipation. Is there anything finer than marching against an enemy at the head of such soldiers?

At 1800hrs, regimental inspection, Colonel Haas followed his thorough inspection of the field-grey-clad regiment with a vigorous talk. Just as we fell out, the mobilisation order came. Now the decision had been made. The shout of German youths eager for battle rang through the ancient grey cloister buildings. The 2nd August, a portentous Sabbath! In the evening the proud Wuerttemberger Regiment marched out to resounding band music and entrained for Ravensburg. (Transcript from General Field Marshal Erwin Rommel, *Infantry Attacks*, Greenhill Books, London, 1990.)

IMPERIAL GERMANY

Rommel grew up in an atmosphere of German nationalism and political confidence. Until 1871 Germany had consisted of a collection of loosely associated states, but in that year Wilhelm I of Prussia was elected Kaiser (Emperor) of a united Germany. This coincided with victory over the French, out of which the Germans gained control of Alsace-Lorraine and planted the seeds of future enmity with their western neighbour. But this did nothing to prevent a surge of German nationalism, based on people associating themselves with an entity greater than their local states. Thus, although the young Rommel would have felt loyalty towards Wuerttemberg – shown by his decision to join the Wuerttemberg Army – he would also have been aware, through his education, of its place in a powerful and influential European country. By 1914 Germany, now under Kaiser Wilhelm II, was dominating the affairs of central Europe and looking beyond the continent for colonies and trade. To its neighbours – France and Britain in the west and Russia in the east – a strong Germany, allied to Austria-Hungary to create a solid bloc of territory from the Baltic to the Balkans, threatened to upset the balance of power. By the same token, German awareness that the country was surrounded by opponents fuelled fears about territorial security. When those fears seemed to become reality with the assassination by Serbian nationalists of Archduke Franz Ferdinand of Austria in Sarajevo on 28 June 1914, followed swiftly by Russian mobilisation in support of the Serbs, war became inevitable. As Rommel bears witness, it was a very popular move throughout Germany.

Chapter II

Mountain Warrior

It was on St Vitus' Day, 28th June 1914, that the opening shots of World War I rang out in the Balkan capital, Sarajevo. The assassination of Archduke Franz Ferdinand, heir to the Austro-Hungarian throne, and his wife Sophie by a Serbian student activist set the armies of Europe on the march. For the young Erwin Rommel, it was the beginning of an illustrious career.

In August 1914, as Europe stood poised on the brink of war, Erwin Rommel was a junior officer in the 124th Infantry Regiment, having recently completed an attachment to the artillery. By November 1918, when the war ended, he was a captain on the staff with wide experience of active service on many fronts. He was also holder of the highest Prussian award for bravery, the Pour le Mérite, gained for operations in the mountains of northern Italy. During those operations he had learnt much about the style of mobile warfare that was to become his hallmark in later years.

Below: Rommel (left), and comrade as young officers in the Wuerttemberg 124th Infantry Regiment. Note Rommel's Iron Cross.

Rommel first saw action on 22nd August 1914, when he was ordered to lead his platoon towards the French village of Bleid. He was tired, having been on mounted patrol for 24 hours, and was suffering from a stomach upset.

August 1914

At dawn, the 2nd Battalion moved out towards Hill 325, 2km (1.25 miles) north-east of Bleid. Thick fog clung to the ground. Visibility barely 50m (164ft). The battalion commander, Major Bayer, sent me ahead to recce the route to Hill 325. I had been on the go for 20 hours non-stop, and could hardly keep in the saddle. Added to this, a gnawing hunger. I rode through a countryside of hedgerows and enclosed pastures. I found Hill 325 by map and compass. The battalion soon followed and took up positions on the northeast slope. Shortly after, the advance guard on our south and west flanks came up against enemy positions in the fog. A brief exchange of fire ensued – I saw and spoke briefly to my friend Bayer (9th Company); it was to be for the last time!

Occasional rifle rounds whined back and forth overhead. Lieutenant Schneckenburger, who had ridden some 100m (330ft) towards the enemy, was shot at from close range. Immediately our troops ran forward and succeeded in capturing a fleeing Frenchman in red breeches.

Then we heard German commands coming from behind us to the left: 'Half-left, March! Dress five paces apart!' The right flank of the 1st Battalion emerged, in line-advance. I was ordered by my company commander to deploy my platoon with the right flank of the 1st Battalion, and advance towards the southeast boundary of the village of Bleid.

I handed Rappen [Rommel's horse] over to Haenle, swapped my automatic pistol for his bayonet, and deployed my platoon. In loose formation we moved out of our hillside positions and advanced on Bleid with fixed bayonets. A thick ground fog battled with the ever-rising sun as we advanced through potato and vegetable plots in 50-80m (165-260ft) visibility.

Suddenly a salvo of shots rang out from close by. We dropped to the ground. Further rounds whistled overhead. Vainly I searched for the nearby enemy with my binoculars. They could not be far away, so I charged forward with my platoon. They fled before we could see them, their tracks clearly visible in the surrounding vegetable plots. We followed them towards Bleid. In the heat of the moment we had lost contact with the 1st Battalion.

More shots were fired at the platoon from behind the dense fog. Each time we charged, the enemy rapidly retreated. For 600-800m (2000-2600ft) we then advanced unopposed. A fence with a tall hedge loomed out of the mist in front of us, while the outline of farm buildings and large trees appeared to our left. Here the enemy footprints we had been following swung right, and disappeared uphill. Had we reached Bleid? I positioned the platoon by the hedge, and sent a detachment ahead to make contact with our neighbours on the left and our own company. So far the platoon had suffered no casualties.

To reconnoitre the farmyard before us, I went ahead with the deputy platoon leader, Sergeant Ostertag, and a pair of artillery rangefinders. Neither sight nor sound of the enemy. We reached the east side of the farm. A track led from here to a road. On the other side, we could make out another farm through the fog. Clearly we were at Mussy la Ville on the outskirts of Bleid. We cautiously advanced towards the road. I looked around the corner of the farm building. There – barely 20 paces to the right – some 15-20 Frenchmen were standing in the middle of the road chatting, drinking coffee, and with their rifles slung. They didn't see me.

FIRST BLOOD

The 124th Infantry Regiment, within which Rommel was a junior officer, left its peacetime garrison at Weingarten late on 2nd August 1914, to be transported by rail to the German-Luxembourg border. Its role was to advance from Diedenhofen (Thionville) towards the Belgian border fortress of Longwy. Skirting the fortress, the regiment would then, in company with other elements of the German Fifth Army, wheel south to outflank French fortifications around Verdun.

This was an important part of the Schlieffen Plan, designed to knock France out of the war in six weeks so that the bulk of German forces could be transferred east to face the more ponderous but numerically much larger Russian Army. The German First Army would advance through Belgium and northern France to outflank Paris to the west and south. Other armies, to the right of the First, would execute shallower advances. The whole campaign would hinge on the Fifth Army which, by definition, had only a short distance to cover. However, in the process it was to prevent the movement of French reserves further south.

The four of us fired. The column again disappeared for a moment, then split into several sections and fled west towards the Gévimont-Bleid road. We chased the fleeing enemy with rapid fire.

Strangely, we had not received any return of fire despite standing upright and surely being in full view of the enemy. Fleeing Frenchmen came running down the road on our left, beyond the bushes where we stood. It was easy to shoot them down at a distance of about 10m (33ft) through a break in the bushes. We divided our fire among the enemy elements. Our four rifles put dozens of Frenchmen out of the fight.

Now the 123rd Grenadiers started up the hill. I signalled my platoon, and with them charged towards the bushes on each side of the Gévimont-Bleid road. Here we found a number of Frenchmen, who had escaped the firefight but who took a long time to come out and surrender their arms. Apparently they had been told that all prisoners would be beheaded by the Germans. From the bushes and cornfields came over 50 men. These included two French officers, an unwounded captain and a lieutenant with a slight arm wound. We found out they were from sections of the 6th and 7th Company, 101st French Infantry Regiment. My men offered the prisoners cigarettes, which made them much calmer.

ABOVE: German infantrymen set up a searchlight by a newly-dug trench in the Argonne forest. Away from the plains of Flanders, much of Rommel's war was to be spent in hilly woodlands and mountain regions.

On the hill to the right, the 123rd Grenadiers had now reached the Gévimont-Bleid road as well. Rifle fire came at us from the direction of the high woods at Le Mat, 1500m (4950ft) north-west of Bleid. I quickly ordered my platoon under cover of a defile, with the intention to mount an assault on Le Mat from there. But suddenly, everything went black and I lost consciousness. The exertions of the day and night before, the battle at Bleid, the fight for the hill to the north and, not least, the state of my stomach, had robbed me of all strength.

I must have remained unconscious for some time. As I came to, Sergeant Bentele was attending to me. Occasional French grenades and shrapnel landed nearby. Our infantry were withdrawing quickly from the Le Mat woodland back towards Hill 325. I took command of an advance formation, and occupied the rise on the Gévimont-Bleid road. From these men I learnt that they had sustained heavy casualties in the wood, had lost their commander and then been ordered to retreat. They had been severely mauled by French artillery as well. Buglers sounded the regimental call and 'Assembly'. Shortly the various sections began to make their way to positions west of Bleid. From where I stood I watched the various companies trudge in. Their ranks were severely depleted. The 124th Regiment had lost a quarter of its officer complement and a seventh of its men dead or wounded during the action. For me it was especially distressing to learn that my friends Bayer and Hotz were among the fallen. Soon the battalions headed off toward Gomery through the southern outskirts of Bleid.

Bleid was an horrendous sight. Dead soldiers and civilians lay among the smoking ruins. In gardens and fields lay numerous cattle and horses, victims of the firefight. The troops were told that the enemy had been pushed back all along the line, and were in retreat. Our joy at victory was tempered by sorrow at the loss of so many comrades. We marched on south. The march was frequently interrupted! Far in the distance enemy columns could be seen. Batteries of the 49th Artillery Regiment trotted ahead and took up positions to the right of our march route. Exhausted, we finally arrived at Ruette around 22.00hrs. The village was already full of our troops. We bivouacked in the open. Straw couldn't be found, and our troops were too tired to look for any. The damp, cold ground forbade refreshing sleep. During the night the temperature dropped sharply, and we were all wretchedly cold by morning. In the latter part of the night, my troubled stomach began to play up once more, keeping me awake. At last day came. Once again, thick fog clung to the fields.

By September, Rommel's unit had been moved to the hills around Varennes, close to the Argonne Forest. The advance was continuing, but casualties were beginning to mount.

During this period, the battlefield itself was still relatively fluid, with infantry charges and counter-charges supported by artillery and cavalry. The machine gun had yet to bring about static warfare and force the soldiers on both sides to dig in. It was in one such machine-gun encounter, in woodland on the edge of the Argonne, that Rommel himself narrowly escaped with his life.

September 1914

To get the company moving, Major Salzman and I went into the front line. A wounded soldier gave me his rifle and some ammunition, and I commandeered a couple of squads. Several times we charged the undergrowth on the next hill with a whoop, assuming the enemy to be close by. We missed him every time. Again and again his rapid fire forced us to the ground. Casualties increased minute by minute as we heard the wounded calling for stretcher-bearers. Flat on the ground or behind thick oak trees we waited for the enemy fire to abate, before making the next attempt to reach his position. It was becoming increasingly difficult to coax the men forward under the relentless fire. Thus we gained ground slowly. The sound

BELOW: German officers look on as their men set about shoring up a trench on the rain- and artillery-battered Argonne front. Rommel was to earn a particular respect from his men by his willingness to lead from the front and to participate in routine chores.

of battle suggested our neighbours were close by on the same hill.

Once more I led the charge against the enemy in the bushes ahead of us. A handful of my former recruits struggled with me through the undergrowth. Again the enemy fired furiously. There – at last – stood five Frenchmen not 20 paces in front of me standing up and firing at will. My rifle went to my shoulder. Two Frenchmen fell. That left three. My men had apparently dropped back to their positions, and couldn't help me. I fired again – nothing! I whipped off the magazine to find it empty. The enemy were too close – no time to reload – and there was no cover to hand. My only hope lay in the bayonet. I had been an enthusiastic bayonet fighter before the war, and had brought the skill to a fine art. Although alone facing three of the enemy, I had complete confidence in the weapon and my ability to use it. As I prepared to charge, the enemy fired. I was thrown head over heels by a bullet to land five paces in front of my foe. A sideways shot had shattered my upper left leg. Blood spurted from a fist-sized wound. Every second I expected the coup de grâce by bayonet or bullet. I pressed against the wound with my right hand, while trying at the same time to roll to cover behind an oak tree. For a few minutes I lay between the two fronts. Finally, my men burst through the undergrowth cheering, and the enemy vanished.

BELOW: Rommel's sharp-eyed friend in the dug-outs of the Argonne in 1915 was – appropriately enough – a young fox cub.

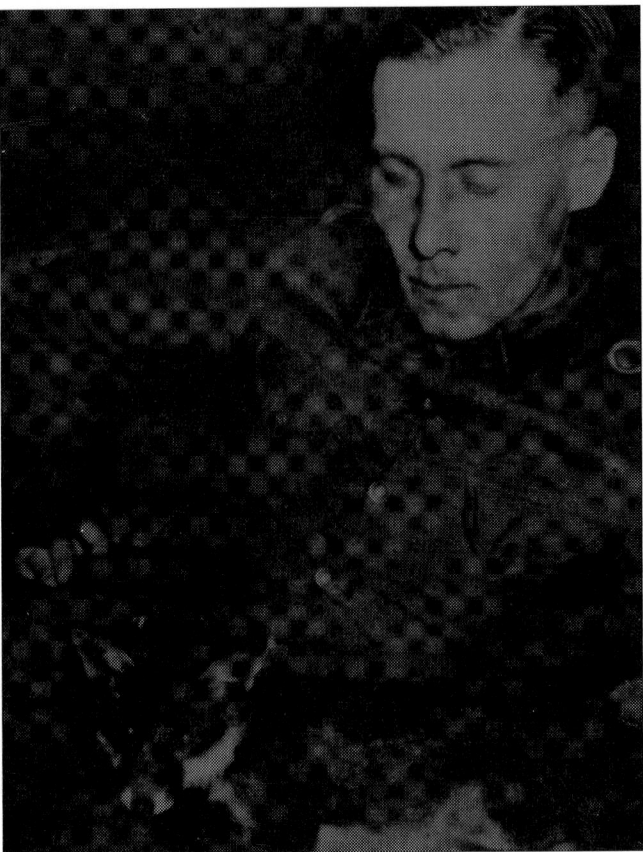

Corporal Rauch and Private Rutschmann took care of me. They used a trenchcoat belt as a tourniquet, and bandaged the wound. Then they carried me through the brush in a sling fashioned from a tent, back to the shelter.

From up ahead came the report that the enemy had been thrown out of the fight – and the wood. They left over 200 prisoners in our hands. Equally, our casualties had been severe: the 2nd Battalion alone had suffered 30 dead, including two officers, and 81 wounded, including four officers. Thus the battalion had for the third time in three days – according to the regimental history – performed its duties with great distinction. The sorrow at parting from these brave men lay heavily upon me.

As the sun went down, I was carried back by two men in the sling, between two poles. They had a trek of 5km (three miles) back to Montblainville ahead of them. I felt little pain, but passed out from the loss of blood. I came to in a barn in Montblainville, to find the staff surgeon looking over me. Haenle had brought him. My wound was dressed again, and I was carried onto a loaded field ambulance. Three men lay next to me, groaning and crying out. We left for the field hospital, riding over sticks and stones. The road had been torn up by shells, and the jolting wagon caused me great pain. When we arrived at the field hospital around midnight, one of the wounded with me was already dead. The hospital was overflowing. The wounded lay under covers in rows by the road. Two doctors worked feverishly. I was again examined, and then placed on straw in a room. The following day, I was transferred by ambulance to the staff hospital at Stenay. There I received, a few days later, the Iron Cross Second Class. Following an operation in the middle of October, I was taken home by car.

Rommel had recovered from his wounds by January 1915, and when he returned to his battalion (still in the Argonne sector), the nature of the front line had changed. Trenches and barbed wire had replaced the open field of battle of the year before.

The end of the war of manoeuvre in the West allowed the combatants time to review their strategy, which was influenced by Turkey's entry into the war. For the Allies, there was an urgent need to re-establish a supply route to Russia, which caused a difference of opinion between those who wished to concentrate efforts on the Western Front and those who believed a more effective blow could be delivered in the East. The decision arrived at was to continue operations in the West, while simultaneously conducting offensives against Turkey. The Central Powers, too, were divided over their strategy: whether to concentrate on the Western Front or deliver further blows against the already battered Russians. In the end, it was decided to have a holding operation in the West and concentrate resources in the East.

It was his close-hand observation of the change from mobile to static warfare, and the consequent large-scale loss of life, that influenced Rommel's tactical thinking for the rest of his military career. At this time, both Allies and Central Powers were reviewing their respective strategies as the 'war of manoeuvre' ground ignominiously and bloodily to a halt, and the war began to take on a larger and more permanent aspect. The German decision to concentrate resources in the East was to tie down their forces on the Western Front for a long time to come.

January 1915

To hold down as much of the enemy's strength as possible, all regiments of the 27th Division were ordered to undertake a variety of diversionary actions on 29th January 1915. The 124th Regiment was to launch an attack with shock troops following the destruction of an enemy mineshaft in the 2nd Battalion sector. In the middle of the action, the enemy line facing 9th Company (to the left) and 10th Company (to the right) would come under artillery bombardment. To this end, Howitzer Battery Hoffman of the Artillery Regiment had carried out ranging shots on the 27th and 28th. It was intended that 10th Company would move out, while 9th Company remained behind to prevent the enemy breaking out on the flank.

At the start of operations, I was positioned with three squads in the new forward embrasure – some 100m (330ft) in front of our own company. We could hear our shells whining overhead, some striking the trees and others falling behind us. Then the mine was blown. Earth and branches cascaded around. Heavy rifle fire broke out, and hand grenades cracked. A lone Frenchman ran up to our position from the left, and was shot down.

A few minutes later, the Adjutant of 3rd Battalion appeared and reported that the

JUNIOR LEADER

By early 1915 Rommel's reputation as a brave and resourceful officer was growing. Already wounded once, during fighting around Varennes in September 1914, he had been awarded the Iron Cross Second Class, and this was followed in January 1915 by the Iron Cross First Class for leading a successful raid on French positions in the Argonne Forest. Theodor Werner, a platoon leader in the 124th Infantry Regiment, was clearly impressed by Rommel at this time: 'In some curious way his spirit permeated the entire regiment right from the start, at first barely perceptibly to most but then increasingly dramatically until everybody was inspired by his initiative, his courage, his dazzling acts of gallantry...Anyone who once came under the spell of his personality turned into a real soldier. However tough the strain he seemed inexhaustible. He seemed to know just what the enemy were like and how they would probably react. His plans were often startling, instinctive, spontaneous, and not infrequently obscure...His men idolised him and had boundless faith in him.' (David Irving, *The Trail of the Fox*, Weidenfeld and Nicolson, 1977.)

RIGHT: A model of pre-war order and precision, this German barricade in the Argonne Forest would have been quickly transformed by the reality of artillery barrage and a war of attrition.

attack to our right was progressing well and asked would we like to join the festivities. Naturally we would.

I was stuck with my company in our positions, unable to move. The enemy had us well pinned down by artillery and machine gun, apparently having us under observation – perhaps from the treetops. Any advance would be met with concentrated fire. I therefore took all my troops along a trench to the right flank of the position, which led forwards. Crawling forwards in skirmish line formation, after about 15 minutes the company arrived some 80m (260ft) in front of the position on the slope facing our enemy. We carefully crawled through the undergrowth towards the enemy.

Before we could reach the dip ahead, the enemy opened up on us with accurate machine-gun and rifle fire that stopped us dead. Bullets slammed into the frozen ground. There was virtually no cover apart from a few thick oaks up ahead. Even with binoculars I couldn't spot the enemy. Clearly, to stay put would cost us dear. Firepower of such strength, even fired at random, would have devastating consequences in terms of casualties. I searched my brain for an answer, for it is in such moments that the hopes and fears of his men weigh heavily on the commander.

I had just decided to make a dash for the hollow 50m (165ft) ahead, since it offered slightly more cover than our present location, when the attack was sounded to our right. My bugler crouched nearby. I ordered him to blow.

As one man the brave 9th Company leapt forward, notwithstanding the continuing hail of fire coming at us. With loud cheers, we charged towards the French positions. Then we saw the enemy – face to face beyond the wire. They were no longer firing, and our cries and the glint of our bayonets sent them fleeing. Red trousers flashed through the undergrowth, with grey-blue coat-tails flying. We pressed on. What did it matter to us that they had left their rifles and machine guns behind in their abandoned positions, as we pursued them fleeing head over heels through the brush? In the rush 9th Company overran two further French positions despite heavy wire entanglements. As proof that the enemy had offered barely any resistance, we had suffered no casualties at all.

The wood thinned out as we cleared a hill. The enemy fled ahead in a herd. We followed on their heels, shooting. A company detachment took about a dozen prisoners while clearing the dugouts, while the remainder continued until we reached the edge of the wood 500m (1650ft) west of Fontaine-aux-Charmes. We were some 800m (2640ft) south of our original positions. The terrain sloped downwards again, and the fleeing enemy had disappeared into the brush. Right and left we were unprotected. Bitter and intense fighting was continuing on both sides and behind us. I deployed my company at the edge of the woods 500m (1650ft) from Fontaine-aux-Charmes before trying to re-establish contact on our flanks. One of my riflemen brought an assortment of women's undergarments he had retrieved from a dugout hurriedly abandoned by the French soldiers, to the general amusement of all.

A little later a reserve company arrived. I ordered it to make contact to left and right, and pushed on with 9th Company to the southwest. The ground here had largely been cleared. Shortly we crossed a hollow. We found ourselves at the Front, and I followed with the company in column formation. From behind and to the left, we suddenly encountered enemy fire which forced us to the ground. Just 50-80m (165-260ft) away, an invisible enemy lay in the bushes. I led the company westwards to bypass the fire zone, and swung south again through the light woodland.

At the southern edge of the wood, we suddenly ran into barbed wire entanglements like none we had seen before. Seventy to 90m (230-295ft) in depth, they stretched as far as the eye could see. The French had cut down the whole forest here. On the other side of the emplacement, I could see three men from my company waving to us from the side of a small hill, under Volunteer Matt. Clearly this fortification was not occupied by the enemy at this point. To stay put and await the reserve company seemed the most sensible thing to do.

As I was following the small track which led through the obstacle, a fierce burst of enemy fire from the left forced me to take cover. At 300-400m (990-1320ft) distance, the enemy could not see me through the thick barbed wire. Nevertheless, bullets ricocheted all around as I crawled on all fours. I ordered the company to follow me. My leading platoon commander lost his nerve, so he and the entire company remained motionless in front of the wire. Shouting and waving was fruitless.

A fierce firefight was taking place by the blockhouse on our right, and we used our last grenades to defend it. Moments later, a French assault squad succeeded in taking it. From its firing positions, they were able to direct rifle and machine-gun fire at our backs. A report reached me just as a battalion runner shouted his orders across the wire: 'Battalion position 800m (2640ft) north and digging in. Rommel

BELOW: Torn trees and hanging branches mark the progress of battle as German soldiers rest up along a track through the Argonne.

Detachment to withdraw, support not possible.'

Decision time! To disengage from the fight and retreat along the two small tracks through the wire emplacement under a heavy crossfire from east and west would surely result in a minimum penalty of 50 per cent casualties, if not the entire company. Surrender? Death sooner! That left one alternative, to engage the enemy at his western end, where the company was strongest. That could and had to work. Indeed, the enemy were superior in number, but the French had yet to experience an attack by the 124th Infantry Regiment. If the enemy could be defeated in the west, it might just be possible to dash back through the barbed wire. We would then only have the more distant fire from the east to contend with. Speed was essential, since we had to be clear by the time the enemy in the west had recovered from his shock.

Quickly, the men under my command were made aware of my intentions. Everyone understood the situation, and resolved to do their best. I charged with the reserve platoon to the right. The blockhouse was seized, and we carried on. The whole line faltered under our attack. Red French trousers flashed through the bushes – the enemy was on the run. For us the moment had come. As the French ran west, we hurried east. Man by man we scuttled through the wire entanglement. As the first of my men reached the northern side, heavy enemy fire caught us from the east. Fortunately the range was over 300m (990ft) and it did little harm. Most of the company had already reached safe cover when enemy fire from the west opened up. Apart from five severely wounded men who had to be carried, the remainder fortunately came through the fire unscathed. Without further incident, the company pushed through dense undergrowth and enemy fire to reach our battalion position.

Below: Mountain troops pose for the camera high up in the Alps along the Italian front.

Bottom: Stony-faced German troops pause during the Isonzo Offensive of 1917.

This was located in dense forest, due south of the three French positions. 9th Company was placed on the right flank. There was no link-up to the left, the 1st Battalion having lost direct contact. We were able to maintain communications with its right flank using messengers. Eighty to100m (260-330ft) into the forest we dug in. Digging in the frozen ground was very difficult.

French artillery had in the meantime directed its fire against our old positions and the areas behind. During the fighting in the woods, they had not fired on us. Now we were subjected to a heavy retaliatory bombardment. The edge of the wood came in for special attention. Our work was seriously disturbed. I prepared an account of the fighting on a blank report sheet.

Rommel's unit remained in the Argonne through spring 1915. The front had now become static and both sides were building ever more elaborate defences. Casualty rates could still be severe, however.

The war of attrition was beginning in earnest as both sides launched offensive and counter-offensive. Vast resources of men and materiel were poured into the pushes at Neuve Chapelle, Festubert and Ypres to little or no avail on either side. Poison gas was introduced to the battlefield at Ypres during April, and the ugliness of the new modern warfare was making itself cruelly felt.

May 1915

Despite the daily casualties and the nerve-racking stress of combat, the morale of the riflemen at Central remained high. Everyone carried out their duties with the utmost self-discipline. We became more and more attached to the blood-soaked Argonne. The hardest thing was taking leave of those comrades killed, or carried away severely wounded. We remained behind to grit our teeth and inwardly resolve to hold out.

I shall never forget a particular young rifleman whose leg had been blown off by a French shell. The sun was sinking as he was carried off down a narrow track. The pain, looking back, is still great. I had taken hold of his hand, thinking to lend him courage, but he said: 'Lieutenant, it is not bad. I will soon be back with the company, even if it is on a wooden leg.' The poor lad never saw the sun again. He died on the way to hospital.

Approaching the middle of July, I began a five-week stint as deputy commander of 10th Company. The 4th and 5th Companies joined us. We company commanders were working together on a shelter plan. The construction consisted of several entrances to an underground dugout 8m (26ft) below the surface. The work went on day and night, from all directions. The officers lent a hand to complete the work, which improved morale. In those days it was often the case that an entire dugout system could be demolished within an hour by concentrated French artillery. The small timber-built shelters were ripped apart like matchboxes by the heavy shells. Happily, the French had a systematic method of firing. Usually they began the bombardment on our left flank and moved right. Not wanting to remain under fire, I moved off as soon as it began and waited

MOUNTAIN WARFARE

In July 1915 Rommel was wounded for a second time. When he recovered, he was not sent back to the 124th Infantry Regiment but to a newly raised unit, the Wuerttembergische Gebirgsbataillon (Wuerttemberg Mountain Battalion), with promotion to Oberleutnant (full lieutenant). After training in Austria, the unit was moved to the Vosges sector of the Western Front, but saw little action. In October 1916, however, it was transferred to the East to take part in the final stages of a campaign against the Romanians, who had declared war on the Central Powers in August and invaded Austria-Hungary. Despite Russian help, the Romanians were outclassed; by the time that Rommel arrived, they were in retreat, opening up the possibility of much more mobile warfare. Rommel adapted brilliantly, leading a self-contained Abteilung (detachment) in attacks behind Romanian lines. In one of these, in August 1917, he captured Mount Cosna after infiltrating four companies between enemy positions without being detected. Once in place, he used his machine guns to lay down heavy fire, then attacked in force on a narrow front.

until it had moved sideways or to our rear. Had the French followed up the bombardment with an infantry attack, we would have thrown them back in a counter-attack. Man to man we were far superior to them in a fight.

Wounded in July 1915, Rommel transferred to a newly raised mountain battalion, and served in the Vosges and then in Romania. In October 1917 his unit was recovering from the hard fighting around Mount Cosna in Romania, wondering where they would be posted next.

October 1917

In beautiful Corinthia, where the battalion had been sent via Macedonia, I resumed command of my detachment in October. Replacements had come to make up the losses from the Mount Cosna battle. Also the unit's firepower was increased with a consignment of machine guns. A short period of rest sufficed to allow familiarisation with the new weapon. What the High Command had in store for us, we knew not. The Isonzo Front?

Rommel was correct. His men were moved to the Isonzo Front, where the fighting for the defences was in full swing. Italy had entered the war in May 1915 on the side of the Allies, despite previous links with the German-Austro-Hungarian Triple Alliance. Hoping to gain territory from the Austrians, they attacked along two flanks into Austria-Hungary, in the Dolomites and along the Isonzo.

The Italian Army was quite large, but was ill-equipped. This, combined with incompetent leadership and indecision, prevented the Italians making any gains against the defending and hard-pressed Austrians, and in the autumn of 1917 Germany agreed to send reinforcements – among them Rommel's own regiment.

By this time the Italian Army had suffered huge losses in its 1917 offensives, first at the Tenth Battle of the Isonzo (from 12th May) and then in the Eleventh Battle. In the latter the Italian Second Army made considerable progress, until it outran its supplies. For their part, the Austro-Hungarians were in a desperate state (their armies were on the point of collapse), until bolstered by Germany.

BELOW: The Italian theatre of operations in World War I.

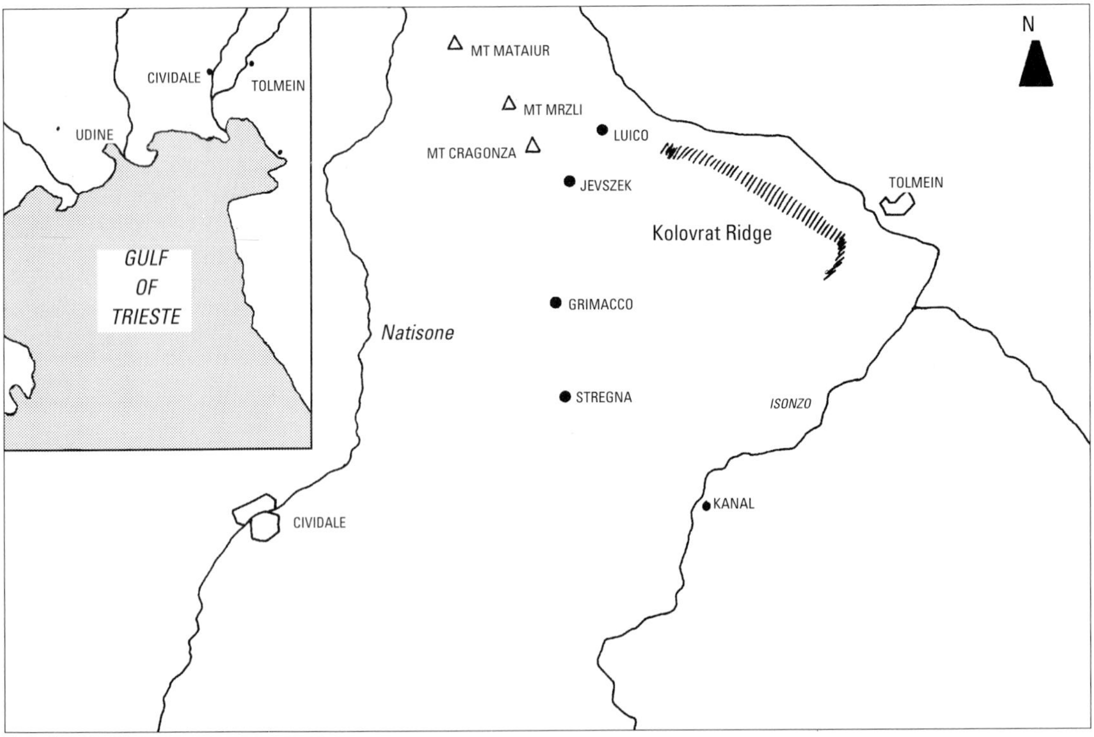

My detachment consisted of three mountaineer companies and one machine-gun company. I usually marched with my staff at the head of the column. Knesa lay 8km (4.8 miles) east of the front, at Tolmein. In the afternoon of 21st October Major Sprosser and his section leaders recced the designated assembly area for the attack: a northern slope of Mount Buzenika which led steeply down to the Isonzo River.

Once in position, his men were soon in the thick of the action, on 25th October, against Italian positions around Hill 1192.

25th October 1917

I had just put down the telephone receiver and was having a piece of white Italian bread for breakfast when a short message arrived from Streicher: 'Patrol broken through. Guns taken. Prisoners taken.' No noise came from the direction of the enemy, not a single shot fired. I hurried off with my detachment in the direction Streicher's men had gone. Each second wasted threatened the success of our undertaking.

It required all the strength of Rommel Detachment to climb out of the hollow in the next minute. A few seconds, and the enemy wire had been reached – and breached. Then we were on top of the enemy position. Ahead lay the long barrels of an Italian heavy artillery battery. Streicher's men were clearing some dugouts. A few dozen prisoners stood by the guns. Lieutenant Streicher reported that he had caught the gunners out at ablutions.

We were in a small saddle. On the bare ridges to each side were numerous earthworks and communications trenches, and the strong fortifications on the north slope were also visible. To the south of the saddle – just 100m (330ft) from the positions on the north slope – was the Luico-Kuk-Hill 1114-Crai road, well camouflaged against ground and air observation.

A third of Rommel Detachment had reached the saddle. The troops were breathless after the rush up the hill. Clearly the Kolovrat garrison were still

Below: Austrian artillery with a mountain gun on the barren slopes of the Italian front. Rommel's regiment was sent to assist its Austrian allies repulse the Italian offensive.

unaware of our occupation of their position. Were they asleep? Judging by the number of prisoners already taken in the 50m- (165ft-) wide saddle, the position was heavily manned. Seconds decided our fate. I wanted to block the east and move west towards Hill 1192 and ordered:

'Corporal Spadinger to take one machine-gun squad from 2nd Company to immediately block the north sides of the enemy position, block the highway, and cover Rommel Detachment's advance to the west.

'Lieutenant Ludwig and 2nd Company to take the enemy position on the northern slope. Avoid shooting for as long as possible. The enemy appear to be still asleep.

'I shall advance with 3rd Rifle and 1st Machine Gun Companies along the road to the west. Lieutenant Streicher assumes responsibility for security.

'Advance rapidly!'

All units of the detachment set about their tasks with speed and efficiency. Stormtroops of the 2nd Company rushed from dugout to dugout and from sentry post to sentry post. The bulk of the enemy garrison were found in the dugouts. One mountaineer sufficed to take over the evacuation, disarming and assembly of an entire enemy position. In the sentry posts the sentries were still gazing at the magnificent spectacle cast by sunrise over the Isonzo and its gleaming twin 2000m (6600ft) peaks.

As 2nd Company had shown, the sudden appearance of a mountaineer behind them frightened the sentries rigid, and they were no more inclined to give the alarm than their comrades of a half hour previously. Rapidly the number of prisoners rose into the hundreds, as we moved towards Hill 1192.

Meanwhile, the main body of the detachment were advancing well along the highway. Fortunately our camouflage screens concealed us from the view of the enemy on the heights east and west. We took several gun emplacements which had been blasted out of the rockface. Our sudden appearance in the quiet of the morning, far from the battle sounds on Hill 1114, caught the garrison out. My

THE BLUE MAX

In December 1917, Kaiser Wilhelm II paid tribute to Rommel's bravery by awarding him the coveted Pour le Mérite – the Blue Max. It was not for a single act of courage but for a series of operations carried out by Rommel's Abteilung (detachment) between 24th October and 10th November 1917 in mountains south of the River Isonzo. The terrain was rugged, with precipitous, trackless mountains, deep ravines and swollen rivers made worse by almost constant rain, yet alpine units of General Otto von Below's Fourteenth Army managed to infiltrate and destroy the Italian defences on Hill 1192, Mount Mataiur, Kolovrat and Hill 1114.

Rommel was always convinced that other officers 'stole his glory', at least in the early stages. For example, he believed two officers, Lieutenants Schoerner and Schnieber, had won Blue Maxes due to his efforts (he believed Schoerner had captured the wrong peak, and that the Rommel Detachment had seized the objective). It was not until early November, when Rommel captured the Italian village of Longarone, along with 8000 prisoners, that his achievements were brought to the Kaiser's attention.

objective now was to surprise any enemy reserves, and to help 2nd Company on the northern hillside in resisting attack. Things turned out differently!

For 2nd Company, the main concern was the 1000 prisoners. Under the energetic Lieutenant Ludwig, the battle-hardened company had cleared all positions on the north slope of Hill 1192. On the highway, 3rd Company were moving towards the saddle 300m (990ft) east of Hill 1192. Suddenly, they came under fire from all sides. Streicher Detachment, having already reached the saddle 300m (990ft) east of 1192, came under machine-gun fire from the south side of 1192, and then received fire from Italian infantry on the southeast slope, who were trying to advance over the road. The unit retreated on the north side of the hill.

Heavy machine-gun fire from 1192 halted 3rd Company and the 1st Machine Gun Company as they tried to advance along the road. Machine-gun squads were quickly set up, but were unable to distract the enemy. To attempt an attack up one side of the road would have left us exposed on the unprotected southern slopes of the Kolovrat ridge. In addition, machine-gun fire was penetrating through our camouflage screens on the left side of the road. In a few seconds, battle sounds swelled in front of us and to the left, where 2nd Company presumably were. Hand grenades in great number were going off, interspersed with the sound of lively rifle fire from the fighting mountaineers. Every last man stood on the firing line.

I could see nothing. It was impossible to reach the bare hilltop to the right of the road without attracting heavy machine-gun fire. Could 2nd Company hold out? They had just 80 rifles and six light machine guns. If they were defeated, the enemy would recover his positions on the north slope of Hill 1192, cutting off the rest of the detachment. I could tell how strong was the enemy ahead by the sound of his firepower. In a few minutes the tables had been turned on us and we now faced a desperate situation. All we could do was hold on to some of the Kolovrat positions gained during our speedy advance, against a superior enemy.

Left: German troops advance through a shattered town in the aftermath of the Battle of Caporetto, during the Isonzo Offensive of 1917.

Clearly, the most important thing for me was to hold the road to the west and aid the beleaguered 2nd Company.

The shortest route northwards over the hilltops was covered east and west by a great number of well-positioned enemy machine guns. Any attack mounted across the road towards the west of Hill 1192 would have been threatened by the same guns, with little chance of success, and heavy casualties. I found a different solution.

A machine-gun squad was already in action against 1192 which, with a section of riflemen from the 3rd Company, was instructed to block the road to the west. I took the rest of the 3rd Company and the machine-gun companies quickly back down the road to the saddle 300m (990ft) east of Hill 1192. Thick camouflage screens prevented enemy observers to the east and west directing fire at us. Occasional sweeps of fire across our screens had little effect on our progress, and we reached the saddle.

Here the capable Spadinger with his eight men were holding the sizeable Italian garrison to the east at bay. As I went by I left two further squads behind to reinforce him. We advanced quickly eastwards through the abandoned Italian positions that had already been cleared by 2nd Company. Some 150m (495ft) west of the saddle were two of our mountaineers, guarding about a thousand disconsolate prisoners. I ordered them to be speedily taken down the hillside past the barbed wire emplacement straight away. They got on with it! Italian machine-gun fire striking the hills to east and west spurred the prisoners on.

Less than 100m (330ft) on, the noise of battle suddenly rose to a crescendo. Exploding hand grenades, continuous machine-gun and rapid carbine fire were all around us. I ordered the companies

Above: The price of a German Pour le Mérite: dead Italians line a rain-soaked trench after the Isonzo Offensive in 1917.

following to move as speedily as possible. Help could not come soon enough – we were running dangerously low on ammunition supplies. I examined the situation from a hillock 350m (1155ft) east of Hill 1192.

2nd Company and Streicher Detachment held a number of trenches on the northeast slope of Hill 1192. They were surrounded to south, west and east by fivefold their number, an entire Italian reserve battalion. The leading enemy elements were stacked up just 50m (165ft) away. Retreat to the north slope behind was rendered impossible by the high and wide Italian obstacles. The men fought hard against the overwhelming enemy. Only unbroken rapid fire held off an attack. If the enemy had attacked nonetheless, the little group would have been destroyed.

I quickly realised that 2nd Company could only be saved by an attack on the enemy flank and rear using the entire detachment. Victory would be assured by the close combat superiority of our mountain soldiers.

The leading elements rushed panting along the deep trenches, followed by the leading men of the machine-gun company with a machine gun. Few words were needed to inform the commanders of the situation and what had to be done. 3rd Company was assembled in a hollow to the left of the trench facing the enemy, and made ready for an assault. A heavy machine gun was set up in another depression to the left, and reported ready for action. An additional heavy-machine-gun squad came up, and on the left the largest section of 3rd Company were now ready for action.

I couldn't wait for the second heavy machine gun to be set up. The massed enemy troops 100m (330ft) ahead were already out of their trenches and heading for the cornered 2nd Company. I gave the signal for 3rd Company and 1st Machine

Below: Italian prisoners-of-war are herded into a hastily built compound outside Tolmein in October 1917. The following month, Rommel captured 8000 Italians in one day.

Gun Company to attack. Then the first heavy machine gun opened up with a steady fire on the enemy, shortly followed by the second, while the mountaineers charged the enemy flank and rear with furious determination. The surprise attack had succeeded. The Italians broke off their attack on 2nd Company, and turned to face 3rd Company. Immediately 2nd Company leapt out of their positions and attacked the enemy right. Hemmed in on both sides, and forced into a tight corner, the enemy laid down their arms rather than fight to the last. Only the officers sought to defend themselves with their pistols once we came within a few metres range. Then they too were overwhelmed. I had to interject to save them from the wrath of the mountain soldiers. A whole battalion of 12 officers and over 500 men surrendered in the saddle 300m (990ft) northeast of Hill 1192. Thus our prisoner count on Kolovrat now amounted to 1500 men. We took the summit and southern slope of the hill, and captured another Italian artillery battery.

Our great happiness in victory was overshadowed by the heavy losses we had sustained. Apart from a number wounded, we had lost two fine fighters, Corporal Kiefner (2nd Company), who had performed so well as stormtroop leader at Hevnik the day before, and Lance Corporal Kneule (3rd Company) both forfeited their young lives.

The Austro-German offensive against the Italians in October 1917 was one of the greatest military successes of the war. From 24th October, General Konrad Krafft von Dellmensingen's 12 assault divisions attacked the Italians in the vicinity of Caporetto (the battle is either known by that name or Twelfth Isonzo). Though they were outnumbered over the whole front, the Austro-Germans achieved local superiority in the sector where they attacked, and quickly pierced the Italian line. The result was the virtual destruction of the Italian Second Army.

Ironically, because the Austro-Germans did not believe they would achieve such success, there was little support for the subsequent attack

BELOW: A pensive Kaiser Wilhelm II looks on as an Austrian officer relives the Battle of the Isonzo for his benefit in November 1917.

LEFT: Rommel the war hero poses with grave intensity, sporting both the Iron Cross First Class and the much-coveted Blue Max in this portrait photograph taken after the Armistice.

from the Tenth and Eleventh Austro-Hungarian Armies. The offensive staggered to a halt when it outran its supplies, and the Italian commander, Cadorna, was able to establish a defensive line north of Venice, though only because the Austrians and Germans could advance no more (they had made no provision for such gains, and were thus unprepared to exploit them).

Nevertheless, it had been a catastrophe for Italy: losses of around 600,000 in prisoners and casualties. To bolster the Italian effort, six French and five British divisions were hastily despatched to the Italian Army, although had the Austrians and Germans possessed the resources to exploit their success, Italy could have been knocked out of the war at a stroke. Only in 1918, when German forces had for the most part been withdrawn to bolster the Western Front, and Austria-Hungary was on the verge of collapse, did the Italians go onto the offensive. As it was, it was actually British and French units that broke the Austro-Hungarian line, which resulted in an armistice being concluded on 3rd November 1918.

THE LESSONS OF EXPERIENCE

When Germany finally collapsed in November 1918 under the twin pressures of domestic unrest and Allied victories, Rommel was 27 years old. Within a month he had been posted back to the 124th Infantry Regiment at Weingarten, as a captain.

But what had he learnt? On a personal level, he had proved that he could lead soldiers in battle and that he enjoyed their confidence even under the most difficult conditions; indeed, he seems to have been idolised by many of his men, who recognised his qualities of courage, initiative and dedication, shown in action from Bleid to Longarone. More significantly for the future, Rommel had displayed many of the tactical attributes that were to be associated with him in later operations. His experiences in the Argonne, in Romania and on the Isonzo all led him to one thing – a belief in the power of shock action to demoralise and paralyse an enemy rather than waste time and resources on frontal, attritional attacks. If small, well-trained and disciplined teams of soldiers, under dynamic leaders, could infiltrate enemy defences, they could gain surprise and open up 'lines of least resistance' that would then be exploited using mobility and speed.

Chapter III

Inter-War Years

During 20 years of peace, Rommel pushed his military career through a succession of regular promotions and training commands, largely unaffected by the political turmoil surrounding him. For Germany, and Rommel, the inter-war period was a time of military change and experimentation, and which also saw the publication of Rommel's World War I memoirs.

When the war ended in November 1918 Germany was in chaos. Spared the disasters of the Western Front in the final months of conflict, however, Rommel himself remained both confident and professional, even though a short period on the staff of an army corps in 1918 had convinced him that paperwork and administration were not for him. He was, essentially, a fighting soldier who felt most at ease leading men into battle, so it was natural that he would wish to return to regimental duties as soon as possible.

In this, he was lucky. While many of his contemporaries were made redundant in the massive military reduction that resulted from the Allied insistence that the German Army should not exceed 100,000 men (of whom only 4000 would be officers), Rommel was allowed to continue his career. Undoubtedly his Pour le Mérite and his reputation for effective junior

Right: Freikorps armed with machine guns, rifles and swastikas rattle across Potsdamer Platz in Berlin in 1920 as revolution grips Germany during the years following the war. Although briefly involved in the suppression of insurgents, Rommel was mostly spared the political warfare of the streets.

LEFT: 'So much for Germany's disarmament' reads the contemporary caption to this 1933 press photo of the Reichswehr on manoeuvres. A machine gun unit takes up position behind advancing dummy tanks as observers look on – the humble birth of mechanised mobile warfare.

leadership helped, but his noticeable lack of political rancour – of the sort that led many other officers and ex-officers to join the Freikorps in order to fight the spread of communism – must have made him an attractive choice. On 21st December 1918, he was ordered to rejoin his old regiment, the 124th Infantry, at Weingarten, as a captain. Three months later he was sent on detachment to Friedrichshafen on Lake Constance to take charge of 32nd Internal Security Company, comprising a collection of rebellious, pro-communist sailors. Their first reaction was to jeer and refuse to obey orders, but by sheer force of personality Rommel soon restored discipline. By the spring of 1920 he was involved in 'operations against rebels in Münsterland and Westphalia', but that seems to have been the full extent of his involvement in the traumas of post-war Germany. In January 1921 he returned to Stuttgart to command a company of the 13th Infantry Regiment, his original unit having been reduced and renumbered in the process of creating the new German Army.

Rommel was to remain in this post for nine years, although there is little indication that he found the situation irksome or boring. On the contrary, he threw himself into his company with enthusiasm, concentrating on the training of his soldiers in the sort of tactical skills that he had practised during the war. He placed great emphasis on physical fitness and sport, taking part in all such activities himself in order to impress his personality on his men. He was also aware that officers in his position were vital for the future, for if the German Army was ever to be expanded, it was their efforts, and those of their NCOs, that would provide the essential link with the glories of the past as well as the professional framework around which new units could be formed. Despite his lack of political involvement, Rommel must have shared the widely held view that the German Army had not been defeated in the war, but had been 'stabbed in the back' by self-serving politicians, not just in Germany itself, but also among Allied powers intent on revenge. The Treaty of Versailles, imposed on Germany in June 1919, was seen as immoral in the sense that its terms had not been negotiated but rather dictated, so it was only going to be a matter of time before its clauses, including the one that reduced the size of the army, would be overturned.

Rommel was not an obsessive officer. He devoted a great deal of time to his family – his only son, Manfred, was born on Christmas Eve 1928 – and cultivated a number of outside interests, including skiing and motorcycle maintenance. He even found time to form an Old Comrades' Association of the Wuerttemberg Mountain Battalion, making contact with ex-comrades and helping those who were finding civilian life difficult. But he did remain fascinated by his war-time experiences, travelling to Italy with his wife in 1927 to revisit the site of his greatest achievements. He was obliged to leave Longarone when local officials, suspicious of a German officer with a camera and obvious memories of incidents they preferred to forget, queried his motives.

Even so, he remained determined to extract lessons from the mountain fighting of 1917 and it was this that led to his next appointment. On 1st October 1929, Rommel was posted to the Infantry School at Dresden as a junior instructor. He was to remain there for exactly four years, during which his lectures on small-scale operations in difficult terrain, based on his experiences in the Argonne, Romania and Italy, were among the most popular on offer. It was these lectures that were to form the basis of his book Infanterie Greift an (Infantry Attacks)*, published in 1937. Rommel, unsurprisingly, looked back to his war experiences, especially the storming of Mount Mataiur, as his finest hour and, as one of his contemporaries noted, 'You can understand Rommel only by taking his storming of Mount Mataiur into account. Basically he always stayed that lieutenant, making snap decisions and acting on the spur of the moment.' It was an astute observation.*

Success as an instructor led to promotion and battalion command. In October 1933, Rommel was ordered to take over the 3rd Battalion of the 17th Infantry Regiment, stationed at Goslar in the Harz mountains. The unit was a Jaeger ('hunter' or rifle) battalion, designed and equipped to move through forests and mountains at speed. Rommel was in his element, taking great pride in outclassing the younger officers in toughness and stamina. A story has been told of his first day in command, when his officers invited him to ascend and then ski down a nearby mountain, thinking no doubt that their middle-aged CO would have problems. Rommel responded by carrying out the exercise three times in succession; when he suggested a fourth ascent, his officers declined. Small wonder that his annual report, compiled by the commander of the 17th Infantry Regiment in September 1934, described Rommel as 'head and shoulders above the average battalion commander in every respect'. It was while at Goslar, on 30th September 1934, that Rommel first met Adolf Hitler, the new Chancellor of Germany, when his battalion provided a guard of honour. There is no

BELOW: A diminutive, helmeted Rommel (right) was part of the guard of honour when Chancellor Hitler visited Goslar in September 1934. It was the first meeting between soldier and dictator, although it is doubtful that they would have spoken much, if at all.

indication that the two men did more than acknowledge each other in a very formal way, although it would not be long before their paths crossed again.

After two years of command, Rommel was posted to Potsdam, just outside Berlin, as a senior instructor in the newly opened School of Infantry. He was no longer training officers for a small peacetime army but for a force that was in the throes of expansion, triggered by Hitler's decision in March 1935 to defy the Treaty of Versailles and reintroduce conscription. Lectures to 250 cadets at a time were not unknown, and once again Rommel's style of presentation proved popular. In September 1936, as a routine and temporary appointment, he was attached to Hitler's escort for a Nazi Party rally at Nuremberg, with responsibility for security. This may have been the time when Hitler became aware of Rommel, but it was not until 1937, when Infanterie Greift an *was published, that his fame began to spread. The book was widely acclaimed as a minor classic – 'one of the best infantry manuals ever written' – and it certainly earned its author substantial royalties. It also led to a degree of hero-worship, particularly among the young nationalist members of the Hitler Youth, to which Rommel was attached as the War Ministry's special liaison officer in early 1937.*

It was a logical but frustrating appointment that brought Rommel into confrontation with Baldur von Schirach, leader of the Hitler Youth. Rommel, under orders from the War Ministry, was determined to introduce military training, seeing the organisation as a vital proving ground for future soldiers. Von Schirach, aware that this would undermine his authority, opposed the plan and managed to secure Rommel's removal. The fact that he was sent immediately to act as temporary commandant of Hitler's headquarters, commanding the military escort that accompanied the Fuehrer into the newly recovered Sudetenland in late 1938, implied that the clash had done no harm to his career.

This was reinforced in November 1938, when Rommel – by now a full colonel – was appointed commandant of the Officer Cadet School at Wiener-Neustadt, near Vienna (Austria having been absorbed into the Reich earlier the same year). Although he threw himself into his new job with customary enthusiasm, he was given little opportunity to develop the school. Twice in March 1939 he was called upon to command Hitler's mobile headquarters, as the Fuehrer entered Prague and the port of Memel, the latter 'returned' to Germany by an intimidated government in Lithuania. Each time Rommel travelled back to Wiener-Neustadt, but it must have been apparent to him that the sands of European peace were running out. In early August he was called again to Berlin, this time to command Hitler's war headquarters for the invasion of Poland, as a major-general. His new command, although smaller than some he had had as a lieutenant, was an important one, as bodyguard to the Fuehrer and his staff. This escort was 380 strong, and included both anti-tank and anti-aircraft batteries. His star was clearly rising.

ROMMEL AND HITLER

Like many of his contemporaries, Rommel viewed Hitler as a saviour of Germany, admiring his nationalistic fervour and welcoming his emphasis on the restoration of German greatness. Although there is no evidence that Rommel supported the National Socialists as they came to political prominence in the early 1930s – he was, like most army officers, non-political at the time – he soon found himself in a unique position from which to judge their policies. His appointment to command a security detachment at the Nuremberg rally in September 1936 brought him into direct contact with the Nazi hierarchy for the first time, and his opinion seems to have been favourable, even though he viewed the SS with some suspicion. The clash with Baldur von Schirach over the military training of the Hitler Youth a year later must have led Rommel to have some reservations – the incident probably reinforced his earlier opinion that, although Hitler and his immediate entourage were to be admired, the 'hangers-on' were less impressive – but this did nothing to prevent him from accepting appointments in 1938 and 1939 that placed him close to the centre of Nazi affairs. To a large extent, this was no more than Rommel doing his duty; as an army officer he had no alternative other than resignation when called upon to command the Fuehrer's headquarters, and he had no intention of ending his career in such an unpatriotic way. But the fact remains that Rommel was close to the Nazi leaders at a critical time and made no particular moral judgement about their aggressive actions.

Chapter IV

Rommel's Ghosts

The astonishing speed of the Blitzkrieg through France in 1940 was, in German eyes, just retribution for the humiliation imposed on them at Versailles in 1919. Among the proponents of this mobile and highly mechanised warfare, such as Manstein and Guderian, was a lesser-known protégé of Hitler, General Erwin Rommel, who had just taken command of his first armoured division.

BELOW: Major-General Rommel beams at the German victory parade in Paris, June 1940. He had played a significant part in making it all possible.

Although he was not directly engaged in the fighting against Poland, it was this brief period which sparked Rommel's career for the remainder of the war. Placed in charge of Hitler's command and communications train during the campaign, the newly promoted general was in daily contact with his Fuehrer, and a clear rapport was soon established between the relatively lowly Rommel and his supreme commander, the self-described 'German Soldier Number One'.

Rommel instantly took to this physically courageous leader, whose grasp of the battlefield seemed more akin to that of the fighting soldier than the staff college lecturer. Hitler, in turn, saw a thrusting field commander unbound by the traditional stiffness of the Prussian Junker caste. In fact, class considerations may have been a consideration in Rommel's favour, in that neither man felt comfortable in the presence of the old-school German military aristocracy.

Rommel's easy relationship with the 'Austrian Corporal' was noted in certain quarters, and this ensured the upstart Rommel would forever remain outside the cherished circle of senior army figures. Rommel, soldier's soldier, apparently could not have cared less. Those early days in Poland brought him to the attention of the man who mattered, and who would seal his fate over the next four years.

In February 1940, Rommel was appointed to command the 7th Panzer Division, at that time based in Bad Godesberg. It seems very likely that Hitler had personally intervened to ensure that Rommel was given this post. The army personnel department had suggested in the previous autumn that any divisional command offered should be of a mountain division (which would maximise his World War I experience), but Rommel made it clear that he wanted to command armoured forces.

Rommel drove his new command hard, subjecting his men to extreme physical exertion. The division was moved to the Rhine, and, together with 5th Panzer, formed part of General Hoth's XV Panzer Corps. Their task was to move rapidly through the Ardennes and then cross the River Meuse north of Dinant, as part of the German plan to lure the French and British forces forward into Belgium and then trap them by a thrust across the Ardennes and into northern France.

Early in the afternoon of 9th May 1940, the code word 'Dortmund' was relayed to Rommel. The German operation to invade France, Fall Gelb *(Case Yellow), was finally under way. This meant that his men were to set off first thing the following morning, blasting a way through the Belgian defences in the Ardennes on their direct route west.*

10th May 1940

For months previously the enemy had been preparing obstacles of every description. In the front line, all the roads had been barricaded, with bridges blown and main routes blocked off by large craters. It was further defended all along with barbed wire, behind which the main positions were surrounded by minefields. In the woods, forest tracks had been blocked with tree trunks for hundreds of metres. Only a few of these defences were manned by Belgian troops. Where this was the case, enemy resistance was quickly overcome. The division was only briefly held up by these obstacles. Usually it was possible to by-pass the defences through open countryside. Where an advance proved impossible, all available troops in

BELOW: Hitler leads a gaggle of cheerful German officers from his Ju 52 aircraft after landing in Poland, his bodyguard Rommel just behind him. Despite their difference in position, both men shared similar military attitudes.

the area were quickly put to work, and the road was thus rapidly rendered passable. Only the long wooden obstacles west of Geilig and in the forest west of Mont le Ban, which were made of exceptionally hard wood, were so difficult they could only be removed with the help of our engineers.

During our first encounter with the enemy west of Mont le Ban, rapid moving fire from a few tanks sufficed to put the enemy to flight. Firing on the move with machine guns, when troops are in the immediate vicinity, especially in the woods during an encounter with the enemy, proved its worth.

Fighting in the woods near Chabrenes was relatively drawn out, until the heavy company was able to join the fray. The motorcycle battalion accompanying the armoured company was only able to contribute a few tanks to the fight. Also, the battery was not yet in action. My opinion was that all these units could have been effective if the junior officers had actually concentrated on the hardest waypoints, quickly using their strength to close off the positions. For the artillery and the tanks these positions posed little obstacle. They could operate in groups. In retrospect I have the impression that the commander, independently calling a halt to the advance, failed to realise that the division he was supporting was continuing its pursuit of the retreating Belgian border troops. In the end the motorcycle battalion succeeded by applying the necessary force.

Losses can be markedly minimised by keeping the defenders under constant and

ROMMEL AND THE NAZI PARTY

There were strong suspicions that Hitler had personally intervened to ensure that Rommel was appointed to the command of 7th Panzer Division. And there is little doubt that Rommel, although not a party member, was sympathetic to the ideals of the party. In February 1940, Karl-August Hanke, a Nazi official and an associate of Goebbels, was attached to Rommel's staff. Given the rank of lieutenant, he was welcomed by Rommel, who realised that he might not be too popular with the other officers. Rommel commented: 'I won't need to watch my tongue, but some of the others will have to be on guard.' The editor of an anti-Jewish newspaper was also sent to 7th Panzer.

On 27th May 1940, Rommel was given control of the two tank regiments of 5th Panzer Division for the advance to Lille. There was a meeting at which these units were briefed as to their objectives, at the end of which Hanke approached Rommel and announced that on the personal orders of Hitler, he was being awarded the Knights Cross. This award made Rommel the first divisional commander to be so honoured during the campaign, and also made it clear that the recipient of the honour had Hitler's personal favour.

heavy machine-gun fire from well-placed enemy positions.

Pushing through the resistance of the heavily outnumbered Belgian Chasseurs Ardennais, 7th Panzer Division was reinforced with two panzer regiments from 5th Panzer Division, and was nearing the Meuse on Sunday 12th May, putting into practice Rommel's theory of advancing and covering suspected enemy positions with an indiscriminate blanket of fire. Above all, the momentum of the advance had to be maintained.

12th May 1940

On our first encounter with French mechanised forces, the immediate opening of fire by Armoured Recce Troop Drews, and subsequently Battery 011, forced the French into headlong retreat. Time and again I have learnt that in close-quarter combat the winner is always he who manages first to envelop his enemy with fire in the shortest time while the one who waits must be the loser.

At the head of the column the motorcyclists must – as I always point out – be

LEFT: The opening round in the play for Lebensraum: Hitler takes the victory salute in Warsaw after the fall of Poland in 1939.

OPPOSITE: Anticipating another war of entrenched attrition, frozen French troops prepare for German aggression during the bitter winter of 1939-40.

ready to open fire with their machine guns the moment an enemy shot is heard.

This opening of fire must come from the leading vehicles. Even if the exact positions of the enemy are unknown, at least the general area where he is expected to be must be sprayed with fire. The following sections of the advance column must deploy instantly and back up their comrades. If this battle rule is observed in close-order battle, one can expect a marked reduction in one's own casualties. It is a fundamental error to halt and seek cover without opening fire. It is equally erroneous to hold one's fire until the enemy positions are known or until rearward sections have caught up.

The tank assault against the enemy near Haverin took a relatively long time to get under way. The landscape was not particularly suitable. Here again it proved an error to hold fire against the enemy. The losses of tanks in the encounter were relatively high. An experience gained from these immediate encounters was that, in tank warfare especially, one must concentrate fire into an area where the enemy is believed to be positioned rather than wait until he has destroyed any of your own tanks – especially in woodland, where spraying fire at enemy positions with machine guns and 20mm mortars is usually so effective that the enemy is in most cases unable to get his own machine guns or anti-tank guns into operation, and usually has to give himself up. Also, in battles against various tanks, often more heavily armoured than German ones, early opening fire has proved effective.

When the leading units of 7th Panzer, armoured cars and motorcyclists, arrived at the Meuse, the bridges had all been blown. The motorcyclists, however, found that an island just north of Dinant had been abandoned. Once on the island, they found that a lock gate gave them access to the far side, and were able to reach the far bank with some infantrymen. But getting more forces across proved difficult. The Belgian and French forces were well dug in, and made it impossible to send boats across the river. How was an armoured division to cross?

13th May 1940

The battle for the River Meuse on 13th May was extraordinarily difficult. The time allocated for planning the assault on the Meuse was too little. As it was, the troops had had no sleep at all since 9th May. Moreover, the division was without support units, without heavy artillery (at least nothing nearby) and had no reconnaissance units for the operation. On the steep west bank of the Meuse, the enemy had numerous carefully placed machine-gun and anti-tank nests as well as observation points, each one of which would have to be taken on in the fight. They also had both light and heavy artillery, accurate and mobile.

The enemy inflicted heavy casualties on the division on 13th May. Also, the supply situation made it exceptionally hard to reach the enemy on the west bank of the Meuse.

Rommel was constantly in the front line during the attempt to cross the Meuse, even being bombed by the Luftwaffe at one point. Investigating the situation both north and south of Dinant, he instructed his tanks to drive northwards from the town, firing across the river. When he reached the northern crossing point, he personally went over in a rubber boat under the tanks' covering fire. Under his inspired leadership, the small bridgehead began to expand, and further north still German engineers rigged up a bridge. Eventually, vehicles began to cross the river, and on 14th May, Rommel raced forward with the 25th Panzer Regiment under Colonel Rothenburg to help in an attack on the woodland north of Onhaye, the first town across the Meuse on his axis of advance west.

14th May 1940

French artillery now opened fire on the wood, and we expected their shells to find us at any moment, since our tank was clearly visible. I decided to abandon it as fast as possible, with the crew. Just then the officer commanding the tank-escort infantry reported a serious injury, with the words '...my left arm has been shot away'. We scrabbled up a sandy ditch, with

ROMMEL'S LEADERSHIP

After the successful bridging of the Meuse, and the advance on the town of Onhaye, a Lieutenant Richter in Rommel's division submitted the following combat report. It shows Rommel firmly at the head of his men, leading from the front with customary vigour. His command vehicle was a specially adapted Panzer III, although he also made use of Colonel Rothenburg's Panzer IV command vehicle. At other times he flew over the battlefield in a Storch light observation aircraft, landing among the leading tanks.

'At 16.00hrs on 13.5.40 I was wounded by a shell splinter on the east bank of the Meuse. About 17.00hrs the company set off under the personal orders of the divisional commander. The general was with the company. [The division had reached the Meuse on 12th May and assault troops had forced a crossing early the next day. However, they had taken heavy casualties, and Rommel crossed the river to be with them and sustain their morale, oblivious to the dangers of enemy small-arms fire. At this time he was hoarse from shouting orders.] The company occupied an abandoned section along the riverbank from a ruined chateau to a point about 400m (1320ft) north.

'At 19.00hrs the regimental commander personally gave the order to begin the attack on Onhaye. At 19.30hrs a tank battle broke out against the French from Somière which lasted until 20.30hrs. Meanwhile it had grown dark. The battalion was to assault Onhaye directly, with 7th and 5th Companies, 7th Company to the right rear and 5th Company to the left adjoining 1st Battalion. 5th Company reached a point 1200m (3960ft) east of Chestruvin. There they broke through the enemy defence line.

'7th Company and 1st Battalion came under machine-gun and rifle fire from positions 1.5km (one mile) behind 5th Company. There it was reported to me that 5th Company had run out of ammunition, and I decided to join up with the regiment, sending 6th and 5th Companies to the Chateau de Mees.

'There I found the regimental commander...who gave the order to advance on Onhaye along the main road.

'It was about 03.30hrs and light was just beginning to break. Before the company had advanced more than 150m (495ft) along the main road, it came under enemy armoured vehicle fire from right, left and in front. One armoured car had even managed to sneak round behind the company. It was repelled by anti-tank guns that had meanwhile been brought up. The company could only advance with anti-tank support, and reached a point some 200m (660ft) in front of Onhaye. Under well-directed enemy shell and machine-gun fire, and without support of heavy weapons, in the growing daylight the company could advance no further.

'Around 14.00hrs the company received instructions to storm and take Onhaye with the tanks which had meanwhile come up. The assault was delayed until 17.30hrs, as our tanks around Haute-Cornue came up against enemy tanks and these had first to be dealt with. At 17.30hrs, the tanks rolled on, and the company plus three platoons marched on Onhaye and took the town. At 18.23hrs I reported to battalion command that the town had been secured.'

artillery shells landing and shrapnel flying all around us. Just in front Rothenburg's tank was clanking along with flames at the back. The Panzer Regiment adjutant had abandoned his tank as well. At first I thought the leading tank had been hit by a shell in the fuel tank, but it transpired the smoke was from smoke canisters which had caught fire, and the smoke was now to our advantage. Meanwhile Most had driven my communications vehicle into the wood where it received a hit and was put out of action. The crew escaped unharmed.

I then gave the order for a tank advance through the wood towards the east. The armoured cars under my command were of course not able to follow. Rothenburg slowly forced his way through the trees which were often large and mature. The unintended smokescreen put down by the tank was the only thing preventing the enemy from taking out any more of our vehicles. If the tanks had sprayed the wood with 37mm and machine-gun fire where the enemy were believed to be during the advance, the French would probably have abandoned their guns positioned at the edge of the wood, and our casualties would have been less. An assault launched in the evening by 25 Panzer Regiment was successful, and we reached our designated area.

Only by staying mobile with his communications troop and keeping in direct contact with the regimental commanders in the front line was the divisional commander able to maintain a firm control over the fighting west of the Meuse. Radio by itself, due to the need to code and decode, would have taken far too long to get reports back to HQ and

BELOW: Rommel and his staff look confidently across to the enemy-held bank, as troops prepare to cross the Meuse in May 1940.

then to issue orders. Radio contact was continuously maintained with the operational staff at Divisional HQ in the rear, and a detailed discussion took place every morning and afternoon between the divisional commander and his number two. This command system was proving entirely successful.

Having crossed the Meuse, pushed forward and prevented any French counterattacks, Rommel now found the physical going for his tanks easier. The countryside was less rugged than it had been in the Ardennes, and roads were not so essential. The advance now careered towards fortifications that were an extension of the Maginot Line, but Rommel did not consider halting, and his tanks were able to move through during the night of 16th/17th May.

By this time, unknown to Rommel, the enemy had already been ordered to start pulling back on surrounding fronts. Holland had capitulated on 15th May, while the next day saw the general retreat of all forces, including the BEF, from Belgium. General Heinz Guderian, who had broken through at Sedan, was being ordered to halt temporarily.

17th May 1940

The way to the west was now open. I gave the order for the leading formation to begin the assault on Avesnes forthwith. The leading squadrons and the artillery were speedily instructed by radio, and then it was high time to climb into the command car of the Panzer Regiment staff and get going. We were soon rolling along in the bouncy 'steel-hedgehog' behind the leading armoured company towards the enemy.

The moon shone from the heavens, and we could not count on darkness in the foreseeable future. For the planned breakthrough, I had already ordered the Panzer Regiment thus: saturate the land right and left of the road on the advance to Avesnes with machine-gun and 20mm and 37mm mortar fire every now and then, to deter

BELOW: German armour rolls on towards Landrecies past carefree French prisoners.

the enemy from laying mines. The remaining part of Panzer Regiment 25 was to follow close behind the spearhead, ready at any moment, on the command of the regiment or section commanders, to provide flanking fire from half-left or right, or fully left and right.

The mass of the division had been ordered to follow Panzer Regiment 25, first the motorcycle battalion and Armoured Recce Squadron 37, then Artillery Section Graseman, followed by the remaining rifle brigades, artillery and anti-aircraft batteries. (In fact this order only reached a few sections of the division, since the command squadron had by this time, about 22.45hrs, lost all radio contact with me, which I didn't myself realise.)

The tanks rolled in a long column through the fortified positions and past the first group of burning houses set alight by our leading elements. To the side one could see Motorcycle Battalion 7 advancing through the moonlight. Here and there an enemy machine gun or anti-tank gun fired, but their rounds came nowhere near us. Our own artillery was directing heavy disruptive fire on the villages and roads well ahead of Panzer Regiment 25, as the speed grew and grew. Soon we had broken through 500m (1650ft), 1000m (3300ft) and 3km (two miles) into the defences, engines roaring, tanks clanking. If the enemy fired it was impossible to tell in the noise. We crossed over a railway line, 2km (1.2 miles) southwest of Solre le Château, after which we swung north towards the main road going from Solre le Château to Avesnes. We soon reached it. Now and then one could hear the spearhead tanks firing as ordered.

We passed groups of houses on the road...The inhabitants were frightened by the tremendous noise of the tanks, the

BELOW: The 7th Panzer Division's route to the port of Cherbourg in 1940.

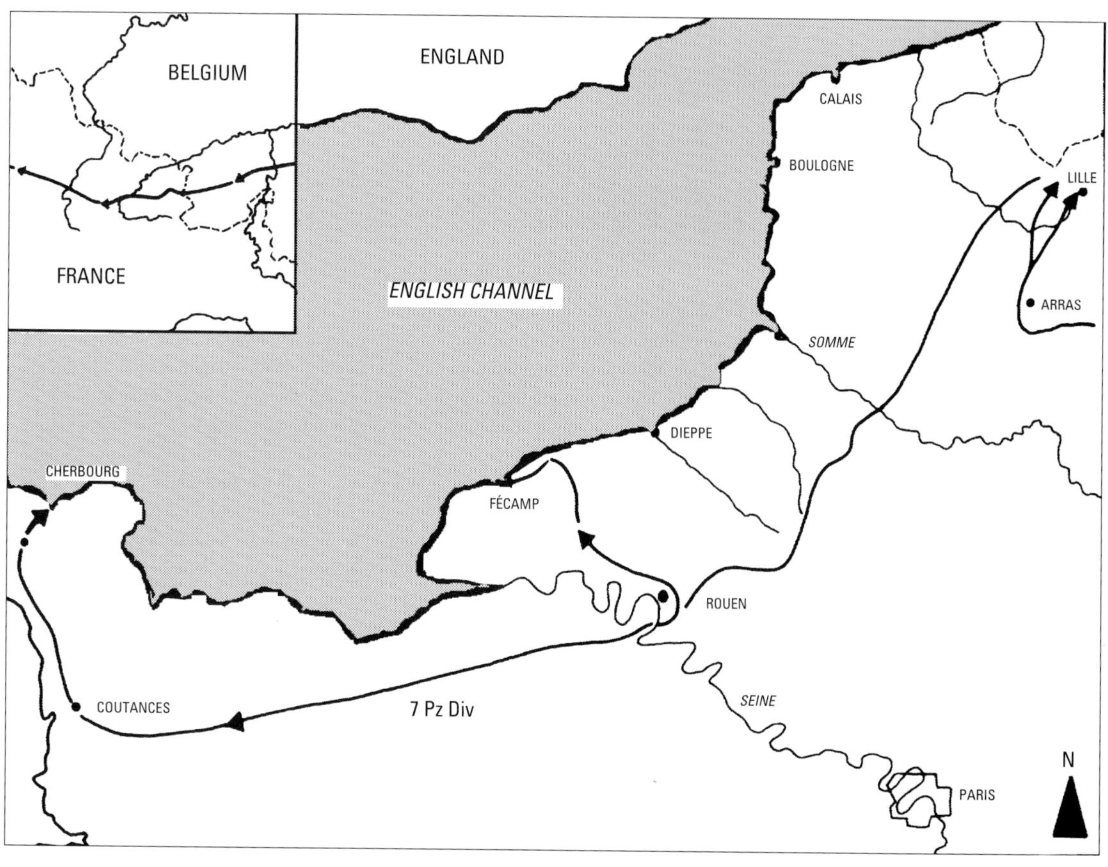

RIGHT: German troops stream west across old battlefields in the wake of Rommel's 25th Panzer Regiment as it heads for the Somme, June 1940.

clatter of tracks and engines. Enemy military vehicles stood in farmyards and sometimes on the road. Terrified-looking civilians and French soldiers lay in the hedges, ditches and hollows beside the road. We overtook refugee columns. The people had abandoned their vehicles in terror and fled inland. We continued towards our goal at an unbroken pace. Now and then a glance at the map by shaded light, and a short radio call to report the current position and the concurrent success of the 25th Panzer Regiment. Head out of the turret from time to time, to listen out for any enemy activity in the night and to ensure the rearguard were keeping up with us.

The flat landscape lay in the pale moonlight. Maginot Line breached! One could scarcely believe it. Four and a half years we had stood here, 22 years ago, facing the same enemy, winning many victories yet finally losing the war. Now we had broken through the notorious Maginot Line, advancing deep into enemy country. Not just a dream, but reality!

Farther on we crossed a range of hills. Suddenly there was a flash from an earth mound 100m (330ft) to the right of the road. No doubt a well-concealed gun-emplacement in a concrete bunker that was now firing on the panzer regiment's flanks. One could also see muzzle flashes coming from other enemy positions. Incoming hits could not be seen. I quickly informed Colonel Rothenburg who was standing next to me in the tank of the danger, and through him ordered the panzer regiment to break through this second defence line with broadsides left

ground, with farmyards brim full with guns, tanks, mini-tanks and various military vehicles. We made our way but slowly towards Avesnes. Finally the firing died down. We drove through Semousies. Right and left, always the same picture: soldiers and civilians in wild flight across the land and down the road.

Now the main road forked, the right going to Maubeuge just 15km (eight miles) away, the left down the valley towards Avesnes. The roads were by now strewn with vehicles and people, whom we directed to get out of the way of our tanks. The closer we got to Avesnes, the tighter the jam of vehicles we had to struggle through. In Avesnes itself, which had been barraged by the artillery shortly before, the entire population was on the run, squeezed between vehicles and guns to right and left of the tank column. Clearly, there had been a sizeable French military presence in Avesnes. I decided not to halt here, but to carry on with the leading tank unit to the high ground west of Avesnes, there to stop and collect prisoners and booty together. I sent a couple of recce tanks deployed in the southern part of

and right, and thus maintain our impetus. Firing commenced quickly as ordered, the crews having been instructed in this form of gunnery before the operation. The majority of the ammunition was tracer, and panzer regiment unleashed an immense torrent of fire to both sides of the defended zone deep into enemy territory.

Soon we had crossed the danger zone, without incurring heavy casualties from the enemy fire. However, it wasn't easy to stop the shooting. We drove on firing through the villages of Poteries and Beugnies. Enemy confusion was boundless. Enemy vehicles, tanks and equipment, plus piled-up refugee carts, were blocking part of the road, and had to be brutally shoved aside. Everywhere there were French soldiers lying flat on the

TECHNOLOGY IN 1940

The astounding successes of Rommel (and other German tank commanders, such as Guderian) in 1940 were due to a concept of warfare rather than any technical superiority. The best Allied tanks were the French Char B (with one 47mm gun, a 75mm howitzer and 60mm of frontal armour, top speed 30km/hr), the French SOMUA S35 (one 47mm gun, and 55mm of frontal armour, top speed 40km/hr) and the British Matilda II (one 40mm gun, 78mm of frontal armour, top speed 24km/hr).

Opposed to these as machines capable of sustaining a tank-versus-tank combat were the German PzKw IIIE (one 50mm gun, frontal armour 30mm, top speed 40km/hr), the PzKw IV (one 75mm howitzer, frontal armour 30mm, top speed 40km/hr), and a number of captured Czech-built 38t models (one 37mm gun, 25mm frontal armour, top speed 40km/hr). Nor were numbers radically different: there were some 500 SOMUAs, 320 Char Bs and just under 50 Matilda IIs against 350 PzKw IIIs, 280 PzKw IVs and 228 PzKw 38ts for the campaign in the West.

Avesnes down the main road to the south, while we stopped about 500m (1650ft) outside Avesnes on the road to Landrecies, to re-group the units and round up the French soldiers in the neighbourhood. Here, too, the farmyards and orchards along the road were filled with refugee vehicles and troops. Whatever came to us down the road from the west was taken. A prisoner-of-war compound was quickly thrown up in the open fields.

Meanwhile, the first sounds of firing had opened up behind us in Avesnes, most likely from tanks. Soon flames were leaping up into the sky, presumably from burning houses or vehicles. Contact with the following Ilgen Detachment and Motorcycle Battalion 7 had been lost. This did not unduly concern me, as it was easy to get held up in the tumult of unmanned carts careering around the road. We had reached our target and that was the main thing! However, the enemy – about a battalion of tanks – made good use of the dislocation between the 25th Panzer Regiment. Heavy French tanks soon cut off the road in Avesnes. Immediately, the II/25th Panzer Regiment tried to tackle the French but failed, losing some tanks, including some heavy Panzer IVs. The fighting in Avesnes grew yet more intense. Intermittent radio contact was established between the regiment and Ilgen Detachment, but the orders to advance and fight to free the road and to send the 7th Motorcycle Battalion ahead were not received. Likewise, contact with divisional command was not continuous. Most messages had to be transmitted blind. It was now about 01.00hrs. The 7th Motorcycle Battalion sent the following garbled message, among others, to divisional HQ: '7th Motorcycle Battalion with tanks front line burning town' – meaning that the 7th Motorcycle Battalion, which is with the panzer regiment, is in the front line at the burning town of Avesnes. That was the only light thrown on the situation. The

Below: A Fieseler Storch reconnaissance aircraft flies low over a column of tanks preparing to move out from cover before crossing the Somme, June 1940.

first HQ knew that it was in Avesnes came through a front-line report at 03.17hrs. For the most part, the radio messages sent by me from the panzer regiment were apparently not received at divisional command. The battle with enemy tanks in Avesnes lasted until 04.00hrs. In the end, on my orders, Lieutenant Hanke advanced from the west with a Panzer IV towards the powerful enemy force, to deal with these heavy French tanks. Meanwhile I myself took a Panzer III and fired a large quantity of anti-armour shells at the house rows, behind which, it had been reported, were the enemy tanks.

Meanwhile, I had been pressing on the radio net that command should let us push on to the Sambre in view of our success in crossing the Maginot Line. I waited in vain for a reply. Despite getting back no response (radio contact had not been established), I decided after discussion with the panzer regiment's commander, Colonel Rothenburg, to resume the battle first thing the next morning, with the objective of seizing the Sambre crossing at Landrecies, and holding it open. I issued radioed orders to all the other units to follow up the panzer regiment's attack on Landrecies. The leading squadron of the Rothenburg Regiment, which incorporated both divisional and regimental commands, began its advance on Landrecies through Marbaix and Maroilles. The 7th Motorcycle Battalion had caught up and followed on.

It was my fervent belief that behind this battalion were also the remaining sections of the division, especially Panzer Detachment Ilgen, and that these would join the battle. I had been unable to determine the exact position of the regiment, however, due to the poor radio link.

Whether Rommel really believed that the rest of his division was following hard on his heels is a moot point. There is little doubt that he was determined to be in the van of the German advance, however, and that he believed utterly in the value of carrying on his drive deep behind French lines to achieve ultimate success. He would be proved right.

The readiness of German field commanders – and their superiors – to accept and act on the theories of mechanised warfare largely put forward by British observers such as Fuller and Liddell Hart before the war, and ignored by the '14-18 brigade', was proving its worth now. Although the risk of a headlong assault being cut off along its extended flanks remained, the reality of a totally confused, overwhelmed and demoralised enemy was to a large extent proof of the validity of the new theories.

17th May 1940

Without firing – we had to be sparing with ammunition since no supplies had come up during the night – we advanced through the growing light of the day towards the west. Soon we came across refugee columns and French troops preparing to march, as we passed the first farmsteads outside Marbaix and carried on into it. Guns, tanks and vehicles of every description, mingled with refugee carts piled high with every possible household article, thronged on and near the road. By not firing, and by driving our all-terrain vehicles sometimes just off the road, we passed these columns relatively smoothly. The French troops, wholly surprised by our sudden appearance, laid down their arms and marched off, on our orders, to our rear. At no point did we encounter any resistance. Enemy tanks, which we encountered on the road, were put out of action. Unhindered, the march pressed on westwards down the road. Hundreds upon hundreds of French soldiers and their officers surrendered at our approach. Sometimes they had to be got out of vehicles driving alongside us.

Particularly angry at this sudden disturbance was a French lieutenant-colonel, whose vehicle was caught in the jam, and whom we overtook. I asked him his rank and position. He gave the impression of being one of these very fanatical officer types. His eyes glowed with hatred and impotent fury. In consideration of the possibility that our column would get split up in the traffic, I decided it best to take him along with us. He was already 50m (165ft) to the east when he was brought

BELOW RIGHT: Rommel and his tank commanders hold an impromptu briefing in a field. All too often these were impossible, since the commander himself had already disappeared ahead with his leading columns, leaving his subordinates to use their own initiative.

back to Colonel Rothenburg's command tank, who motioned him to climb up. The French officer bluntly refused to come along, and there was nothing for it but to shoot him after three times ordering him to get up.

We drove through Maroilles. The market square and the streets were awash with troops and refugees. It was very difficult to get across our shouts of 'à droite' (move to the right). In a light morning mist, with the rising sun behind us, the tank column rolled on towards the west. Once again the roads outside the villages were filled with troops, vehicles and refugees. One could only get one's tanks past slowly, using the fields alongside the road. We reached Landrecies, the town on the Sambre. Here again, vehicle after vehicle, French soldiers in every alley. No resistance. We rolled over the Sambre bridge, on the far side of which we found a French barracks full of soldiers. While the tank column rattled by, Lieutenant Hanke drove to the yard and ordered the French to muster the troops, collect together their weapons, and march off towards the east.

It was still my belief that the whole of the division was rapidly advancing on Landrecies, and I ordered the march onwards towards Le Cateau. We came across a long wood, in which there was a large munitions depot. With the sun in their eyes, the sentries didn't recognise us until the last moment and gave themselves

up. Pommereuil was also full of troops who laid down their arms and set off back eastwards. Not until the hill east of Le Cateau did we halt the advance. It was 06.15hrs. First of all I wanted to confirm that contact with the following troops was established, before making a final attempt to get in touch with headquarters.

Having got to within sight of Le Cateau, Rommel told the senior officers with him that their line of advance was now to the Channel – along the line Le Cateau, Arras, Amiens, Rouen, Le Havre. This particularly astonished the tank commanders, who were almost out of fuel. The rest of his division, far from following hard on his heels, was back in Belgium, and his chief staff officer had decided that Rommel and Rothenburg were probably lost. They almost were – because, having halted, the French attacked them and almost cut them off. But support did arrive, and the advance could begin again. The aim was for Rommel's division to drive south of Arras to cut off Allied formations in Belgium. At Arras, 7th Panzer experienced the severest resistance of the campaign, as British armoured forces equipped with heavily protected Matilda tanks struck south, to avoid being isolated.

ORGANISATION OF 7TH PZ DIV.

Rommel's 7th Panzer Division was a converted 'light' division – that is, it had been intended as a mechanised support division before conversion. It was still light on tanks, having only one tank regiment (25th Panzer Regiment) rather than the two that the other panzer divisions possessed. Its three tank battalions possessed 218 tanks, but of these half were the lightly built Czech models.

The panzer regiment was, however, led by an extremely able commander, Colonel Karl Rothenburg. Like Rommel himself, he had won the Pour le Mérite in World War I, as a company commander in 1918. He was personally fearless and had absorbed totally the fluid rhythm that the tank brought to the battlefield. He died in 1941 on the Eastern Front.

Apart from the Panzer regiment, 7th Panzer Division consisted of two motorised infantry regiments, each of three battalions, an armoured reconnaissance battalion, an engineer battalion, a field artillery regiment with 36 guns and an anti-tank battalion with 75 anti-tank guns, mainly the standard 37mm model.

21st May 1940

Meanwhile, violent and costly fighting was under way in the Tilloy-Beaurains-Agny area. A powerful enemy armoured formation had thrust out from Arras, attacking 1st Battalion, 6th Rifle Regiment, causing heavy losses in men and materiel. The anti-tank guns we quickly brought up turned out to be ineffective against the heavily armoured English tanks, and most were put out of action along with their crews by gunfire, and quickly overrun by the tanks. Many of our vehicles were ablaze. SS forces to the south were also pushed back by the force of the tank attack. In the end, divisional

Right: An advance column from the 7th Panzer Division stops to examine an abandoned French SOMUA 35 tank for possible booby-traps.

artillery and 88mm anti-aircraft guns were successful in bringing the enemy to a stop south of the Beaurains-Agny line. Twenty-eight enemy tanks were destroyed by the artillery itself; the anti-aircraft guns took out one heavy tank and seven light.

While this heavy battle raged about the 6th and 7th Rifles, Rothenburg with his 25th Panzer had reached his objective in a rapid advance, but waited vainly there for the reconnaissance battalion and the rifle regiments to arrive. About 19.00hrs, I issued an order for the panzer regiment to push to the south, to catch enemy tanks moving south from Arras in the flanks and rear. In this operation, the panzer regiment encountered a superior enemy force south of Agnez, comprising heavy and light tanks supported by many artillery pieces. A fierce fight soon ensued, tank against tank, in an exceptionally hard engagement in which the panzer regiment destroyed seven heavy tanks and six anti-tank guns and spectacularly broke through the enemy line, at a cost of three Panzer IVs, six Panzer IIIs and a number of light tanks.

The enemy were put in such confusion by this skirmish that despite superior numbers, they retreated to Arras. By night the fighting had died down. Meanwhile, the situation northwest of Wailly had been recovered.

The Allied counter-attack had fizzled out by 24th May, but Hitler ordered his eager panzer units to halt – probably swayed by advice that as the Allied forces in Belgium were effectively cut off, the armoured forces should be husbanded in case a sudden drive south were needed. 26th May was a good day for Rommel: he was formally decorated with the Knights Cross of the Iron Cross, and Hitler lifted the halt order. Calais had surrendered, and Operation Dynamo, the plan to evacuate the British Expeditionary Force from the beaches at Dunkirk, was put in hand.

Instead of driving due west, however, 7th Panzer was to push north towards Lille, as part of a plan to envelop Allied forces in Belgium and northern France. Rommel now began to push forces across the next obstacle facing him, the La Bassée canal. A small bridgehead was established, but not until he got some of his tanks across could he make good progress. His division was now reinforced by a tank brigade (Panzer Brigade Harde) from his neighbouring formation, 5th Panzer Division.

27th May

Meanwhile, the 25th Panzer Regiment had made a long sortie ahead and reached the neighbourhood of Lorgies. In this advance, the regiment had encountered heavy and costly fighting against a heavily defended front, which they eventually succeeded in breaking through. Enemy guns which had until then been raining shells on our bridgehead now hastily withdrew in the face of oncoming German tanks. The panzer regiment continued, its gunnery smashing a visible breach in the enemy front line, through which the division reinforced by Panzer Brigade Harde then moved. As the tanks fought across the country, the advance was slow enough for the infantry to follow in loose formation across a wide stretch. Soon Panzer Regiment Werner drew level on our right with other 5th Panzer Brigade elements following up. I was deeply impressed by the number of top-rate tanks the 5th Panzer Brigade had – far more than the tank complement of my division.

Dusk was already well established as I reached a barnyard 1km (0.6 miles) east of Fournes and caught up with Rothenburg's command vehicle on the Lille road. Fighting in Fournes seemed to have stopped. About 1km (0.6 miles) to the east, lead elements of 5th Panzer could be seen regrouping. Despite nightfall I now ordered the 25th Panzer Regiment to continue their assault and shut off the western exit from Lille and the Armentières road. The regiment was to form a 'hedgehog' near Lomme and wait until I could send reinforcements.

Rothenburg asked if I would accompany the attack personally, but I was forced to refuse because it was difficult enough at this time managing the division. Radio was useless again and it appeared more

BELOW: Resting troops look on as a requisitioned Czech PzKw 38t rolls across a pontoon bridge over one of the canals in northern France. The barge was probably sunk to block the waterway. Blown bridges and sunken barges, however, failed to impede the German advance.

important that I position my force around our ultimate goal at Lomme, and ensure personally if necessary that this was actually done. I also had to make certain that substantial reinforcements for 25th Panzer arrived by first light, and make certain they had an ample supply of ammunition and petrol, which was not a light task. I wanted above all to be sure that the regiment did not find itself in the same unfortunate situation it had faced outside Le Cateau. [Halted outside Le Cateau on 18th May, and with divisional support lacking, Rothenburg's men had almost been cut off by a determined French counter-attack.]

Since radio contact with General Harde had proved impossible, I attempted to pass orders to him through the divisional staff to advance immediately to Englos following the 25th Panzer Regiment. But I was not able to move the main bulk of the brigade, and the assault on Englos had to go ahead with only a company initially, followed later by a battalion. Unfortunately I was unable to drive across the country myself under cover of darkness to deliver the orders personally, as my battle staff was not properly equipped with cross-country vehicles. Anyway, it would have meant risking the danger of being mistaken for a British recce vehicle, and being fired on by one of 5th Panzer's tank detachments which were scattered around the countryside.

Rommel's division was instrumental in the capture of Lille and the surrender of a large part of the French First Army. It now enjoyed a few days' rest, and Rommel himself had time to attend a conference of senior officers with Hitler at Charleville. The Allies had completed their evacuation of Dunkirk on 4th June, and the Battle of France was to begin in earnest. Then 7th Panzer moved south. Hoth's panzer corps was directed to attack across the Somme, carrying the offensive deep into France. On 5th June, the first of Rommel's units crossed the Somme, to find French positions that were organised in depth and difficult to crack. The French now expected deep tank thrusts, but Rommel employed a new tactical formation: what he described as 'area march' (Flaechenmarsch), in which the whole division advanced in a huge box formation, over 1.5km (one mile) wide and over 20km (12 miles) deep. The advantage was that all-arms support was always available when resistance was met.

7th June 1940

The tanks moved out. Following some initial delays caused by mistakes in our map-reading, the panzer regiment's attack carried smoothly on. The advance continued directly across country over trackless fields, up and down hills, through hedges, fences and tall cornfields. The route taken by the tanks was picked so that vehicles of the 37th Reconnaissance Battalion and 6th Rifle Regiment, which were less capable of cross-country travel, could follow in their track furrows.

We encountered no enemy troops, apart from stragglers, but much to indicate, by way of abandoned vehicles and horses in the open fields, that they had fled shortly before we arrived. Four French soldiers were taken near Feuquières. One of them, despite severe wounds, continued to fire at us until the last moment. Fleeing civilians

BRAVERY ON THE BATTLEFIELD

Not only was Rommel always near the front; he was also often directly in the line of fire. He displayed a personal bravery that had great influence on his troops, but which put both himself and his staff at great risk. During the desperate search to find a way across the Meuse on 13th May, for example, his aide de camp, Major Schraepler, was wounded as they drove through heavy fire. Rommel then crossed the river in a rubber dinghy, again under French small-arms fire.

Once across the Meuse, the action did not cease. On 14th May, during the action near the village of Onhaye, Rommel's tank was hit and immobilised by anti-tank gunfire, and he had to scramble clear.

Major Schraepler's arm was better by 22nd May – and he rejoined Rommel because his replacement had been killed at the divisional commander's side during the fighting near Arras. The British counter-attack of 21st May had seen Rommel at his most dynamic, as he urged his anti-tank gunners to fire at maximum range to break up attacks by the heavily armoured British Matilda II tanks.

and soldiers were on all roads. Sometimes we came across surprised refugee vehicles in open country whose occupants – men, women and children – cowered underneath them. We passed them shouting at them to go home.

East of Villers, two enemy infantry guns and a light tank fired on us. They were quickly dealt with. Their crews, at least the survivors, ran for the woods.

The Somme having been crossed successfully by the Germans, the next target was the bridges over the River Seine.

8th June 1940

Now the main bulk of the division received deployed forward and brought into action in the open. A motorcycle company arrived, and anti-aircraft guns got into position. The roads were cleared, and our vehicles took cover along a railway embankment. Meanwhile, I recce'd the possibilities for getting tanks across the river, and found a place 400m (1320ft) south of Sigy where it could be crossed.

Although the water was more than a metre deep near the eastern bank, the first tanks got over without difficulty and soon overtook the infantry. However, when the first Panzer II tank tried, its engine conked out midstream, blocking the crossing to any other vehicles. Meanwhile, a number of British soldiers had waded

ABOVE: Tanks of the 7th Panzer Division roll down towards the Somme, hatches open and apparently untroubled by enemy action.

orders to move out, and it proceeded apace until Sigy, where the panzer company, which had in the meantime assumed the lead, encountered enemy fire, to which it responded immediately in force.

During this short action, the enemy mined the bridge over the Andelle. We were watching the whole engagement from a few hundred metres off. The howitzer battery situated just behind us was rapidly across to us with their hands up, and they helped our motorcyclists to make the crossing workable. Sections of a demolished railway bridge nearby were hurled into the deepest part of the river. Willow trees along the riverbank were cut down to make the crossing easier. A Panzer III which had crossed before was brought back to tow the stalled Panzer II clear.

At that point I received a radio message announcing that Lieutenant Sauvant's reconnaissance section had succeeded in preventing enemy attempts to blow the road and rail bridges at Normanville. Sauvant had both bridges securely in his control, and had created a bridgehead across the river.

With this good news, I immediately ceased action at Sigy and switched all forces south at top speed to cross the Andelle at Normanville. The divisional assault group crossed the bridge and continued advancing west. Sigy was taken from the west at 14.00hrs, with 100 British prisoners.

The route we took now by-passed all towns wherever possible. Good results had been achieved in the preceding few days by attacking away from the roads. The 25th Panzer Regiment's attack started on time. At first we found no enemy troops in the hamlets through which we drove. After some time we suddenly discovered that enemy despatch riders and cars were travelling in our tank column. Here and there a single shot rang out.

Towards 20.00hrs, a company of the panzer regiment was sent along the Rouen road to capture a crossroads 8km (five miles) east of the town, to provide protection for the artillery and anti-aircraft batteries that were to be deployed there. It was my intention to confuse and alarm the enemy by firing a long-range barrage, hiding my true plans to take the Seine bridges at Elbeuf later in the evening. The panzer company arrived at the crossroads by 20.00hrs, but was not as far forward as I wanted, since the rearguard had appar-

RIGHT: Victor and vanquished... Rommel stands proudly contemplating the fortunes of war after the fierce battle for St Valéry-en-Caux, 12th June 1940. High-ranking British captives include Major-General Victor Fortune and his staff, who glare balefully at the German press corps.

ently become involved in fighting around Martainville, and we could not get a rapid deployment of artillery and anti-aircraft batteries around the position as a result.

In Elbeuf, there was total chaos among our vehicles in the narrow streets north of the Seine, and I had to go forward on foot to reach the head of Motorcycle Battalion 7. I found there that the assault teams had not yet made any attempt at the crossing, although they had been in position over an hour. I was told that when the battalion entered Elbeuf, they had found a busy traffic of civil and military vehicles using the bridge. An officer also reported shooting near the bridges.

The situation was uncertain, and the likelihood of success was getting slimmer since the battalion had been standing in the town for a whole hour just a few hundred metres from the bridges. There might still be a chance, though, I thought. I ordered the battalion commander to commence the assault on the two bridges forthwith. Under cover of darkness, I crept closer to the bridge. Civilians were standing about in the street, and a dead French soldier lay across one of the sandbagged barricades at the crossroads. Valuable time was still being lost as the storming party regrouped. At last they moved out – it was just before 03.00hrs. They never reached the bridge, however, since the enemy blew it up before they had advanced 100m (330ft). The same happened again with the second storming party. Further heavy explosions came from west and east, from far and near. The French were blowing all the Seine bridges.

I was exceptionally angry at the failure of our enterprising operation. I had no knowledge of the whereabouts of the bulk of the division. We had left behind us numerous enemy-held towns that we passed in the night, and at first light we saw two observation balloons in the sky over Rouen. It would appear we were going to have a fight on our hands. I therefore decided to pull out of the stretched position we had advanced into. The troops moved out at speed. Fortunately, the Seine basin lay shrouded in mist and we had no fear of enemy fire from the far bank.

The bridges across the Seine may have eluded Rommel, but the Allies were thoroughly defeated, and looking for a route to escape. With Dunkirk fresh in their minds, the German High Command ordered Rommel to make for the coast, to prevent ports such as Le Havre being used for evacuation. Riding with Röthenburg's 25th Panzer Regiment, Rommel reached the sea at the village of Dalles.

10th June 1940

The sight of the sea with cliffs either side was a thrill and a spur to each one of us; as was the thought that we had reached the French coast. We dismounted from

Above: Still waving white flags of surrender, a ragged assortment of French and British troops are led away from the French coast, 10th June 1940 – the end of the road for friend and foe alike.

our vehicles and walked down the shingle beach to the water's edge, and let it lap against our boots. Some despatch riders in long waterproofs waded out to their knees, until I had to call them back. Close behind, Rothenburg came up in his command tank and ploughed through the beach wall, driving on down to the water. Our work was done. The enemy's route to Le Havre and Fécamp was shut.

Rommel's Panzers moved past Fécamp and then headed for St Valéry, and met resistance en route.

10th June 1940

We started out on the return journey at 23.00hrs. With the road still solidly blocked by the motorcycle battalion, only the 1st Panzer Company could leave with us. We drove behind the third tank. En route we passed numerous enemy vehicles, which apparently had been driven into the motorcycle battalion column in the darkness, their crews taken prisoner. Some of them looked as if they had first of all put up a fight. Suddenly there was anti-tank fire coming from a village ahead, hitting a lead tank in the track. The enemy gunners then rapid-fired along the road just over our heads. Without returning fire, the tanks ahead of us drove straight up onto the embankment on either side of the road. The lead tank remained where it had been hit. My vehicle was now left standing just 150m (395ft) away from the enemy battery, with shell after shell whistling a hairsbreadth overhead, not a comfortable situation. After two or three minutes like this our tanks still hadn't opened fire, so I jumped down from my vehicle and hurried over to the tank up on the left embankment, where I also found the commander of the stranded tank. I gave him a piece of my mind for failing to open fire and for leaving his tank. I then ordered the Panzer II tank commander to open fire immediately with gun and machine gun, so that the column could have a chance of getting away through a cutting to the left of the road we were now in. When the

Panzer II tank finally did open fire, its 20mm shells and tracer caused such a fireworks display that the enemy ceased firing as I had anticipated. We were then able to get my command vehicle up the embankment, but it was too steep for the staff car, armoured cars and dispatch riders, so I sent these back to spend the night with the motorcycle battalion.

Then we drove off with panzer company. It was not an easy task in the pitch darkness picking our way across country, where we might at any moment come across another enemy force, and it required strenuous vigilance.

St Valéry was full of Allied troops, and defences had been organised. In an effort to spare unnecessary bloodshed, Rommel called on the enemy to surrender. However, he would have to fight for the town.

11th June 1940

That evening I sent a number of German-speaking prisoners into St Valéry, which was still full of enemy troops, calling on them to surrender by 21.00hrs, and to march under white flags to the hills west of St Valéry. For the most part it was the British, with some French officers, who refused to contemplate surrender, and sent our negotiators back empty-handed. They kept their men busy building barricades and getting large numbers of guns and machine guns positioned all around St Valéry, especially in the harbour. The British were probably hoping to resume their embarkation in the night.

Given the circumstances then, the concentrated fire of the division was let loose at 21.00hrs, including the panzer regiment and the reconnaissance battalion which had arrived in the meantime. A Panzer IV crashed through the heavy barricade on the pier, where there were numerous guns, and set it aflame. Fires soon raged everywhere. After a quarter of an hour, I directed the entire division's fire on to the northeast sector of the town where, we saw next day, the effect was really devastating. The tenacious British, however, still refused to give up.

Rommel kept up the pressure on the defenders of St Valéry, who now knew they had little hope. Everywhere, French and British troops were surrendering to the Germans.

12th June 1940

As the tanks were moving round the southern side of the harbour towards the eastern quarter of the town, I followed the infantry across a narrow bridge to the square. The town hall, and many buildings all around were either burnt out or still ablaze. Barricades constructed by the enemy from vehicles and guns, also showed the effect of our barrage. French and British troops were now pouring into the square from all directions, where they formed up in column and marched off west. The infantry were mopping up the town house by house and street by street.

Shortly afterwards an NCO reported that a high-ranking French officer had been taken prisoner on the eastern side of the town, and had requested to see me. A few moments later, the French General Ihler approached me wearing an ordinary unmarked military trenchcoat. When I asked the general which division he

ROMMEL'S COMMAND STYLE

The style of command that Rommel had developed in World War I – of pushing ahead, of 'bouncing' a surprised enemy into surrender – was perfectly suited to armoured warfare. The Wehrmacht had adopted the precepts of Heinz Guderian during the 1930s, and had created armoured divisions that contained a suitable mix of arms to support a spearhead of tanks that could penetrate an enemy front and carry on advancing, ignoring minor threats to their flanks and rear.

Guderian's ideas accorded perfectly with Rommel's feel for warfare. There are four elements that should be emphasised about his command during the advance into Belgium and France. The first was his absolute insistence on pushing on. The second element was the weight he gave to manoeuvre rather than destruction of enemy men and materiel. The third element lay in Rommel's ability to adapt. The fourth element was his imaginative coordination of his resources. This was shown at its best in the attack south across the Somme from 5th June, when he organised his division into an enormous box in which support was always available to the tanks at the front.

commanded, he answered in broken German – 'No division. I command IX Corps.'

He announced his readiness to accept my demand for immediate unconditional surrender of his forces. But he added that he would not be standing there in surrender if his forces still had any ammunition remaining.

The general's ADC, who spoke German, informed us that the number of divisions at his disposal was five, including one British. I requested that the general now return to his HQ and issue orders through his regular channels, that his troops surrender and march off immediately towards St Valéry under prominent white flags. I wanted to be sure our troops would be able to see clearly that the enemy had laid down their arms.

I then requested that the general present himself with his staff in St Valéry square and agreed to his request to be allowed his own vehicle and kit. Orders were issued to the artillery to cease all fire on St Valéry and neighbourhood, and only to engage shipping. The 5th Panzer, which had reported an action at 11.40hrs against enemy tanks near Manneville, was advised of the enemy surrender at St Valéry. Over the next few hours no fewer than 12 generals were brought in as prisoners, four divisional commanders among them. A particular catch for us was the inclusion among them of General Fortune, commander of the 51st British Division, and his staff. I now agreed divisional boundaries between us and our neighbour, General Cruewell, commanding the 2nd Motorised Division. In the meantime, the captured generals and staffs were being assembled in a house south of the square. A Luftwaffe lieutenant, recently liberated from captivity himself, was given responsibility for the guard. He relished the reversal of roles.

We were particularly struck by the sang froid with which the British officers met their fate. The general, and his staff officers in particular, strolled around the street in front of the house laughing. The only thing that seemed to irritate them was the constant photography they had to suffer at the hands of our Propaganda Company and other photographers.

The captured generals were now invited to join us for an open-air lunch at a German field kitchen, but they declined politely saying they still had supplies of their own. We ate alone. Arrangements still had to be made for the transportation of so many prisoners, especially the large number of officers, and for salvage, securing the shoreline and the evacuation of St Valéry. Around 20.00hrs we returned to Divisional HQ at Chateau Auberville.

It was impossible at that point to estimate the total count of prisoners and booty. 12,000 men, of whom 8000 were British, were carried off by the 7th Panzer Division's vehicles alone. The total number captured at St Valéry is reputed to have numbered 46,000 men.

The capture of St Valéry was not the last serious fighting for 7th Panzer Division in 1940. Rommel did manage one more feat. There were fears that a French 'redoubt' would be set up in Brittany, supplied through the port of Cherbourg. To forestall this, 7th Panzer moved back inland and crossed the Seine on 17th June. By the evening of 18th June, Rommel had artillery covering Cherbourg, having covered over 320km (200 miles). There was strong resistance fire from French troops at La Haye du Puits to overcome, and some shelling from the forts around Cherbourg, but on 19th June the port surrendered.

The rolling up of France was by this stage all but complete. De Gaulle fled Paris with General Spears on 14th June, the day the city was entered by the advancing Germans. The country's government had hurriedly evacuated south from Tours to Bordeaux. With the resignation of the premier, Reynaud, Marshal Pétain formed a new government and promptly called for the Germans to state their own terms. By 17th June Guderian's leading panzers were already at the Franco-Swiss frontier at Pontarlier. The whirlwind assault on France was drawing to a close. On 21st June, Hitler and his staff met a delegation from the French at a clearing in the Compiègne woods near Paris. The Germans had pointedly retrieved from a local museum the railway carriage which was the site of their own capitulation in 1918. The French were to be spared no humiliation, and the Fuehrer's glee was palpable that day. All fighting ceased on 22nd June, with the armistice coming into effect.

Rommel's achievements during the invasion of France were little short of phenomenal, and he was the darling of Hitler and of the German people as a whole. 7th Panzer had captured an estimated 90,000 prisoners; more importantly, it had been the spearhead of the German Blitzkrieg. It had suffered 2328 casualties (682 dead), with 296 men missing in action. Only 42 of its tanks had been lost.

However, it was not all good news for Rommel. Many fellow officers were jealous of him, while others had reservations. His corps commander, Hoth, wrote in a confidential report that his subordinate would be suitable for a corps command only after he had more experience and a better sense of judgment. In addition, Rommel tended to play down the part of other units in the campaign, in order to increase the 7th Panzer Division's reputation. In a manuscript written by him after the campaign, Rommel virtually ignored the part played by the Luftwaffe. This was pointed out to him by Kluge, the Fourth Army commander, whom Rommel had approached to write a foreword to the manuscript. Other criticisms included Rommel's inaccuracies concerning the 32nd Infantry Division, which he portrayed as making slower progress than it actually did.

Nevertheless, to the Nazi government Rommel's achievements were the stuff of legend, and he and his 'ghost division' were quickly turned into heroes. His exploits were re-lived in the propaganda film *Victory in the West*, in which his tanks rolled over the French countryside again, this time for the cameras.

Rommel's star was certainly in the ascendant after France, and he did everything he could to help it on its way up. More importantly, the campaign as a whole was confirmation of the potency of the German panzer divisions, and what they could achieve if handled by commanders such as Rommel. Above all, the campaign had demonstrated the importance of retaining the initiative. To this end Rommel urged his subordinates on at every stage to keep up the momentum of the advance.

BELOW: A distant oil fire spews black smoke into the summer sky as Rommel forces the surrender of Cherbourg on 19th June. The last major port in northern France was now in German hands, and the French capitulation just 48 hours away.

Chapter V

Storm in the Desert

The year 1941 was an inconclusive one in North Africa, marked by battles to and fro across the Libyan desert. With the Japanese attack on Pearl Harbor, and the consequent widening of the war, storm clouds were looming on the horizon for Germany's favourite general.

*On 6th February 1941, Rommel, now a lieutenant-general, was summoned to Berlin and told he had been selected to command a German force of two divisions that was to deploy to North Africa in spring 1941 as Operation Sunflower (*Sonnenblume*) to help the Italian forces that had been thrown out of Cyrenaica and back to Tripoli by a British offensive from Egypt. The Axis intelligence was that British forces were about to attack Tripoli*

BELOW: Rommel and his Afrika Korps parade in Tripoli, 31st March 1941, prior to deploying against Wavell in the Libyan desert. Considerable publicity was given to this visible act of Axis cooperation, which Hitler saw as necessary to keep the Italians in the war and on the right side.

itself, and the Germans were to salvage the Italian position. Although of some strategic importance to Germany, the North African campaign was primarily embarked on so as to keep Italy in the war and on the Axis side. Rommel was ostensibly under the command of the Italian Commander-in-Chief in North Africa, General Italo Gariboldi, although he was given the right to appeal to Berlin in the event of any serious disagreement. His orders were to recapture Cyrenaica.

6. Feb. 41
Dearest Lu! [Rommel's wife]
My plane landed at 12.45hrs. The car ordered by Major Oppel was ready. We first went to the Supreme Commander of the Army who informed me of my new task, then to the Fuehrer. It's all terribly urgent. My baggage will be sent here. I can only take articles that are absolutely necessary. You can imagine how my head is buzzing because of all these new developments. What will come of it?

The new man arrived in North Africa on 12th February 1941, and the first German troops two days later. As a mark of Hitler's support, Rommel was accompanied by Colonel Schmundt, one of the Fuehrer's close aides. Characteristically, Rommel's first act was to get into an aircraft and fly towards the enemy positions to get a feel for the ground over which he would be fighting. He disagreed with Gariboldi over the strategic course to follow: whereas the Italians wanted to defend near Tripoli, Rommel wished to push forward, and wished to get things moving right away. He made his views known in Berlin and Rome, and, again characteristically, soon got his way.

13. Feb. 41
Dearest Lu!
Arrived and quartered very well. Made a 1000km (600 miles) flight yesterday. Everything worked out fine. Schmundt will fly back tomorrow and bring you mail.

The British had already been made aware of Germany's intention to reinforce their Italian allies in North Africa. The decoding of top-secret German Enigma signals, although still a rather hit-and-miss affair in 1941, had been successful in revealing details of Operation Sonnenblume.

February 1941
That evening when we met with General Gariboldi to report on our reconnaissance flight, General Roatta was already there with the Duce's orders. Nothing more stood in the way of my plans. In the course of the next few days, the Italian X Corps, made up of the Brescia and Pavia Divisions, was to advance to the Sirte-Buerat area and take up defensive positions. Following it, the Ariete Division, which then had only some 60 tanks of ancient design (they were too light, and had been used only for chasing Abyssinian natives around the desert), was to deploy west of Buerat. These were all the forces at our disposal. Moving even these units was a headache for the Italian High Command. They did not have enough transporters, and the Tripoli-Buerat road was 400km (240 miles) long.

I couldn't count therefore on these formations being available in good time. Apart from the light Italian garrison at Sirte, the only means we had of containing

ROMMEL ARRIVES IN NORTH AFRICA

Rommel arrived in North Africa, in Tripoli, as part of Germany's effort to shore up the armies of Mussolini. The Italians had entered the war in June 1940, when France was about to fall, hoping to profit from an Allied defeat.

In the Mediterranean, Italian ambitions were to invade Greece from Italian-occupied Albania, and to invade Egypt from the Italian colony of Libya. The attack on Greece, in autumn 1940, was thoroughly repulsed, while the attempt to take over Egypt led to a full-scale disaster. A weak Italian offensive was easily repulsed, and, in December, British forces in Egypt commanded by Major-General Richard O'Connor rolled across the Italian front line and advanced almost 800km (480 miles).

On 11th January 1941, Hitler ordered the Italians to be given help: 'The situation in the Mediterranean makes it necessary to provide assistance...Tripolitania must be held.' On 6th February, Rommel, a lieutenant-general, took command of one armoured and one light division and on 12th February landed at Tripoli.

the enemy was the German Luftwaffe. Therefore it was necessary to ask the Luftwaffe's African commander and X Corps' air commander to undertake this action so vital to the African theatre. Notwithstanding the limited resources at their disposal, they did all they could day and night, and in this endeavour they were successful. Under constant pressure from the Luftwaffe, General Wavell's army stayed put at El Agheila.

A few days later I flew to Sirte, to inspect Italian troops positioned there. The troops, well led by Colonel Grati and Major Santa Maria, amounted to about a regiment in strength. This was the only ground force available to face the British and our very real fears were understandable. The rest of our troops were some 300km (180 miles) away.

Above: Mobile warfare comes to North Africa. Greatcoats are still needed as the first Panzer IIs of Rommel's Afrika Korps are unloaded at Tripoli harbour in the early spring of 1941.

At my urging, an Italian division was marched out for Sirte on 14th February. On the same day, the first German units arrived in Tripoli harbour – the 3rd Reconnaissance Battalion and an anti-tank unit. In view of the time situation, I ordered that the disembarkation be continued throughout the night, if necessary by lamplight. Even if that meant the risk of enemy air attack.

The night-long unloading of this 6000-ton transport turned out a record for Tripoli harbour. Early the next morning, tropical kit was issued to all the men, and they were assembled on the square in front of Government House by 11.00hrs. An air of victory emanated from the men, and this did not pass unnoticed in the port. After a brief parade, Baron von Wechmar moved out with his men towards Sirte, arriving there 26 hours later. On the 16th, German reconnaissance troops in company with Santa Maria's column made contact with the British. I took over command at the front. Colonel Schmundt had already returned to HQ several days before.

17. Feb. 41
Dearest Lu!
I am on excellent terms with the Italian command and could not hope for better cooperation. My tanks are now at the front which has moved 560km (350miles) east. The enemy can only run away from us.

Having got everything going, Rommel was then ready to meet the British in battle. In particular, his chief aim was to take Benghazi, the main town in Cyrenaica, which had been taken by Major-General O'Connor. Although it was a small coastal town, Benghazi was an important facility as a small port. As Rommel's writings continually stress, the establishment of an effective supply line was vital to the continuation of mechanised combat in the severely inhospitable climate and terrain in North Africa. The British realised this, of course, so the fighting tended to concentrate around small but vital harbours along the coast.

February 1941

To make us look stronger and to make sure the British were cautious, I got the workshops 5km (three miles) south of Tripoli to produce dummy tanks, in large numbers, based on Volkswagen cars and looking very like the real thing. On 17th February the enemy was very lively, and I feared he was about to press home his attack on Tripoli. The likelihood increased on the 18th, when we ascertained the presence of further British formations between El Agheila and Agedabia. To impress on them that we too were active, I resolved to send out the 3rd Reconnaissance Battalion and the Santa Maria Column, including the 39th Anti-tank Battalion, to the edge of the Nofilia area, with orders to engage the enemy.

On 24th February came the first clash between German and British troops in the African theatre. Without casualties ourselves, we destroyed two enemy scout vehicles, a truck and a car and took three British soldiers, among them an officer, prisoner. Meanwhile, further elements of the 5th Light Division continued to the front as planned.

We were still wary of the British activities, and to stabilise the situation General Streich, commander of the 5th Light Division, and who was now in command at the front, advanced up the Mugta defile and sowed it with mines. He saw no enemy.

25. Feb. 41
Dearest Lu!
I returned from my trip. Everything went well and I am quite satisfied with what I have seen. Yesterday we took the first British prisoners, a lieutenant and two men. A good omen. We suffered no casualties.

3. Mar. 41
Dearest Lu!
Major Grunow returned from Berlin and brought greetings from the Fuehrer. He reported that the Fuehrer was extremely pleased with the change that has taken place here since my arrival and the beginning of my activities. He endorsed my measures in every respect. This sort of thing pleases you and gives you energy to go on. Every morning at 06.30hrs the typewriters start rattling away. First thing in the morning, I dictate the important events of the previous day for the historical record.

Rommel was looking to push forward, as he realised that the British forces were weaker than he had first estimated, and he resented being tied down by orders from Berlin. What he did not know was that the planning for Operation Barbarossa, the invasion of the Soviet Union, took precedence in the minds of his superiors, who did not want a small sideshow to soak up supplies. The implications of a war against the Soviet Union far outweighed any considerations as to the success or otherwise of the war in North Africa. Rommel returned to Germany in March, determined to argue his case.

LEFT: Plumed helmets bent against a sandstorm, these Bersaglieri struggle to follow an armoured car advancing towards enemy positions. Italian alpine troops found the combination of British military tactics and unfamiliar desert conditions overwhelming.

March 1941

I was unhappy with the intentions of Field Marshal von Brauchitsch and Colonel-General Halder to send the least number of troops to Africa as possible, leaving the fate of the African theatre to chance. The momentary weakness of the British should have been exploited with utmost rigour, so as to take the initiative at the outset.

I also believed it was a mistake not to risk the invasion of England in 1940-41. If this undertaking were ever to succeed, it would have been after the defeat of the British Expeditionary Force in France, and the loss of most of its equipment. The longer it was left the harder for Germany it would be, though the invasion would have to be initiated if the war against England were to be won.

Before I departed, I ordered the 5th Light Division to make ready to attack El Agheila on 24th March, capture the airfield and the small fort, and force out the garrison. Shortly before, a mixed German-Italian force had occupied the Marada Oasis, some distance to the south. These units had to be maintained, and our supply columns were being constantly harassed by the British at El Agheila.

On my return to Africa, the 3rd Battalion took the fort, the water stores and the airfield in the early hours of 24th March. The garrison, composed of light forces, had the whole area mined and retreated skilfully on our attack.

With El Agheila taken, Rommel could see that Mersa el Brega was vulnerable to attack; and once he had Mersa el Brega, then he could attack into Cyrenaica. Typically, Rommel was impatient to continue the momentum of success when the opening domino had been seen to fall. He was supposed to wait until May to attack; but he decided to move off in March, and was himself in the forefront of the action...

31st March 1941

On 31st March we began our attack on the British positions at Mersa el Brega. A fierce battle broke out in the early hours with British reconnaissance troops at Maaten Besker. In the afternoon, troops of the 5th Light Division attacked the Mersa el Brega position itself, which was solidly defended by the British. Our advance came to a halt.

I myself, with my Chief of Staff Lieutenant-Colonel von dem Borne and Aldinger [Rommel's ADC], spent the whole day on the battlefield, trying in the afternoon to find a possible way to attack north of the coastal road. There in the evening the 8th Machine Gun Battalion made a fierce attack through the rolling sand dunes, and succeeded in pushing the enemy back to the east, capturing the defile at Mersa el Brega.

Rommel's intelligence showed that the British were drawing back rather than strengthening their positions, and so he decided to disobey the

BELOW: A field commander in his element. Rommel aboard an armoured car among his soldiers. He managed to instil a sense of élitism into an otherwise unremarkable fighting unit.

orders that he was not to advance into Cyrenaica until May. On 3rd April he initiated a three-pronged advance, and urged speed on his forces – brooking no dissent. Tactically, this was somewhat at odds not only with conventional military methodology, but also with Rommel's own exhortations elsewhere in his writings never to split one's forces.

3rd April 1941
At about 18.00hrs, I returned to my forward HQ to learn that the 5th Light Division wanted four days to refuel. I considered this excessive, and ordered the division to unload all its vehicles and take them to the divisional pool near Arco dei Fileni, and to bring up enough fuel, rations and munitions for the advance on Cyrenaica within 24 hours. It didn't escape my attention that our men would be exposed for 24 hours, but with the enemy already in retreat this was a risk worth taking.

Meanwhile it was becoming clear that the enemy was greatly overestimating our strength. At all costs it would be necessary to keep up this illusion by generating the appearance of a major offensive. Naturally, I was not in a position to push the enemy hard with my main force, but we were probably able to maintain enough pressure with our advance elements to keep him on the run. Within 24 hours, I hoped, I would be able to move up a stronger force to reinforce my troops. I intended to aim for the south flank, with the object of advancing through Ben Ganaia to Tmimi, thus cutting off and isolating as many British troops as possible.

On my return to Corps HQ, I met the Italian Commander-in-Chief, General Gariboldi, who was not at all pleased with the turn of events so far, and berated me severely, mainly because our actions were in contravention of instructions from Rome. He said that supplies to the Italo-German troops were so limited that no one could assume responsibility for such an undertaking, or answer for the consequences that might ensue. He demanded that I discontinue all such operations forthwith, and undertake no further action without his authority.

I had already made up my mind to seek the greatest tactical and operational freedom, and was determined not to let good opportunities go by. The atmosphere became rather heated as I made my views as clear as possible. General

BELOW: Sir Archibald Wavell (left) and his successor, Sir Claude Auchinleck.

ROMMEL'S FIRST OFFENSIVE

When Rommel arrived in North Africa, he overestimated British strength. He did not realise that the British had only two divisions rather than two corps in Cyrenaica, nor that 7th Armoured Division, whose Matilda tanks had cracked the Italian morale, had been withdrawn.

The first of Rommel's divisions – 5th Light Division – had arrived at Tripoli in February 1941. His orders were to wait until his second division – 15th Panzer – arrived before he considered offensive action. But in March, it became clear to Rommel that the British were not preparing an offensive; and his advance units were able to push on past El Agheila, meeting little opposition. At the end of the month his forces moved up to Agedabia – and now he could see an opportunity opening up.

By speed and dash, German forces had put themselves at a strategic advantage, and Rommel would not refuse it. He sent three columns across Cyrenaica. Flying in his Storch light plane, Rommel flogged his few troops and even fewer armoured vehicles on. He pushed the British back into Egypt – but failed to take the vital port of Tobruk.

BELOW: Rommel and a less confident-looking aide in a Fieseler Storch reconnaissance aircraft, a type used extensively throughout the North African campaign. From his very first days in Tripolitania, Rommel regularly took to the air to acquaint himself with the elusive landmarks of the desert and the disposition of enemy forces.

Gariboldi wanted to get the authority from Rome first. That could take days. I wouldn't stand for that so I explained that I would continue to react to each situation as it arose as appropriately as I thought at the time. This brought the argument to a head when, like an avenging angel, a message arrived from the German High Command giving me the complete free hand I demanded. This brought our fierce confrontation to an end, with the result in my favour.

The key to Rommel's attack across the Cyrenaican 'bulge' was the taking of Mechili, against which he intended to concentrate units from all three of the columns he had sent across the desert on 3rd April. The plan would prove a stunning success. Rommel was again fortunate in this. Not only had he seized the initiative by disobeying orders, and by flouting military convention, but he also risked stretching his supply line beyond its limits. In fact, some tanks did run dry on the advance to Mechili.

8th April 1941

The attack was due to be launched the following morning. On the 8th April at about 06.00hrs I flew off in the Storch to the front east of Mechili, to follow the course of battle. Flying at about 100m (330ft), we approached a Bersaglieri battalion which had been brought up by Colonel Fabris the day before. Apparently the Italians hadn't seen a Storch before, and were so taken aback by our sudden approach over their heads that they began firing at us from all directions.

It was truly a miracle that from a range of 50-100m (165-330ft) we were not shot

down, and it didn't say much for Italian marksmanship. We immediately turned round and put a hill between ourselves and our allies. Not wishing to be shot down by our own troops, I straightaway ordered the pilot to climb to 1000m (3300ft), where we could safely observe the situation without being shot down.

Clearly, the attack on Mechili was gaining headway. A large column of enemy vehicles was rolling westwards from Mechili, and we flew on expecting to find Olbrich's force which was surely due. Still no sign of them. We did see an 88mm gun positioned about 2-3km (1.2-2 miles) from the British vehicles. I expected to find more German troops there, and as we came in to land, the Storch struck a sand dune and nosed in. The gun commander reported that his gun had been attacked and damaged by tanks the day before. There were none of our troops in the area. A man had been despatched by truck to try and make contact with our troops. I asked him if at least he could fire at the dust cloud being raised by the British vehicles. He could – but then realised that the man with the truck had driven away with the firing pins. The English column, in open deployment, was getting nearer and nearer. It was high time for us to be off, if we didn't want a trip to Canada! By chance, the gunners still had a truck left and we made off in it to the southeast, where we soon found a salt-marsh that I recognised from my flight the day before. From there, we finally found our way back to Corps HQ.

When Mechili was taken, the British were forced to withdraw from Cyrenaica. Rommel had won his first desert victory, and could express his future ambitions.

April 1941

The re-taking of Cyrenaica was now complete. However, I still deemed it necessary to keep up the pressure on the enemy's heels, and to keep him on the run. Although we could not expect to isolate and destroy any significant part of the enemy army, we would have an ideal springboard in Marmarica for an Alexandria offensive in the summer, not to mention the propaganda and psychological lift that the reconquest of the Italian colony would provide, especially among the Italians themselves. It was also looking hopeful that normal supply routes could be established along the coast road.

Several of our units had already gone missing during our desert raids. We sent out search parties to find and return them.

Above: Rommel lends a hand pulling an MB 340 personnel carrier out of a sand dune. Although notorious for driving his troops and their commanders hard, the vigorous general often led by example, sparing neither himself nor his men.

I ordered aircraft to comb the desert. A large fire was started at Mechili, giving off clouds of thick smoke.

Having cleared Cyrenaica, Rommel was determined to carry on into Egypt, and to take the port of Tobruk on the way, even though there was little intelligence about the defences or the intentions of the defenders. He had also been specifically instructed by his immediate superiors not to extend his advance into Egypt.

On 10th April I left for Tobruk at first light. I found 3rd Recce Battalion 50km (30 miles) west of it, and not yet repositioned to the right for the flank attack. Straightaway I gave General von Prittwitz the order to begin his attack on the Tobruk road, with the 3rd Recce Battalion to advance on El Adem through Acroma. I drove off again towards Tobruk, and found the leading elements of Machine Gun Battalion 8 in battle 16km (10 miles) outside. The sky flashed and a sandstorm blew up. Heavy artillery fire from Tobruk brought the attack shuddering to a halt. At that time we had no knowledge of the enemy's defensive positions. Shortly the visibility deteriorated. At midday Count Schwerin reported to me that the courageous General Prittwitz had been killed by a direct hit from an anti-tank gun a few hours earlier. He was a great loss in the fight.

I ordered the 5th Light Division, after they had been relieved by the Brescia, to push on with all speed with all elements towards the Via Balbia east of Tobruk and encircle the fort. Meanwhile the Ariete had been stationed at Bir Tengedier. I therefore ordered the division to re-position to El Adem.

The situation was relatively unclear. Next day I took a fire-damaged English command vehicle [Mammoth] up to the front, to try and get a better picture. For the commander to have a good understanding on the battlefield of his own and the enemy's dispositions is of utmost importance. It is often more important to have an accurate overview of the actual battlefield than to be intellectually more qualified, or to have more experience. This is especially true of a situation where developments cannot be foreseen. A man must observe and learn for himself, since reports from second-hand sources cannot be relied upon as a base for important military decisions.

On 11th April, Tobruk had been surrounded and the first attack got under way. Stukas dive-bombed the defences, details of which were still unknown to us. On 12th April, reinforcements arrived, and it was decided to mount the first main assault on the fort that afternoon. On the same day, the 3rd Reconnaissance Battalion took Bardia. The Brescia, which had meanwhile taken over the western front of Tobruk, began the afternoon attack. The 5th Light Division was unhappy with its orders for the attack, and

Below: Making tracks for the desert...Panzer IIIs and IVs lead an armoured column on a reconnaissance patrol during the fighting for Tobruk in spring 1941.

I had to overrule a number of objections its staff raised. British artillery fire would not be accurate on a day of gusting sandstorms. The division's attack was finally launched about 16.30hrs. The enemy fired shells all over the area, causing few casualties. The tanks came under fierce fire when they slowed at the point of attack, and halted in front of the anti-tank ditches which we were not yet able to breach. The defences around Tobruk's fort stretched further than we had anticipated to the west, south and east. We had requested plans of the defences, but these were yet to be seen.

After we left off the attack, I decided to try again in a few days after more artillery and the Ariete had arrived. Under no circumstances could we allow the enemy time to organise his defences.

I ordered a reconnaissance battalion from the 5th Light Division on 13th April to advance to the crossroads inside the Tobruk defences, and if possible to blow the anti-tank ditches. The Brescia was to contain the enemy west of the fort, and to raise enough dustclouds to make it look to the enemy as if a major assault was being prepared.

Because of the failure of the earlier raid on Tobruk, the 5th Light Division was lacking in confidence and was unrealistically critical of my plan to get the main attack under way on the 14th. The leadership of the division did not understand the tactic of making a breakthrough, securing the flanks and then pushing deep into the enemy rear before he has a chance to retaliate. My understanding of the enemy was that we had the necessary troops to undertake such an operation. Realism and initiative were all that were needed. It was unfortunate I had not had the opportunity to train my divisions personally before the raiding in Cyrenaica, otherwise we should have been much more successful at Tobruk.

22. Apr. 1941
Dearest Lu!
I stayed 'at home' all day yesterday, in my quarters at a hotel. I had, however, several very important conferences, the outcome of which will be felt in about 10 days. A few quiet days do you good. Looking back, it is safe to say now that our unexpected offensive was a grand success, about which the world's press is talking. It is true the British expected us to attack but they never expected the attack to be carried out with such power and striking speed. That we were able to bypass Tobruk and take Bardia and Sollum was a woeful surprise for them. 'Garibaldi' [Rommel's nickname for his Italian superior, General Gariboldi] will arrive today and I will expound my new plans to him. He will, I am sure, be very pleased.

April 1941

During the attacks on the southwestern flank of Tobruk, we lost over 120 men killed, wounded or missing. Clearly it can be seen that the casualty curve rises steeply when one goes from mobile to static warfare. In a mobile war, what is of importance is the materiel, as the essential ingredient for the combat soldier. In a mobile war, the best soldier is useless without vehicles, tanks and ordnance. If you destroy the enemy's armour, he can be

PAULUS' VISIT

The advance across Cyrenaica and the attacks on Tobruk worried Halder, head of the Army High Command (OKH). To rein his subordinate in, Halder sent Lieutenant-General Paulus, Rommel's equivalent in rank, out to Africa, arriving on 27th April. He described his role: 'As the delegate of the Commander-in-Chief of the Army, charged with the elucidation of the situation in the African theatre of war and having been invested with the right to advise the German Afrika Korps, I reserve my attitude to the decisions of the Korps imparted to me until I have examined the situation.'

Paulus agreed with Rommel's plans to make another attempt on Tobruk, but suggested that some German forces be detailed to cover the Egyptian frontier, which was masked only by Italian troops. Rommel agreed and detached a German combat group to the frontier.

Paulus left Africa in early May. His report stressed the problems of supplying forces in Africa, expressed doubts that the taking of Egypt was possible, and suggested that a further attack on Tobruk should have OKH's permission.

rendered useless without heavy loss of manpower. The opposite applies in static war. There, the trooper with rifle and hand grenade is as important as ever so long as he is protected by anti-tank weapons or obstacles against enemy tanks. His number one enemy is the attacking infantryman. It follows that static warfare is always a struggle to destroy men, as opposed to mobile war, where destruction of the enemy's materiel is the key.

The heavy losses we suffered during the assaults on the southwest front of Tobruk were not least due to lack of training. Even in a minor skirmish, there are tactical skills which can be used to spare casualties and these the men have to learn through the proper training. On some occasions, speed was employed where caution should have prevailed. On the other hand, there were instances when the men were over-cautious when boldness was called for. In these small infantry tactics there is one rule: maximum caution allied to boldness exercised at the right time.

The captured Ras el Madauer positions were under continuous enemy artillery fire. Because the rocky ground was impossible to dig into properly, our defences were very shallow. By day, therefore, our troops were forced to remain still and endure thousands of flies. A majority of the men had dysentery, and the conditions were unspeakable. In order that troops could be trained in the ways of static warfare, a stormtroop school was subsequently set up at Acroma.

To disrupt the enemy artillery fire, dummy tanks were placed on my orders in the area held by the Brescia. They soon began to draw heavy enemy fire. Unfortunately, the men did not know how to operate these devices, which needed to be kept on the move and not just left sitting for a week in the same places. I made numerous visits to the front line to instil some modern thinking about static warfare into the troops there.

The Italians had acquired a severe inferiority complex. This was not surprising, as their infantry had almost no anti-tank weapons and their artillery was obsolete. Their training also fell well short of modern standards, so we faced more and more serious disruptions. Many Italian officers had thought of war as an amusing diversion. They had been bitterly disillusioned, and faced very dire

RIGHT: This German press release photo reads: 'Between palms and wells, with our troops in North Africa. A pause in the advance on Benghazi is the opportunity for a refreshing wash at a desert well...'. Such welcoming oases also offered booby-traps and poisoned water to the unwary.

consequences if they didn't wake up to the reality of war.

Rommel was forced to besiege Tobruk, and in order to prevent British forces relieving the port he set up his front line along the line of Sollum and the Halfaya Pass near the frontier with Egypt. The success of this enterprise soon dispelled the depression he had felt after the failure to take Tobruk, although his ambitions in North Africa, and the logistic and air support he demanded for them, were still not to the liking of his seniors in Berlin, who were pre-occupied with planning Barbarossa, the invasion of the Soviet Union. These preoccupations, however, probably enabled Rommel to act with a freer hand in North Africa than might otherwise have been the case. A high command busy planning a major invasion had less time to get involved in the tactical affairs of an essentially political, rather than strategic, campaign.

23rd April 1941

Heavy fighting at Tobruk yesterday. We succeeded in regaining control over a very difficult situation. The Italian troops are very unreliable [he would suggest their removal from Africa altogether, leaving the fighting to the Afrika Korps]. They are very sensitive to enemy armour and – as in 1917 – they give up easily...I have many worries these days. Every day we have to patch up another spot. Much work is to be done and I don't get the right kind of co-operation from all the divisional commanders. I am requesting the relief of some of them.

Whether the officers of the 5th Light Division had been 'unrealistically critical' of Rommel is a moot point. But Rommel's appreciation of the dangers of static warfare for his troops was acute.

ABOVE: Mottled desert camouflage adorns the airframes of these Ju 87 'Stuka' dive-bombers en route to British positions around Tobruk. This long-range 'airborne artillery' was a proven means of softening up the enemy prior to a ground assault.

26. May. 41
Dearest Lu!
Last night I received quite a snub from Berlin, from the Army High Command, the reason for which is beyond my comprehension. It seems that my reports about the actual situation over here do not suit the gentlemen up there. The result will be that we over here will become taciturn and report only the absolutely necessary. Things are rather quiet here as well as on the front near Sollum. Up there, however, you can never tell whether it isn't the calm before the storm.

In June 1941, the Commonwealth forces, reinforced with 400 tanks, launched a major offensive against Rommel's forces – Operation Battleaxe, the brainchild of General Wavell, Commander-in-Chief Middle East. It had not been part of Wavell's plan to launch an offensive against Rommel at this point, but Churchill had received a decode of Paulus' report to headquarters the month before and decided to press Wavell into an assault while there were light enemy forces on the Egyptian border.

THE SIEGE OF TOBRUK

Rommel had believed that the British wished to evacuate Tobruk, and that if they tried to hold it, it would deliver vast numbers of prisoners into his hands. These assumptions were grave mistakes.

The first attempts on Tobruk, by troops that had raced across Cyrenaica and were ignorant of the strengths of the defences, were a total failure and a shock to the Germans. While Tobruk held out, there could be no advance into Egypt – and besieging the port exposed Rommel's weakness. His main supply base was Tripoli, over 1500km (900 miles) from Tobruk. The British, in contrast, enjoyed a short communications link with Alexandria and Cairo.

Tobruk became the focus of the war in North Africa from April 1941 until the end of the year. The defenders, the tough Australian 9th Division under the even tougher Major-General Sir Leslie Morshead, fought brilliantly.

British forces made a major attempt to raise the siege in June 1941, in Operation Battleaxe. The three-day battle was a defensive victory for the Germans. Typically, Rommel himself took direct command of some of the battle. His forces absorbed the attack and threatened to cut off British forward units – Wavell ordered his forces back.

While certain of his forces – most notably a unit under Captain Bach at Halfaya Pass – held the assault, Rommel showed his mastery of armoured warfare in organising a swift counter that made the British break off their attacks after just three days.

11. Jun. 41
Dearest Lu!
The situation here is a bit tense. The British took off 65 kilometres into the desert and I don't know whether that is just a defensive measure or preparation for an attack...

16. Jun. 41
Dearest Lu!
As you will have read in the communiqué there was heavy fighting all day yesterday in the eastern sector. It's 02.30hrs now and I believe there will be a result today after a hard struggle. I don't sleep under these circumstances.

June 1941

Soon the 5th Light Division was engaged in heavy fighting against the 7th British Armoured Brigade in the desert 10km (six miles) west of Sidi Omar. Strong British forces separated the 5th Light and the 15th Panzer Division, and neither unit was in contact with the other, which was hardly desirable.

During the heavy fighting which followed, the 5th Light Division was able to swing the odds in our favour, and continued to battle through the desert northeast of Sidi Omar towards Sidi Suleiman. This was a decisive moment in the onslaught against the British position. I immediately ordered the 15th Panzer Division to leave just a minimum force holding the line north of Capuzzo, and advance with all mobile units as quickly as possible on the northern flank of the victorious 5th Light. The decisive moment had come. One can often influence the outcome of a battle by simply moving one's point of concentration.

At this point, General Gambarra, Chief of Staff to the Italian High Command, North Africa, arrived at my field HQ. After a brief description of the battle and its tactical problems, I explained to him in no uncertain terms that the German troops, however positive in outlook, were in no condition to carry on into Egypt. I painted as black a picture as I could of the strategic position, to convince him to bypass the Tobruk road and bring up further Italian divisions as quickly as possible. General Gambarra seemed quite impressed, and promised all would be done to enable the Sollum position to be held.

The enemy appeared unwilling to let go of the initiative so easily, and concentrated the bulk of his armour north of Capuzzo, intending early the following morning to launch a heavy attack on the elements of the 15th Panzer Division remaining in the north, to achieve a breakthrough there. To impose my plans on the British, I ordered the 5th Light and 15th Panzer Divisions to get their assault on Sidi Suleiman under way by 04.30 hrs.

So, on 17th June, the 5th Light set off at the appointed time and succeeded in reaching the environs of Sidi Suleiman by about 06.00hrs. The 15th Panzer left shortly after and reached its destination with equal dispatch. A large number of destroyed British tanks were to be seen during the course of the operation.

Clearly, the British were taken entirely by surprise. Their position was now serious. It was obvious to me that the British could not undertake any action for the moment, that they had lost their drive and I could get them in the bag by continuing on to Halfaya. About 09.00hrs, the 5th Light and 15th Panzer Divisions were ordered to continue their march on Halfaya, to forestall a breakthrough by British armour from the north. I hoped to bring the British into direct combat and annihilate them, since they were seriously low on fuel and ammunition.

The enemy's radio net was reporting continued shortages of ammunition. They shortly set fire to their stores at Capuzzo and retreated, the desert behind strewn with vehicles abandoned through lack of fuel. They complained angrily at their tank losses.

Below: Rommel confers with Marshal Cavallero, Chief of the Italian General Staff. Relations between the German popular hero and his Italian counterparts were strained. Technically answerable to the Italian Commando Supremo, Rommel tended either to ignore them or to report direct to Berlin.

RIGHT: Major-General Sir Leslie Morshead, commander of the resilient 9th Australian Infantry Division defending Tobruk, was forced to spend an undue amount of time defending his valiant troops against British accusations of indiscipline and breaches of military etiquette.

17. Jun. 41
Dearest Lu!
Still heavy fighting up front and I hope a decision will be reached today. You have no doubt read the details in the communiqué and can read between the lines.

Shortly after 16.00hrs, the 5th Light and 15th Panzer Divisions reached the Halfaya Pass, where they turned into line to advance northwards. This was a misjudgment, the result being to stretch out the pocket instead of closing it and preventing the enemy from escaping. The enemy was therefore able to pour back through the huge gap left between Sidi Omar and Halfaya. I was furious at the lost opportunity. Both divisions should have deployed facing the enemy directly they reached Halfaya; this would have brought them to battle and so prevented their escape. That way we should have destroyed their offensive strength.

So the three-day battle of Sollum came to an end. It ended in total victory for the defenders, though we could have inflicted more damage on the enemy than we in fact did.

In total, British losses accounted for more than 220 tanks and very heavy casualties among their troops. For our part, we lost only some 25 tanks completely written off.

18. Jun. 41
Dearest Lu!
The end of the three-day battle was complete victory. I am going up front to the troops now to thank them and give them further orders...

22. Jun. 41
Dearest Lu!
I was gone for three days visiting the battlefield. There is tremendous joy in the ranks of the African fighters over the

latest victory. The British thought they could crush us with 400 tanks of the heaviest type. We could not mount that quantity of armour against them...

29. Jun. 41
Dearest Lu!
We must expect the British to make another try before long, especially while we are tied up in Russia. I am preparing thoroughly for our next encounter. Churchill admitted to the House of Commons: 'The Battle of Sollum from the 15th to the 17th of June was a painful affair.' If that fellow is driven to such an admission it must have been quite a success!

Wavell's strategic planning for the offensive had been first rate. His considerable strategic courage and sense of balance distinguished him from other commanders, allowing him to concentrate his resources without having to consider his opponent's likely moves. He well knew the need to avoid an engagement which would enable his opponent to fight along his inner front and destroy his elements bit by bit with locally superior forces. However, his main disadvantage was the slowness of his heavy tanks which could not be deployed quickly enough to counter our faster armour. So we were able to exploit this weak spot – the slow speed of the main element of his armour.

The enemy plan was simple in the extreme, but simple plans are often a greater threat than complex ones. While the Italian and German forces were holding the Sollum-Halfaya position against frontal attack, the British planned to advance their assault units round the escarpment and then northwards. The Halfaya Pass was to be taken by an attack on both flanks, which would have seemed a certain success after their experience in

BELOW: Tobruk's defenders divide their faith between a well-dug-in anti-aircraft gun and their padre during an open-air field service in the summer of 1941.

May. Having opened the road through the passes, the British planned to concentrate their strength and move up to the north to unhinge our entire Sollum-Halfaya line. They would most probably have gone all out for Tobruk and attempted raising the siege there.

The crucial point in this battle was the Halfaya Pass itself, which Captain Bach and his troops held throughout heavy fighting. Pardi's artillery battery also performed with distinction in this engagement, and showed that Italian troops could give of their best when they had good officers. If the British had succeeded in taking the Halfaya Pass as planned, the situation would have been very different. They would have been poised to push both to the front and the rear along the coast, and would have been better placed to make tactical use of their armour under whatever circumstances. The British armoured divisions were unable to slow the advance of 5th Light and 15th Panzer Divisions on Halfaya, having been decimated by anti-aircraft, anti-tank and tank fire. It would now have been possible to destroy a large part of the British forces north of Sidi Suleiman, if the commanders had been aware of the possibility and taken the initiative themselves.

Wavell had been unable to shift his main force from Capuzzo to the Axis battle area, owing to the lack of pace in his tanks and the slowness of the British infantry at the moment of the German attack out of the desert north of Sidi Omar. There was nothing left for him but retreat, and this he managed with a minimum of British casualties.

This was particularly welcome news to the defenders of the main attack points on the Sollum Front, sections who had withstood the British onslaught to the last breath.

The assault had left a considerable impression on our higher commands. General Roatta, who after some time had finally set foot in North Africa, brought news of reinforcements: German strength in Libya would be increased to four mechanised divisions, and the Italian

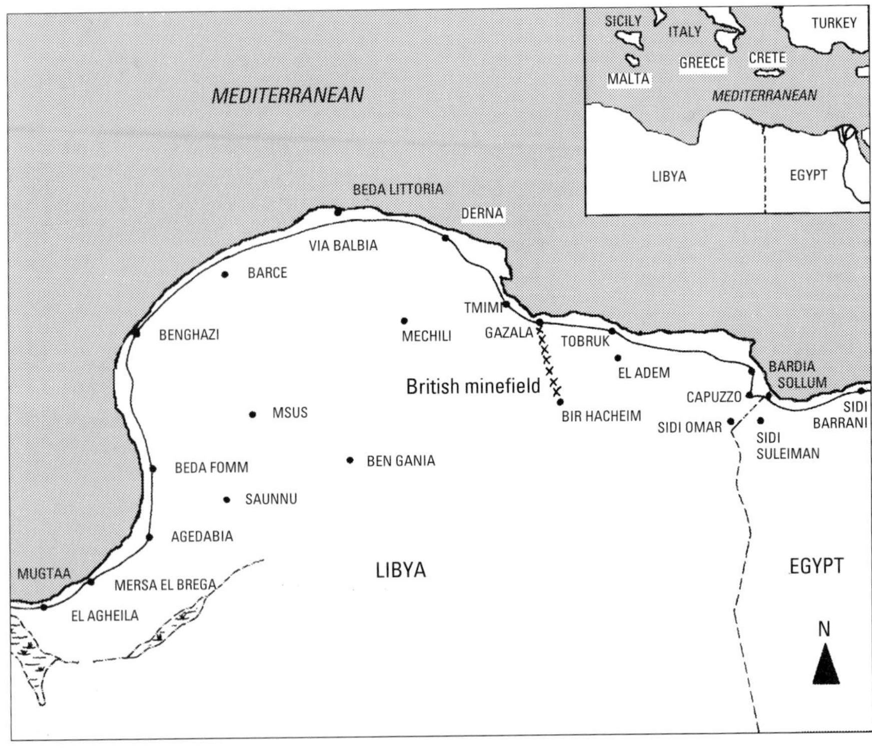

RIGHT: The area of the first period of the Rommel's war in North Africa. OPPOSITE: Italian gunners with a World War I artillery piece in 1941. Rommel acknowledged that Italian soldiers, well motivated and equipped, proved as able soldiers as any. But often badly led, with obsolescent weapons, they became a hazardous ally.

strike force would be brought up to a corps of three divisions, plus some two to three motorised divisions for overall increased mobility. Their enthusiasm was temporary, however.

Had these reinforcements arrived in Africa in the autumn of 1941 with fully guaranteed supplies, we could have fought off the British offensive in Marmarica, always assuming Auchinleck would have begun it under such circumstances.

At this time, Rommel was beginning to gain fairly detailed impressions of the commanders he was facing across the battlefield. His high opinion of Wavell, which Rommel was to reiterate in later writings, was not shared at this time by Churchill, who replaced him with Auchinleck following Sollum. After his own recall from North Africa, Rommel made a number of comments about his opposite numbers based on observations made during these relatively early encounters.

THE AFRIKA KORPS

Rommel's command was originally the Deutsches Afrika Korps (DAK) – a name dreamt up by Hitler. The DAK originally consisted of 5th Light Division and 15th Panzer Division. Rommel also had some degree of control over various Italian divisions.

In August 1941, Rommel's command was redesignated 'Panzer Gruppe Afrika'. This consisted of the Afrika Korps itself, under General Cruewell, which now comprised 15th Panzer, 21st Panzer (5th Light renamed) and 90th Light (essentially a division formed out of existing units in North Africa – it was not formally named 90th Light until November); and two Italian corps, Ariete and Trieste, over which Rommel's authority was informal. The final German formation that joined the Afrika Korps was the 164th Light Division, which came out to North Africa in August 1942.

The men of the DAK showed themselves to be extremely adept, especially in their ability to combine their armoured vehicles with anti-tank guns and mobile infantry. For his part, Rommel drove them hard, and many officers, especially in 1941, were aghast at his methods.

BELOW: Bearing the palm and swastika emblem of the Afrika Korps, this short-barrelled 75mm Panzer IV is being patched up in the field for rapid return to service. Greedy in fuel and difficult to service, the tanks that made mobile warfare possible also speedily drained the available resources they needed to remain mobile.

The ills affecting the excellent British motorised forces could not be removed simply by quickly retraining the officers and commanders, without the whole command structure – with the English this was an inordinately cumbersome affair – being changed. Up to the summer of 1942, British tanks and anti-tank guns had very poor range, and the tanks at first had no grenade launchers. It was also true that the highest-ranking British commanders had a certain methodical, rigid and bureaucratic outlook.

The exception was Wavell, a man of genial character. Auchinleck was a very good commander, but he handed over the majority of his tactical operational command to his subordinates (General Cunningham, General Ritchie), who soon allowed me to set the rules of the game, reacting rather than taking the initiative. This was wholly unnecessary. Neither Cunningham nor Ritchie were tank commanders and could not undertake the training of their men in modern mobile tactics...When General Auchinleck took over the tactical initiative himself at Alamein, he conducted the operation personally with skill and courage.

30. Jun. 41
Dearest Lu!
Work at our firmly rooted front is making good progress. I see that our armies are advancing very rapidly in Russia, apparently even faster than we had thought. This is of particular importance to us in Africa, since we must hold back during the Russian operations.

1. Jul. 41
Dearest Lu!
A pity we can't celebrate the second star together [Rommel had just been promoted

to 'General der Panzertruppen', roughly equivalent to lieutenant-general]. Aldinger reported the good news quite officially.

2. Jul. 41
Dearest Lu!
Much work, much travel. Roatta left here today. Unfortunately he could not do much of importance or even promise. The British seem very perturbed by our firm stand and probably wish they had not launched their last offensive.

By the autumn, the British, now commanded by Auchinleck, had launched their Crusader offensive, totally against Rommel's confident predictions. Oblivious to warnings about a British build-up, the general was busily preparing his own plan of attack. Having celebrated his 50th birthday in Rome while on a visit to the Duce, Rommel was away when the storm broke. However, Crusader was ineptly handled by both sides, and the result was more confusion than any outright gain, although it ended in tactical defeat for Rommel. Reports from Rommel and his staff, and his letters home, give an idea of the situation as fortunes swung to and fro.

18th November 1941
In the continuous heavy fighting between 18th November and 1st December, some 814 enemy armoured fighting vehicles and armoured cars have been destroyed, and 127 aircraft shot down. No estimate can be given yet of the booty in terms of weapons, ammunition and vehicles. Prisoners number over 9000, among them three generals.

At this point, unknown to Rommel, Major-General Ritchie had been sent to relieve Lieutenant-General Cunningham as commander of the Eighth Army. At 44 he was the youngest

BELOW: The opposition: British cruiser Mk VI Crusader tank knocked out in the fighting, and trailing a track. A solid vehicle that sacrificed speed, manoeuvrability and firepower for defensive armour, it was a poor tank in mobile operations.

RIGHT: A formation of battered Afrika Korps Panzer IIIs in the scrub desert of Cyrenaica after the failure to take Tobruk. The desert was an ideal arena for tank battles, providing rugged terrain with few obstacles, little cover and no risk of damage to civilian population or property.

general in the British Army, and he was instructed not to 'lose his nerve'. Ritchie was a methodical member of Auchinleck's staff, considered more reliable than Cunningham who, the commander decided, had lacked the authority to assert himself on the battlefield. Meanwhile, the fighting continued its inconclusive course.

2. Dec. 41
Dearest Lu!
Yesterday we succeeded in destroying one, or rather two, British divisions at T[obruk]. The tension has thus been eased, but if I know anything about the British, they won't quit yet.

3. Dec. 41
Dearest Lu!
It was somewhat quieter yesterday. There are indications that the enemy is breaking off his attack. Yesterday's communiqué probably gave you an idea of the magnitude and gravity of the fighting in the last few days.

4. Dec. 41
Dearest Lu!
The past night was disturbed by enemy air-raids. The staff and I are all right, so far as we can make out. I am moving! Let's hope the new place will be quieter...The battle continues. As it moved further to the west we had to regroup completely last night. I hope we succeeded. I cannot describe to you the bitterness of the fighting, but I hope to master it.

The attack of our two combined battle groups on the Bardia-Sollum line had failed. By 4th December, the army had a clear picture of the enemy deployments. A new force was being formed near Bir el Gobi, clearly intended to push past our flank and penetrate deep in our rear to unhinge the siege lines at Tobruk.

The Germans and Italians were hard pressed. For the first time since April 1941, the British had clearly taken the initiative and shown a determination to stick with it. However, once again Rommel saw the attack as an opportunity to try to seize the initiative by launching a counter-strike. On 6th December, he is unusually too preoccupied even to write home – a job deputed to his batman, Guenther:

6. Dec. 41
Dear Frau Rommel,
The present fighting takes up all of the general's time. We hope to clean up these attackers as we did the last ones. It will be

hard, though, as their superiority is very great...

The Afrika Korps began their attack on the 6th December, once again alone. The Italians reported that their troops were exhausted, and no longer fit for duty. The enemy retreated but slowly as far as Bir el Gobi, yet we could no longer hope to destroy, or even outflank and surround any worthwhile part of his force. Indeed, there was real risk of our own elements being encircled by the more numerous enemy units. Despite this, the attack was continued on 7th December, again meeting with no success, and casualties were high.

Not just a fateful day in the western desert, 7th December also saw the surprise Japanese attack on Pearl Harbor, followed a few days later by the precipitous declaration of war on the United States by Germany, a move that was to have profound consequences for Rommel's subsequent career. Interestingly, Rommel does not even refer briefly to this momentus event in his diaries – distant fronts were not the main preoccupation of the desert commander.

Rommel finally decided that further defence of his position was untenable, and sought to begin a full-scale withdrawal. The Italians, whose contribution of late had been less than visible, were up in arms. Both sides describe a stormy meeting between Rommel and the Italian Commander-in-Chief in Libya, General Bastico, the same day.

I also received a visit from Excellency Bastico...He is very upset at the way the campaign here is progressing, and is particularly worried about the Agedabia area, to which he wants to deploy an Italian division as soon as possible. It grew into a very stormy argument, in which I said, amongst other things, that I was not prepared to allow any of my Italian divisions to be taken and re-deployed by him. In addition, I assured him that I would have no hesitation in retreating through Cyrenaica with only my German formations, leaving the Italians to await their fate...Excellency Bastico thereupon became much more flexible.

The more vivid Italian record described Rommel as 'very excitedly and in an uncontrolled and impetuous manner' laying all blame at the Italians' door, and that he 'very heatedly, and acting like an overbearing and uncouth boor, yelled that he had struggled for victory for three weeks and had now decided to withdraw his divisions to Tripoli – and to have himself interned in Tunisia'.

Whatever the truth of the matter, Rommel was for the first time on the run in the North African campaign – and it was not an experience to his liking.

Following four bruising weeks of sustained and costly combat, the fighting strength of the men – notwithstanding tremendous individual achievements – is beginning to falter badly, in particular because the flow of equipment and ammunition has totally dried up. If the army intends to maintain its grasp of the Gazala sector during 16th December, withdrawal through the Mechili-Derna line will be unavoidable, at the latest by the night of 16th December, if it is to escape encirclement and total destruction by a superior enemy.

THE CRUSADER BATTLES

Rommel built up his strength during the summer and autumn of 1941, intending to launch an assault that would deliver Tobruk into his hands late in November. He ignored intelligence reports that the British were preparing their own offensive.

A new British commander in the Middle East, General Sir Claude Auchinleck, had established a new formation – the Eighth Army under Lieutenant-General Sir Alan Cunningham – and his attempt to relieve Tobruk was codenamed Operation Crusader.

Crusader showed both the best and worst of Rommel. His refusal to believe good intelligence about Allied intentions was wrong; and even when the offensive began he would not at first believe a major offensive was under way.

When the battle did begin, Rommel took personal command of counter-attacks, and at once virtually put paid to the Eighth Army's spearhead, 7th Armoured Division. His subsequent attack nearly came to grief, but he recouped the situation by brilliant command of armoured forces in the mobile battle. By early December his men were exhausted and he had to retreat, falling back to Mersa el Brega.

Further stormy encounters with his Italian counterparts and theoretical superiors were inevitable. Although more accustomed to the glow of military success, Rommel was adamant and competent in his recognition of the need to withdraw, sparing both men and materiel for the inevitable counter-offensive.

At my meeting with Marshal Cavallero, I stated that as things had turned out there was only one option left to me, that is to say, to disengage from the fight south of Gazala Bay near Tmimi at night, and pull our men back to Tmimi and Mechili respectively. The enemy had encircled this position entirely and the only escape route left to us was a narrow defile through Tmimi. The Italian troops now had little fight left. Cavallero made no objections at the time.

However, at 23.00hrs he re-appeared at my HQ, accompanied this time by Field Marshal Kesselring, Excellency Bastico, and General Gambara. In emotional tones, he demanded that the retreat order be immediately withdrawn. He could not see that it was necessary and was fearful for the political difficulties the Duce would suffer at the loss of Cyrenaica. Kesselring supported him forcefully saying that it was unthinkable for him to give up the airfield at Derna. I stood my ground saying it was too late to reverse the decision, the orders were issued and in some places being carried out already. Either the panzer group could face total annihilation, or it would have to fight its way back through enemy lines at night. I was fully aware this meant the loss of Cyrenaica and that a political fallout would result. But I faced a choice. Either to stay put and sacrifice the panzer group, losing both Cyrenaica and, inevitably, Tripolitania in the process, or to commence withdrawal overnight, fighting our way through Cyrenaica back to Agedabia to be able to defend Tripolitania at least.

I could only do the latter. Bastico and Gambara were so fraught in my room that evening that I finally had to ask Bastico how he himself proposed to deal with the situation, as commander-in-chief of African forces. But Bastico dodged the question, saying that as such it was not his affair. He would only repeat that we had to keep our forces together. In they end, they all left. Nothing had been achieved.

Once again, circumstances were to come to Rommel's aid. The British, doubtless aware through Ultra of the pressure being put on Rommel to hold the Gazala Line by his superiors in Rome and their German liaison counterparts, were therefore quite unprepared for the precipitous withdrawal that followed. Impulsive and often disobedient of direct instructions from above, Rommel was not an easy commander to anticipate, especially when his actions ran counter to the gist of intercepted and decoded signals between his field command HQ and Rome or even Berlin. Dynamic even in retreat, Rommel speedily drew his forces back under cover of darkness and bad weather to his chosen defence line at El Agheila, leaving the British advance columns floundering around his evacuated positions.

A combination of factors, including confusion, poor weather and transportation blockages with their attendant supply problems,

COMMAND IN THE MEDITERRANEAN

Rommel's position within the command structure of the Axis was complex and ill-defined. He was officially reporting to an Italian superior – Gariboldi and then Bastico – and through this superior to strategic direction from the Italian High Command. The direction of the Italian war effort was headed by Mussolini and Marshal Cavallero. Rommel believed the latter had no grasp of realities. A German staff officer, General von Rintelen, was the senior German attached to Commando Supremo, and with him Rommel did not enjoy good relations.

Effectively, Rommel did as he wished, arguing, cajoling, concealing and disobeying in order to get his way against Italian resistance. But his situation within the German command system was also somewhat anomalous. The Army High Command (OKH) was the final authority on his actions, but on occasion he sent his reports back to Hitler's personal structure (OKW). Rommel's status as a favourite of Hitler added to this confusion.

Field Marshal Albert Kesselring was placed in charge of German forces in the Mediterranean in late 1941, but he did not have operational control over Rommel's forces!

LEFT: Standing in their armoured car in the middle of the desert, Rommel points in one direction while Lieutenant-Colonel Fritz Bayerlein, Afrika Korps Chief of Staff, peers in another. Bayerlein and Cruewell managed occasionally to hold Rommel back from some of the more ambitious plans he was liable to initiate.

made it impossible for the British spearhead to pursue the withdrawal to the west of Rommel's DAK and Italian divisions. Apart from a couple of brushes with the 1st Armoured Division's advance 22nd Brigade, which were fought off successfully, Rommel's forces reached their defensive line unmolested and effectively intact.

Thus the impetus of Crusader trickled away in the desert sands of Cyrenaica. Tactically a defeat for Rommel, it was not on the other hand an obvious victory for the British, who had lost the opportunity to strike any sort of decisive blow against the Axis forces.

The cost of Crusader had been high on both sides. Axis losses totalled 38,000 men, although the majority of these were Italians listed as missing, while the British lost some 18,000 men, the majority, however, killed or wounded.

Chapter VI

Desert Magician

The early months of 1942 brought a sea change in Rommel's leadership of the Afrika Korps. From his tactical defeat after the Allied Crusader campaign, Rommel turned the tables on his foe and snatched his finest victories in the North African campaign.

The Crusader campaign of November-December 1941 had seen Rommel at his worst. He had been unwilling to believe that a major offensive was in the offing, his 'dash to the wire' had been a failure, and he had undone all the good work of Cruewell, whose steady control of the Afrika Korps during the opening of the Allied offensive had promised to bring victory. Forced to raise the siege of Tobruk, Rommel had extricated his forces and pulled them back to the Gazala position, 80km (50 miles) west of Tobruk, by 8th December.

Having shown himself at his worst, Rommel spent the next two months showing himself at

BELOW: Rommel gesticulates with characteristic impatience as an Italian ally looks on sceptically during the assault on Derna.

his very best: taking unpopular but realistic decisions and then seizing upon any opportunity that presented itself to turn the tables. He showed both great moral courage and great skill in manoeuvre, and completely confounded his unimaginative opponents.

The moral courage lay in the way that he decided, and stuck to, his belief that having abandoned the siege of Tobruk he should not try to hold on to Cyrenaica. He knew that, militarily, the ground was valueless, and that his chances of retaking it were much greater if he could pull back to Tripolitania to reinforce and replenish his army. This was a decision that ran counter to the wishes of the Italian High Command. This would be their second abandonment of Cyrenaica – and Cyrenaica was an Italian colony. This was not a situation in which Rommel could pull the wool over his superiors' eyes – as he had during his first spring offensive. But he stuck to his opinion, resisting all attempts to make him change his mind. At a meeting on 15th December, for example, where both his nominal superior (Bastico) and the Italian Chief of Staff Count Cavallero were pushing for him to try to hold on to Benghazi, he refused to make any compromise. All arguments – that the Axis garrisons near the Egyptian frontier (at Bardia and Halfaya) would probably be lost; that the airfields of Cyrenaica gave the Luftwaffe greater operational freedom and put more pressure on Malta – were ruthlessly disposed of.

Rommel got his way, and was given permission to pull out of Cyrenaica. On Christmas Eve, Axis forces abandoned Benghazi, and although the Allied forces tried to harass his retreat, the tough Afrika Korps armoured units turned and gave British forces a bloody nose at Agedabia. Rommel had got his way again.

Moral courage having brought him out of Cyrenaica, Rommel's military genius, his feel for the enemy and for his own chances, soon brought him back. There were various aspects to the change in the balance of forces. First, his losses in armour during Crusader were made up, to a certain extent, by two ships carrying tanks, one arriving in December, another early in January. Secondly, Luftwaffe strength in the Mediterranean had grown. Hitler had ordered an air fleet to the area, under Field Marshal Albert Kesselring. The additional air power had its effect: the very arrival of the extra panzers in North Africa owed much to the extra pressure put on Malta – cruisers from Malta were attacked and forced to abandon the chase just as they were setting off after the first of the convoys. The relative ease with which ground targets could be located and targeted in the open and often featureless desert made air power an important ingredient in the North African campaign.

The third factor creating the window that Rommel saw opening before him lay in the Allied dispositions. All Allied plans were overlaid, from 7th December, by concerns over the Far East, where Japan had begun its great offensive and opened the conflict out into a true world war. Some Allied forces – an Australian division, the British 70th Division, and the 7th Hussars – were moved out to the Far East. But quite apart from concerns in the Far East, the British High Command was complacent after Crusader. The most experienced armoured formation – 7th Armoured Division – was back in Egypt refitting. Auchinleck intended to attack Tripolitania, but believed that he had a breathing space to build up his forces. So he left

'ROMMEL – WHATEVER MATTERS BUT BEATING HIM?'

Rommel's reputation among the British and Commonwealth forces owed much to Winston Churchill's decision to use the German commander as a reason for the failure of the British in North Africa. The success of the audacious German attack that retook Cyrenaica in January 1942 – after Allied propaganda had described the Afrika Korps as being on the verge of annihilation in the wake of the Crusader battles – had to be explained somehow, and Churchill suggested: 'We have a very daring and skilful opponent against us and, may I say across the havoc of war, a great general.'

Auchinleck, commanding Allied forces in the Middle East, felt impelled to send out a memorandum to senior officers, because 'the real danger is that our friend Rommel is becoming a kind of magician or bogeyman to our troops, who are talking far too much about him.' Auchinleck finished his memo by insisting that he was not jealous of Rommel – which caused great hilarity among Rommel's staff when a copy of the document was captured and translated. For the British troops, however, there was little doubt that the successful German counter of January 1942 ranked as something almost magical.

1st Armoured Division, fresh from the UK, in Cyrenaica. Effectively, immediately facing Rommel were an armoured brigade never tested in combat, and a weakened infantry division. The Afrika Korps' intelligence soon recognised that – and once Rommel himself knew, his instinct, his genius for seizing the moment came into play. His letters home make clear how his satisfaction early in January in completing his retreat turned to elation as he realised that there was a new opportunity on offer.

4. Jan. 42
Dearest Lu!
Movements proceed according to plan. Full moon nights! Field Marshal Kesselring is coming up again today. We cooperate very closely now.

6. Jan. 42
Dearest Lu!
Cold and storms are setting in over here. The operation is going according to plan, which has the Duce's approval.

10. Jan. 42
Dearest Lu!
One loses all sense of time here, yesterday's letter was dated 10th as well.

Our mines and our air force give the enemy trouble. Just think of it: the bulk of our forces is still intact and I was able to lead them back to good positions after a withdrawal of 500km (300 miles) without their being greatly weakened. I can understand why the dyed-in-the-wool strategists screw up their faces. Criticism is cheap. Today, for the first time since 18th November, the Afrika Korps has been pulled back to secondary positions. Cruewell has a severe case of jaundice. I don't know whether he will pull through. Now I am the only officer of the German forces who has stood up from beginning to end...

17. Jan. 42
Dearest Lu!
The situation is turning out well and my head is full of plans which I may not even mention to those around me. They would think I am crazy. But I am sure I am not...

21. Jan. 42
Dearest Lu!
Two hours from now the army will launch its counter-attack. After thorough weighing of all the pros and cons I decided to risk it. I firmly trust that the

BELOW: Rommel peers through binoculars from an SdKfz 250 armoured half-track at smoke billowing up from the fighting along the horizon.

LEFT: A panzer unit bivouacked in the desert. Spartan conditions, poor rations, unreliable drinking water and primitive sanitation led to a high level of dysentry, jaundice and sundry gastric complaints among desert soldiers.

Lord will hold his protecting hand over us and give us the victory...

Rommel knew he had to strike before the British could build up their forces. He kept his intentions completely secret: by now he had developed a fear that the Italians would reveal his intentions to the Allies. In fact, it was Ultra intercepts, not treachery, that lay behind British intelligence; but his desire for secrecy had the right effect. There was no reconnaissance of enemy positions, and even the German divisional commanders were not told of the offensive until 19th January. So when the first German units moved into the attack on the 21st, surprise was almost complete; and the day was made even better for Rommel because he received yet another honour in the course of it, while waiting for his tanks to drive off.

22. Jan. 42
Dearest Lu!
How did you like the award of the Swords to the Oak Leaves of the Knights Cross? I was very pleased. It showed me that the Fuehrer fully approved of my actions during the past grave weeks. And what do you think of the counter-attack that we launched at 08.30hrs yesterday? Our opponents took off as if stung by a hornet. Have high hopes for the next few days...

25. Jan. 42
Dearest Lu!
We had four days of absolute success. Our blows struck the enemy between the eyes! One more to go. Then we'll become meek again and lie in waiting...another two weeks and I'll be able to leave here to report and receive the Swords. It's wonderful for a general to have his capabilities recognised and to have an opportunity to make a contribution for Fuehrer, nation and idea...

Rommel had not, of course, told Bastico, his nominal superior, about the offensive, and first Italian reactions were of fury. But as before, success brought approbation. On 26th January, Mussolini himself congratulated Rommel on driving the Allies back from the frontier of Tripolitania. Rommel was worried about fuel shortages, which constrained his natural urge to push directly across the Cyrenaican 'bulge'; but a feint towards Mechili and a drive towards Benghazi had the desired effect. British forces withdrew as far as the Gazala position.

This retreat was not a serious defeat for the British: indeed, Auchinleck had contemplated such a manoeuvre before the German attack. Like Rommel in December, he could see no point in holding ground that was strategically vulnerable and merely extended supply lines. To the outside world, however, and to the British soldiery, the way the Axis had bounced back was astonishing, and could only be put down to a rare display of military genius.

By the German people, too, Rommel's military genius was now taken for granted, and when he took his predicted leave in Germany in March, his investiture with the Swords to the Oak Leaves of the Knights Cross was a fitting cap to his triumph. Meanwhile, his force had been upgraded in status to 'Panzerarmee Afrika', and he himself promoted to colonel-general. In conversation, Rommel and the Fuehrer talked about the possibilities of taking Egypt, which Rommel felt was perfectly feasible with a modest reinforcement, especially if the island of Malta was taken.

While Rommel's troops moved towards the Gazala position, and their commander enjoyed the limelight in Germany, Auchinleck, who had been confidently expecting to launch his own spring offensive, found that the balance of forces had now swung away from him. He had lost material during the retreat; Far Eastern concerns were denying him priority, while Malta, under concerted air bombardment, was no longer offering the threat it had to Axis supply lines. Auchinleck reported to Churchill that German technical superiority meant that he needed a superiority of 2:1 in tanks to undertake the offensive himself – and he did not have this in May when Rommel, having built up his forces, took the offensive again. In general, Rommel considered himself hard done by so far as supplies went, because he was far down the Axis order of priorities (wrongly, as he saw it), but he recognised that spring 1942 did offer him an opportunity, in spite of Allied logistic superiority, as he described in 1943, when reflecting on the North African campaign:

BELOW: Rommel congratulating and exhorting his ragged but victorious troops after the capture of Benghazi in January 1942.

After the end of our counter-offensive, which at the outset of 1942 had led to the re-conquest of Cyrenaica, there were serious shortages of supplies.

Aside from the lack of interest shown in the North African theatre by the German High Command who had failed to recognise its importance, the blame for this lay in the lacklustre war conducted by the Italians at sea. The British navy on the other hand was extremely active in the first months of 1942 and sank a number of ships. The RAF was also particularly troublesome.

My superiors still failed to see that the African theatre occupied a position of any importance. They did not realise that we could have won victories in the Near East, which would have overtaken the Don Bend conquest in Russia in strategic and economic significance. Before us lay a land rich in raw materials – Africa and the Middle East which could have spared us further worries about oil shortages. The strengthening of my army by just a few more divisions and adequate supplies would have been enough to ensure the complete defeat of the British armed forces in the Near East.

But – it has to be said – in the absence of strategic foresight the Afrika Korps suffered. The results were serious: for a year and a half we kept the British busy in North Africa with just three German divisions – which were often ridiculously reduced in strength – giving their troops a proper mauling until our strength finally gave way before Alamein.

With six German divisions, we could have smashed the British so thoroughly in the summer of 1942 that the threat from the south could have been be eliminated for a long time to come. Sufficient supplies could have been organised to support these formations if the will had been there. Later, in Tunisia, when it was altogether too late, it became possible to double the supplies. By that time it had become clear even on the mainland that we were up to our necks in trouble.

After March 1942, when out of a total requirement of 60,000 tons just 18,000 tons reached the Panzer Army in Africa, the situation changed thanks to the initiative of Field Marshal Kesselring, who succeeded in gaining air superiority over the Mediterranean with the Luftwaffe in the spring of 1942. The heavy air raids on Malta, for example, effectively neutralised the danger to our shipping routes for a time. On account of this, an increased flow of materiel into the ports of Tripoli, Benghazi and Derna became possible. The reinforcement and re-equipping of the German-Italian forces thereafter proceeded apace.

Despite this, it was clear to us that the British Eighth Army was being re-supplied faster still. Great efforts were made by the British commanders to ensure that all possible war materiel necessary was made available to the Eighth Army. Large convoys were constantly pouring into the Egyptian ports unloading war supplies brought around the Cape from England or America. Naturally, this 12,000-nautical-mile voyage, which could only be undertaken by the British supply ships at most once or twice a year, must have been a severe drain on their organisational staffs, on account of their having to cope

TANKS AND ANTI-TANK GUNS

There has been considerable debate about the relative merits of the key equipment used in the desert battles, and the two sides themselves had different perspectives. The Crusader tank that Allied crews thought was an unreliable death trap in 1941-42 was felt to be a good weapon by German observers, for example. It is difficult to deny, however, that the German Mk III and Mk IV tanks were better than anything the Allies could put against them until the Grant and Sherman tanks came into service in summer 1942, and even then an up-gunned Mk IV was still the best tank in North Africa until Mk VI Tigers arrived in Tunisia.

Where the Germans did have an advantage was in their 88mm anti-aircraft/anti-tank guns. In the anti-tank role, these packed a punch that the Allies could not match.

The Afrika Korps' major advantage, however, lay in the way it combined its various arms – especially anti-tank guns and armour. It developed a method of advancing using tanks to clear a way and then leapfrogging anti-tank guns forward to deal with enemy counter-attacks.

with the considerable hardship imposed by our U-Boat warfare. Despite this, the British navy and merchantmen were able to maintain supplies to the British forces in the Near East at a rate far superior to ours even over such great distance. The British could obtain all their petrol from the refineries in the Near East.

Only occasionally did the British supply ports receive serious attention from German bomber attacks. From these [ports] the British had three routes to follow for sending supplies down the line to the front:

a) A well-built rail-track from the Suez area to the outskirts of Tobruk.
b) The British navy had established an admirable coastal shipping organisation, and occupied the ports of Mersah Matruh and Tobruk, the latter being one of the best ports in Africa.

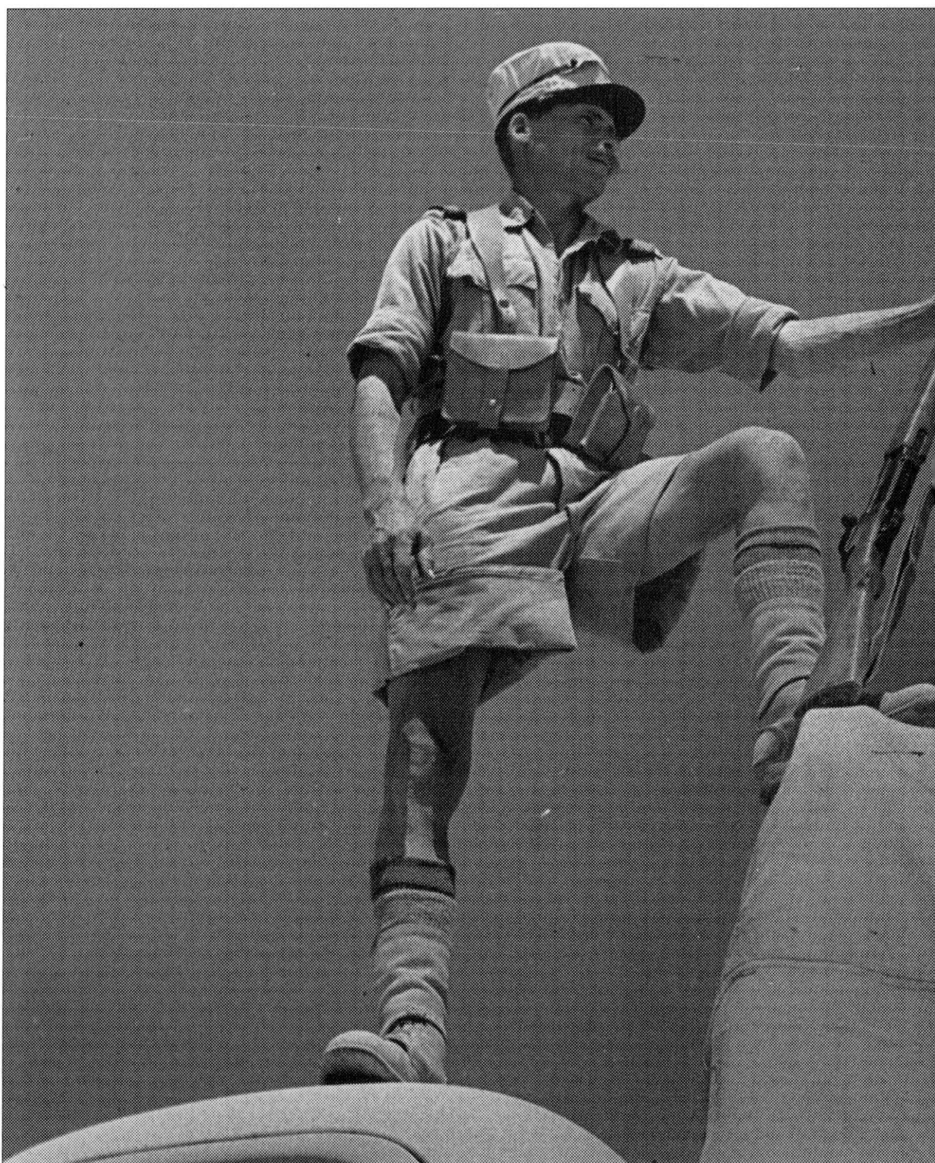

RIGHT: 'Gaullists, swashbucklers and criminals of twenty different nations' was how Alfred Berndt, Rommel's chief aide, described the defenders of Bir Hacheim. Free French troops, mostly in the Foreign Legion, stubbornly resisted every effort to oust them by artillery, air raids and blockade until finally capitulating on 11th June 1942 after 16 unrelenting days of hell.

c) The coast road and the numerous transport vehicles at their disposal.

Above all, however, the British had on their side people with greater influence and considerable insight, who did all they could to organise the efficient provision of supplies. My enemies benefited from this:

a) The British considered the North African theatre to be decisive in the war.

b) North Africa was the key theatre of war for the British Empire.
c) The British had in the Mediterranean a powerful and excellent navy and air force, while we had to contend with the unreliable Italian naval staffs.
d) The whole British Eighth Army was motorised down to the last unit.

It was quite clear to us that the English would try by every means possible to annihilate our army as soon as they felt sufficiently strong. Our southern flank was open. The enemy had a wide range of possible options open to them. Our supply lines would be under continual threat. If we were compelled to withdraw owing to the danger of being outflanked we would be in very serious difficulties, for most of my Italian divisions were not motorised. But Ritchie was not to have the chance to exploit his many opportunities, for I had decided to anticipate his attack.

Major-General Ritchie, commanding Eighth Army, had set up an extensive defensive system along the Gazala Line, but if the intention was to deny Rommel mobility, it was fatally flawed in that it could do nothing about the wide-open southern flank; and although the British were aware that they needed to concentrate their armoured forces to counter-attack when the Germans came, such concentration had not been achieved. Rommel was well aware of these weaknesses in dispositions and doctrine, and also of the strength of the defensive 'boxes'.

The groundplan for the British defence of Marmarica was based on the intention to impose on the attacker a means of warfare more amenable to the British leadership than was manoeuvring in the open desert. The technical execution of this plan was faultless.

The British were altogether wrong in their approach to the solution of the problem. Given any position with an open southern flank in the North African desert, a rigid defensive stance will lead to catastrophe. The defensive fight has to be taken on to the offensive. Self-evidently, defended positions can be of great signifi-

RIGHT: German artillery awaits the order to open up with 105mm howitzers during the bombardment of Bir Hacheim, June 1942.

cance, if the enemy is to be prevented from carrying out operations. But the manning of them must on no account be at the expense of the mobile force.

The deployment of British troops in Marmarica was as follows:

From the coast near Gazala a heavily mined defence line stretching away to the south was occupied by the 50th British and 1st South African Divisions. From the southern point a deep minefield continued on as far as Bir Hacheim. This location was the southern stronghold of the British Gazala position and was built as a fortress. Its defences were festooned with mines. It was occupied by the 1st Free French Brigade.

The whole line had been built with great skill. It was the first time such a line had been set up so far into the desert. Around 500,000 mines had been sown in this defence area alone.

At a crossroads some kilometres east of the centre of the Gazala Line was the 'Knightsbridge' strongpoint, held by the British 201st Guards Brigade.

The area near El Haitan and Batruna was heavily reinforced to cover the southern approaches to Tobruk. The El Adem Box, as this was called, was occupied by troops of the 5th Indian Division. Tobruk itself served as supply base and as support position for the Gazala Line as a whole. From 1941 the British had been carrying out improvements in the defences at Tobruk, particularly in laying extensive minefields in the defensive position. These defences were manned by the reinforced 2nd South African Division.

All fortified positions were supplied with powerful artillery, infantry, tanks and armoured vehicles. The whole line had been constructed with consummate skill. Positions and strongpoints had been built according to the concepts of modern warfare. Countless mines – over a million around all the Marmarica area – had been laid by the engineers. To judge from the 150,000 or so more mines which my troops recovered from the British rear areas, they had plans to distribute yet more.

Besides these fully motorised forces, the British held powerful tank and motorised formations in reserve behind the main defence works (1st and 7th Armoured Divisions and several freestanding mechanised brigades and units).

Although it was basically a second-best solution, especially given the motorisation of their whole force, the British defence plan was cunningly constructed and extremely hard for us to overcome.

THE BALANCE OF FORCES

At the outset of the battle, the German-Italian Panzer Army consisted of one Italian and two German panzer divisions, plus one German and one Italian motorised division. The German-Italian High Command had under its command a further four Italian non-motorised infantry divisions and one non-motorised German rifle brigade. During the battle, Commando Supremo also sent us the Italian armoured division Littorio.

In total we had three German divisions and one German brigade, plus seven Italian divisions, out of which only three were motorised and therefore of any use in a mobile battle. Many German and all Italian units were below full strength. The 90th Light Division, for example, had a company strength of only 50 men. The Italians were hardest hit, to the extent that an Italian motorised division could be considered a brigade, and an Italian infantry division a regiment.

Until May 1942 our tanks had for the most part been superior to their British counterparts. This was now no longer the case. During the summer campaign, the American-built Grant tank appeared and was a certain match for our long-barrelled Panzer IV. But only four of this type were available on African soil, and in any case we had no ammunition for them so they could play no practical part in the battle. Our short-barrelled Panzer IV was clearly superior to the Grant in speed, but the Grant with its longer-range gun could brew up a short-barrelled Panzer IV at a distance from which the latter's rounds could not hope to penetrate the American tank's heavy armour. Whereas the British had 160 Grant tanks, we had only 40 short-barrelled Panzer IVs.

Our Panzer III, with which the bulk of our armoured units was equipped, was primarily armed with a 5cm gun (the majority of them being short-barrelled) and was even less competition for the Grant. The British tanks, which were armed with a 40mm gun, were inferior to the Panzer III. However, a large proportion of the older British tanks had been re-equipped with a 75mm gun, making them very potent. The 240 Italian tanks could in

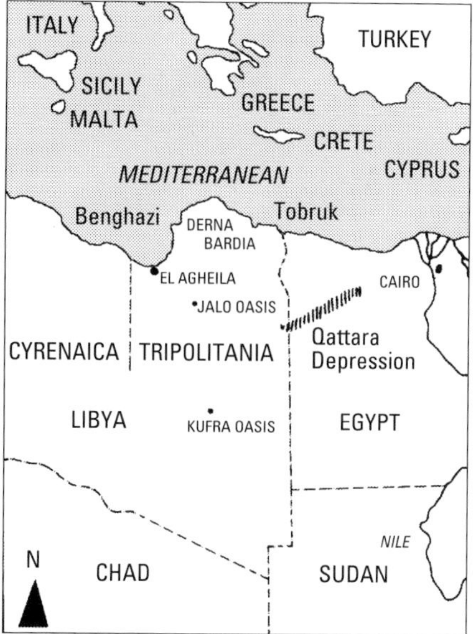

LEFT: The North African theatre of operations.

ROMMEL'S METHOD OF COMMAND

Rommel's method of command involved him in taking personal risks, and risking losing contact with his command structure. He preferred being at the front, and if he was not actually at the front he was likely to be flying around in his Fieseler Storch light aircraft trying to get a feel for the way the battle was developing or visiting some outlying sector.

At the Battle of Gazala, for example, the chain of command effectively collapsed early in the battle because he insisted on being in the front line, and the Luftwaffe could not support the ground attacks because there was no information from army headquarters. And yet the feel for the battle that being in the front gave Rommel was, in the end, invaluable at Gazala. On 28th May he led Italian armoured forces up in support of the Afrika Korps to maintain the momentum of the offensive, and on 31st May he was with the panzer grenadiers in the front line, urging them on, when the British infantry defending the box in the 'Cauldron' surrendered.

At his best, Rommel embodied the Napoleonic quality of being able to control the timing on a battlefield, and to bring together seemingly disparate forces to surprise an enemy.

no way match the British ones. For some time the troops had been referring to them as 'rolling coffins'.

It was the same situation with the artillery: the British had superiority (8:5).

The German-Italian air force, despite variations from time to time, was on a level par with the RAF at first. Later things were to change considerably.

In quantity and quality the British armoured forces enjoyed considerable superiority over the Panzer Army.

Rommel hoped to fool his enemy into believing there would be an attack in the north or centre of the positions, while he in fact intended to lead the Afrika Korps in a great sweep round the Allied southern strongpoint at Bir Hacheim.

The following plan prepared by myself and my colleagues must be judged from all these viewpoints. It should be seen as the best decision under the most favourable circumstances. The fate of my army was in no way dependent on the success of this plan since, following my given principles, I assumed throughout the possibility of failure, of things not going as well as they should. But even in that case, the situation at the start of the battle would, as far as one could tell, be not wholly unfavourable. We anticipated the coming battle with optimism, trusting the excellent tactical training of our troops and their experience and initiative.

The opening move of the offensive was to be made in the form of a frontal attack by the Italian infantry divisions occupying the Gazala positions against the 50th British Division and the South Africans. A powerful force of artillery was earmarked to support this attack. The impression was

BELOW: Orders of the day. Rommel confers with Major-General Bismarck (left), commander of the 21st Light Division, while Colonel Fritz Bayerlein, Rommel's Afrika Korps Chief of Staff, looks on beneath his desert goggles.

to be created both by day and by night that tank assembly positions existed behind the front. For this purpose tanks and lorries were to be driven round in circles in this area. The British command was to be made to expect our main attack in the northern and central part of the Gazala position. What we wanted to achieve was for the British tank formations to deploy behind the infantry on this sector of the front. To the British command, the idea of a German frontal attack against the Gazala position could not have appeared too far-fetched as it was by no means impossible that we should prefer such an attack to the risky right hook round Bir Hacheim...

During daylight hours all movement of my motorised forces was to be directed towards the point of attack of the Italian infantry. But after nightfall the motorised group was to drive into its assembly area. This group consisted of the German Afrika Korps with the 15th and 21st Panzer Divisions, the XX Italian Motorised Corps, and the 90th Light Division with the three reconnaissance units. The beginning of the advance, which was to take the form of an enveloping attack on Bir Hacheim, was fixed for 22.00hrs. From there the German Afrika Korps and XX Italian Corps with the Ariete Tank Division and Trieste Motorised Division were to push on to the coast via Acroma, in order to cut the supply line and smash the British division located in the Gazala position, together with the tank forces which were assembled there .

The 90th Light Division was ordered to push into the El Adem-El Hamed area together with the three reconnaissance units in order to prevent the withdrawal of the Tobruk garrison and the bringing up of reinforcements into the Acroma area. In addition the British were to be cut off from the extensive supply depots which they had established in the area east of Tobruk. In order to simulate the existence of massed tank forces in that area, the 90th Light Division had been equipped with lorries on which were mounted aero-engines fitted with propellers, which were intended, by stirring up large quantities of dust, to suggest the approach of strong tank forces. We wanted to keep the British forces in that area from intervening in the Acroma battle, so long as our tank units were trying to achieve a decision there.

Following upon the destruction of the British forces in the Marmarica we had planned for a rapid conquest of the fortress of Tobruk. My freedom of operation had been limited by the Duce to the area bounded by the Egyptian frontier.

It had actually been intended that Malta should be taken by Italian and German parachute and landing forces before the offensive started, but for some unaccountable reason our High Command abandoned this scheme. Unfortunately, my request to have this attractive little job entrusted to my own army had been turned down back in the spring. Consequently, in view of the steady increase in British war potential, we fixed the date of the attack for 26th May 1942.

The fighting, which was to end in a stunning German triumph, was hard – partly because Rommel had miscalculated the strength of positions such as the strongpoint at Bir Hacheim. He was fortunate that his opponents were unable to take full advantage of this.

May/June 1942

During these three weeks a war of attrition was waged in the Western Desert in its most violent form. The fighting began badly for us, but in the struggle that followed we were successful in defeating the enemy units one after the other despite the courageous fight they put up.

World opinion was taken by surprise at this success of my German-Italian troops in the light of such superior British strength. The actions of my opponent, Lieutenant-General Ritchie, received strong criticism. Was it really true that the British commander's errors were responsible for the defeat?

After the battle I saw an article by the British military critic Liddell Hart, who put the shortcomings of the British command during the African campaign down to the British general's close familiarity with infantry warfare. I was of the same opinion. The British commanders had failed to learn from the consequences of their defeat in 1941-42.

Prejudice against novel methods is a phenomenon typical of an officer corps raised in a proven system. The Prussian Army was defeated for this reason by Napoleon. The same phenomenon showed up in this war, in German as well as British officer circles, where complicated theories obstructed the capability to see things in reality. A military dogma had been worked out in every last detail, and this was taken to represent the very peak of military wisdom. In their minds, the only military thought acceptable was that which followed their own doctrine. Everything other than the rule was a game of chance; and it followed that success could only be the result of luck or accident. This attitude leads to fixed ideas, the consequences of which are incalculable.

I believe that my old opponent, General Ritchie – like many generals of the old school – had not fully appreciated the consequences of having fully motorised operations conducted in the open desert. Despite the good detailed nature of his plans, they were bound to fail, since they were in effect a compromise.

26th May 1942

On 26th May at 14.00hrs, the Italian infantry under General Cruewell launched a frontal assault on the Gazala Line following a softening-up by heavy artillery. To deceive the British who – as stated – were to be given the impression that the main Axis thrust was to be at this point, so bringing up their armour, one Afrika Korps panzer regiment and one from the XX Italian Corps were attached to the assault groups, to be returned to their own formations in the evening. The British forward reconnaissance posts in advance of the Gazala Line offered little resistance, and drew back to their defence positions.

The strike force, the DAK, 90th Light Division, and XX Italian Corps, assembled at their appointed locations. On the

RIGHT: Auchinleck stops his jeep for a word with an Indian sentry in the summer of 1942, shortly before he was relieved by Churchill. The rugged, all-terrain jeep – newly arrived from the United States – proved a popular and efficient desert vehicle much admired by the Germans in North Africa.

evening of 26th June elements of this force moved off towards the Italian attack point and were spotted as intended by the British evening air reconnaissance patrols. They then turned around and hared back in great haste to the assembly positions.

At 20.30hrs I gave the order for Operation Venezia [the 'right hook' around the south of the Allied positions] to begin. The 10,000 vehicles of the strike force set off.

In the moonlight my staff and I left with our DAK unit for the great tank battle. Far in the distance one could see lights glowing now and then. It was probably the Luftwaffe, trying to locate Bir Hacheim with flares. I had felt tense and impatient waiting for the day to come. What will the enemy do, what has he already done were the questions which raced through my head. Only the next day could tell. The thousands of vehicles rolled on without pause. The drivers had considerable difficulty not losing sight of the man ahead.

Shortly before daybreak there was a one-hour break in the desert some 20km (12 miles) southeast of Bir Hacheim. Then the great formation started to move again, and amid swirling dust and sand the units pushed on into the British rear. British minefields and decoys offered some difficulties, but an hour or two after daybreak saw all units of the Panzer Army in headlong advance towards their allotted objectives. Already by 10.00hrs the 90th Light Division reported having reached El Adem. Numerous supply dumps of the British XXX Corps, which had its stores depot here, had fallen into their hands. Around midday, the British command reacted, and a mighty battle with the British strike force broke out.

As I and my staff tried around midday to reach the 90th Light Division, our column was attacked by British tanks and we were forced back. Contact between DAK and the 90th Light Division was broken. We attempted to fight our way back to DAK. Suddenly, we were faced with a British battery that was apparently moving up from Bir Hacheim to Tobruk. Although not much of a fighting force, we took on the British on the move and rounded them up. Clearly, they were completely surprised.

In retrospect on our first day of the battle it was clear that our plan, to overrun the British units behind the Gazala Line, was a failure. Also the push towards the coast was not successful, and thus we had been unable to cut off the 50th British and 1st South African Divisions from the remaining elements of the Eighth Army. The main reason for this was the fact that we had underestimated the strength of the British armoured divisions. The arrival of the new American tank had torn great holes in our ranks. Above all, our forces now were locked in heavy and destructive combat with a superior enemy.

28th May 1942

I cannot deny but that by the evening of that day I was full of worries. Our severe tank losses were not a good start. The 90th Light Division under General Kleeman had been split off from the DAK and was now in a very serious position. Through

WHAT HAPPENED IN THE 'CAULDRON'?

The Battle of Gazala was Rommel's greatest victory. The battle began on 26th May 1942. Rommel's plan was to outflank the British positions and then to engage the enemy in an armoured battle behind their main defensive line. The outflanking manoeuvre worked, but the British position was stronger than anticipated. There was confusion. On 28th and 29th May, Rommel kickstarted the attack, and on 31st May took a British brigade 'box' in an area known as the 'Cauldron', on the British side of the Gazala front-line. But to continue his plan, he needed to break through the defensive position of Bir Hacheim (held by a Free French brigade) at the south end of the Gazala Line.

Bir Hacheim held out until 11th June – which should have left Rommel and his Afrika Korps units isolated and vulnerable in the 'Cauldron'. But in severe fighting on 5th and 6th June, British attacks on Rommel's troops were severely defeated. Using a screen of anti-tank guns, the Germans destroyed over 100 British tanks and launched accurate counter-attacks to send a numerically superior enemy reeling back. On 12th and 13th June, after the fall of Bir Hacheim, there were more large armoured battles that finished the British armour.

RIGHT: Rommel and his staff gleefully pick over a knocked-out British light tank during the lull between taking Benghazi and the assault on the heavily defended fortress at Tobruk, early summer 1942.

the open gap streamed British motorised units hunting for our transport columns, which had become separated from the rest and which were for us a lifeline.

Despite the serious position on the evening of 27th May, which promised severe problems, I looked forward to the coming battle full of hope. For Ritchie had thrown his tanks into battle a bit at a time, thereby giving us the opportunity at each engagement to counter them with a near parity of armour. This dividing up of the British armoured strength was incomprehensible, since no strategic or operational gain whatsoever was to be had from the sacrifice of their 7th Armoured Division south of Bir el Harmat, since it was the same to the British whether my panzer divisions were brought to battle here, or at Trigh el Abd, where the rest of the British armour was subsequently engaged. The main aim of the British should have been to bring all their armoured units into the action at the same time. They should never have allowed themselves to be fooled either into splitting their forces before the battle, or by our diversionary attack on the Gazala Line. The full motorisation of their forces enabled rapid deployment across the battlefield to wherever a threat appeared. Desert warfare has often been compared to sea warfare, and rightly so. It is equally incorrect at sea to engage in battle with half the fleet left in port.

The first days of the offensive had seen the Germans push well into the British rear areas: but the strong Allied boxes of Sidi Muftah, 'Knightsbridge' and Bir Hacheim were formidable obstacles, threatening their communications and supply lines, while, as Rommel realised, the diversion of 90th Light from the main thrust line had weakened his position. What would the next day bring?

28th May 1942

At first light on 28th May, I scoured the horizon through my binoculars to see what was happening in our neighbourhood. In the northeast, I saw British forces retreating towards the west. We still had no contact with the main section of the Panzer Army. Shortly after daybreak, British armour opened fire on my command post. All around us shells were falling. The windscreen of our command bus was shattered. Luckily we were able to get out of the Tommies' range in our vehicles. Later that morning I drove to the Italian XX Corps. I ordered them to march out following the DAK.

I was getting anxious and wished to make contact with the two panzer divisions. I set out that afternoon with General Gause, my chief of staff, to try and find a passable way to them. Meanwhile a radio signal had been received, with the alarming information that a section of the 15th Light was out of ammunition and unable to continue the fight. Bringing up the supply columns was of the utmost urgency. By late afternoon we were able, with some vehicles and anti-tank units, to climb a hill about 15km (nine miles) north of Bir el Harmat, and from there we could see the DAK. A typical picture of desert warfare presented itself. Black smoke rolled skywards, giving the landscape a haunted, curious beauty. I decided to bring up the supplies for the DAK early next morning through this way.

On the way back to our command post, however, we had a short engagement with both a British and an Italian column. The latter also took us for the enemy and opened fire widly; we escaped by rapidly retreating.

I myself formed up the supply columns later that night ready to go up to the DAK. In view of the shortage of cover available to us, on this journey through a sector predominated by British units, a risky operation was in store.

As we arrived on the battle scene, the DAK was directly attacked from the north and east by British tanks. Through lack of petrol and ammunition, the Korps had been severely restricted in its ability to fight. Now at last this situation could be eased. I set my command post up that afternoon.

Under these conditions, it was much too risky to continue our attack to the north, as originally planned. I saw the consequences of this. Of outstanding importance to us at the moment was to ensure a safe supply line to our army strike force. To this end, elements of the 90th Light Division and sections of the DAK were to be sent against the minefields to the east. To assist this operation, the remaining units were to take up defensive positions along a shortened front. Once the Gazala defences had been penetrated, I intended to squeeze Bir Hacheim, the southern strongpoint of the British front.

I went ahead on the basis that with strong German motorised forces positioned south of the coast road, the British would find it too risky to use any large part of their armoured forces against

Left: South African troops at Sollum, 1942. Like the Australians in 1941, these Commonwealth soldiers fought with determination and distinction to keep Tobruk from German hands. This time round, however, they were overwhelmed.

the Italians on the Gazala Line, as a counter-attack by my forces would have placed them between frying pan and fire. On the other hand, I hoped that the presence of the Italian infantry in front of the 1st South African and 50th British divisions would help to persuade the ever-cautious British commanders to leave those units whole on the Gazala front. It was perfectly impossible, to my mind, that Ritchie would order both these divisions to attack the Italian corps without support from other units, such an operation not coming up to the British expectation of 100 per cent certainty. So as I saw it, the British motorised brigades would continue to hammer our panzer units head on until they wore themselves out. The defence was to be conducted with extraordinary elasticity and mobility.

Having personally sorted out the supply situation by leading from the front, and being directly involved in the critical sector, Rommel had now also reorganised his battle plan. Once again, he underestimated the resistance of Allied defensive positions – but his basic belief that enemy armour was no match for the Afrika Korps proved absolutely correct.

30th May 1942

At first light on 30th May each of the divisions moved into the area assigned to it and took up a defensive position. During these movements we noticed the presence of strong British forces with tanks in the Ualeb area. This was the strengthened 150th British Brigade from the 50th Division. In the meantime part of the X Italian Corps had succeeded in crossing the British minefields and establishing a bridgehead on the eastern side of them, although the lanes the Italians cleared through the minebelts were subjected to heavy British artillery fire, which had a most upsetting effect on our moving columns. All the same, by noon, contact had been established between the striking force and X Italian Corps, and thus a direct route opened to the west for supplies and reinforcements. During the day the British brigade was encircled in Got el Ualeb.

In the afternoon I drove through the minefield to X Corps headquarters for a meeting with Field Marshal Kesselring, the commander of the Italian corps, and Major von Below, the Fuehrer's adjutant, and told them my plans. The British minefield was to be shielded by the Afrika Korps from all attacks by British formations from the northeast. Meanwhile I intended to smash the whole of the southern part of the Gazala position and subsequently to resume the offensive.

The operation would include the destruction of, first, the 150th British Brigade at Ualeb, and then the 1st Free French Brigade at the fortified position of Bir Hacheim.

The enemy had only hesitatingly followed up our withdrawal. The falling back of the German-Italian formations had evidently come as a surprise to him, and besides this the British command didn't react very quickly. Already on the morning of 30th May we had noticed the British taking up positions with 280 tanks on the

ROMMEL AND THE GERMAN HIGH COMMAND

While he was in North Africa, there was always tension between Rommel and the chiefs of army staff in Berlin. There were many reasons for this. Partly, they mistrusted him because they considered him to be able to circumvent the 'proper' lines of command by appealing directly to Hitler, who considered him a favourite general. Rommel himself believed that his rapid promotions created problems: '...I've leapfrogged over enormous numbers of my comrades, and this is bound to attract a lot of envy.'

Rommel's biggest problem with senior Wehrmacht command, however, was that he did not obey orders. He would not do what he was told, preparing offensives when he should have been obeying orders to stay put.

The distrust came out in various ways, some rather petty: mention of Rommel's 50th birthday was forbidden by army censors in Germany, to the annoyance of Minister of Propaganda Goebbels, who wished to make an event of it. But this distrust was also expressed in a stream of telegrams to Africa, many of which were direct reprimands. Rommel generally ignored them. While he was winning, he was confident that he alone knew how to play his hand.

east and 150 infantry tanks on the north of our front. We kept waiting for the British to strike a heavy blow. But in the morning only a few British attacks were launched on the Ariete and were beaten off easily by the Italians. Though there were some slight British advances on the rest of the front, by the end of the day a total of 57 British tanks had been destroyed.

In the afternoon I myself reconnoitred the possibilities of an attack against the forces occupying Got el Ualeb; and I detailed part of the Afrika Korps, part of the 90th Light Division and the Italian Trieste Division for an attack on the following morning against the British positions there.

courage. As usual the British fought stoically to the last round of ammunition. They used a new anti-tank gun of 57mm calibre [the 6-pounder]. Nevertheless by the evening of the 31st we had penetrated a considerable distance into the British positions. On the next day the British occupying forces were to receive their final knock-out blow.

One after another the sections of elaborately constructed British defence system were taken by my troops, and by early afternoon the position was in our hands. The last British resistance was at an end. We took 3000 prisoners, and destroyed or captured 101 tanks and scout cars as well as 124 guns of every kind.

BELOW: Aglow with mutual admiration, Rommel and Hitler shake hands at the Fuehrer HQ in 1942. Rommel was still winning, but the promises of improved supplies and air support were more easily delivered than the actual goods.

31st May 1942

The attacking formations advanced against the British 150th Brigade on the morning of 31st May. Yard by yard the German-Italian units fought their way forward against the toughest British resistance imaginable. The British defence was conducted with considerable skill and

At this stage in the battle, the British commanders were optimistic that they had Rommel trapped with his back to their minefields. They interpreted his attacks through the minefields as looking for a way of escape rather than a search for supplies.

Even in the heat of battle, Rommel's regard for the rules of war was maintained. When his

intelligence brought him a British order on the treatment of prisoners, he made sure, by publicising it, that it was countermanded:

At this time an order fell into our hands from the 4th British Armoured Brigade to the effect that German prisoners were to be given nothing to eat or drink until interrogated. We considered this to be very bad since the war between German and British nations was tragic enough without being made worse by increased bitterness. The British command were apparently of the same opinion, since the order was rescinded after our intervention.

Contrary to the optimism of British commanders, Rommel was was in no sense beaten as May gave way to June. True, he was in a vulnerable situation and exposed to Allied attack, but he had set up communications with his main line of forces, and now set about redressing the situation in his favour. Leaving the bulk of his armoured forces to face the probable British counter, he himself moved south to take out the main position to the south, the still unconquered fortress of Bir Hacheim. The DAK diary continues the narrative:

On the night of 1st/2nd June, the 90th Light Division and the Trieste Division moved out towards Bir Hacheim. They crossed the minefields without heavy casualties. The 90th Light Division reached their battle positions against enemy scout cars in the desert southeast of Bir Hacheim, and cut off the fortress to the south. The Trieste Division swung sharply north of the fortified area. Our offer of surrender terms was rejected. Around midday, the attack on the fortress began, although little progress was made due to a sandstorm during the afternoon. The Free French put up stiff resistance.

To deceive the enemy, a feint attack to the east was mounted by sections of the DAK. A number of enemy tanks and a gun position were thus destroyed. The combat units then returned to their battle order positions.

At about 18.00hrs, the 4th Armoured Brigade of the Ariete Armoured Division and the east flank of the DAK came under heavy preliminary artillery barrage. The attack was fought off, and in the subsequent counter-attack some 22 tanks and seven guns were destroyed or captured.

Review: over the next days, the ring around Bir Hacheim tightened. Intelligence reports indicated an enemy action would be attempted from the east.

BELOW: The British counter-attack. An American-built Stuart Mk II light tank overtakes a deliberately sabotaged Panzer III, which meanwhile provides shelter for a temporary radio communications post.

3rd June 1942

On the east and north fronts, the Panzer Army found little significant reconnaissances or artillery activity. Time and again the enemy tried to disrupt traffic on the supply route...

Observation units 3/33 and 580 were deployed west into the desert to reinforce the 90th Light Division and bolster the stranglehold on Bir Hacheim. The 90th Light Division and the Ariete tightened their ring around the fortress. The Free French brigade continued tenaciously to hold out in their much-reduced positions. The enemy deployed the 10th Indian Brigade – clearly in an action to dislodge the forces blockading [Bir] Hacheim – into the desert west of el Gubi.

Review: the enemy had done nothing about the [Bir] Hacheim attack up to now, limiting themselves merely to harassing the supply traffic. Bringing forces up from El Gubi to the west implied that the enemy

Left: Lifeline in the desert. A German supply column struggles through the inhospitable terrain to bring desperately needed fuel, ammunition and stores up to the front line. Battles in the Western Desert were routinely won and lost through the availability or otherwise of adequate supplies on both sides.

commanders sought to get involved in the fighting for Bir Hacheim only from outside the area.

4th June 1942

At 06.00hrs, following a heavy preparatory artillery barrage, the 90th Light Division moved out to press home its attack on the fortifications at Bir Hacheim. Enemy return fire from various defence positions deployed around the fort was so intense that the attack had to be called off. The division was then ordered into the area south and southeast of Bir Hacheim, around the defences, so as to forestall any attempt at a breakout or other action. In the afternoon, the division was attacked from the southeast by an armoured column. The attack was thrown off. A lively firefight followed after the 90th Light Division's reconnaissance units west of [Bir] Hacheim encountered enemy reconnaissance and armoured units. The enemy were gradually pushed back away from the supply route, so that re-supply operations could proceed unhindered.

DAK was safely with the 21st Panzer Division, until now deployed to the east and the north, while the 15th Panzer Division was being held as a combat reserve west of Bir el Tamar...

Review: the enemy had during these days held off in waiting. The anticipated major assault against Bir Hacheim had not materialised. Nevertheless it had to be assumed that the enemy would either attack the blockade around Bir Hacheim, or attempt to relieve it by launching an attack on other positions.

The British forces were indeed about to launch an attack on the Axis positions; but during 5th June they were thoroughly worsted – so much so that Rommel was himself able to launch a counter-attack and, typically, to head part of that counter.

5th June 1942

In the night of 4th/5th June the 15th Panzer Division was let loose in the area north of Got el Ualeb as ordered. The division was ordered to build a bridgehead to the south of Bir el Harmat against possible enemy attacks either south- or northeastwards.

Around 06.00hrs following an hour-long heavy artillery softening-up barrage, the enemy attacked the Ariete Division from the east. As a deception, they put up a heavy artillery attack plus smoke in the area of the 21st Panzer Division, to the north. The enemy attack was undertaken by the 2nd and 22nd Armoured Brigades, plus the 10th Indian and 201st Guards Brigades. Shortly after, an attack was also launched by the 4th Armoured Brigade and the 42nd Armoured Division against Eluet et Tamar.

The Ariete Armoured Division was forced by heavy enemy pressure to fall back to behind the army's artillery line, whereupon the attack was brought to a halt by the DAK and artillery. The enemy suffered heavy losses as a result.

Panzer Regiment 8 of the 15th Panzer Division pushed through to Bir el Tamar to relieve the Ariete.

In the afternoon the DAK, its northern front secured, began the counter-attack. The enemy was finally forced to retreat through heavy loss of armour. By evening, they had suffered 56 tanks destroyed. Combat Group Wolz, located with the army reserves 10km (six miles) northeast of Bir Hacheim, thrust forward, led by the commander-in-chief, against the enemy rear in the crossroads area north of Bir el Harmat. This supported the attack by the 15th Panzer Division, and reached its objective 10km (six miles) northeast of the crossroads by evening.

Around 19.00hrs the 21st Panzer Division launched an attack from the southern flank with two battalions supported by tanks, but this was beaten off. In the 10th Afrika Korps sector, an enemy tank attack led to the loss of a reinforcement Italian battalion.

In the struggle for Bir Hacheim, the noose was strengthened and tightened.

6th June 1942

The northern forces of the DAK, largely comprising the bulk of the 21st Panzer Division, moved into the attack at 05.45hrs towards the east. By 09.00hrs, the enemy had already begun to give ground. At the same time, the 15th Panzer Division began its advance in the general direction of the northern perimeter of the minefields. The enemy positions there were taken by 10.00hrs, a number of guns captured, and 600 prisoners taken. Especially important was the blocking-off of the area northeast of Bir el Harmat, so preventing an enemy withdrawal to the southeast. Panzer Regiment 8 was deployed here.

The DAK assault continued successfully. The enemy had suffered heavy losses in armour.

Below: A German small-arms ammunition dump, probably at the small harbour of Sollum, on the advance towards Tobruk. Supplies at this stage were stretched, since few of the Italian merchant ships survived the murderous crossing to North Africa unscathed.

Battle Group Wolz closed to the south of Bir Bellefaa towards the west, but was itself outflanked to the south and attacked by the enemy from the east.

By midday the weight of fire from the east against 15th Panzer Division and Battle Group Wolz had increased considerably. Enemy attacks during the day were twice beaten off, and overnight the battle group was withdrawn to the area north of Bir el Harmat. Bir el Harmat remained in enemy hands.

The number of prisoners taken on the 5th and 6th June now reached above 4000; they consisted for the most part of 201st Guards Brigade, and the 10th Indian Brigade. The 10th Indian Brigade was wiped out in this battle.

The 90th Light Division moved out against Bir Hacheim at 10.15hrs, with the spearhead coming to within 800 metres of its objective by 13.00hrs. Then the attackers came under withering defensive fire across the flat and rocky landscape. The assault was called off that evening, with the noose tightening around the fortress. Strong sections of the 7th British Motorised Brigade attempted to storm the south front of the division; however they were thrown back.

Review: the attack by the northern sections of the Panzer Army against British armoured units had resulted in heavy losses of men and armour to the latter, thereby seriously reducing their overall fighting capacity. The British offensive of of 5th June had led to a much greater victory in the resultant counter-offensive by 6th June. A yet fiercer relief battle, to make the situation easier for the taking of [Bir] Hacheim, could no longer be held off. The battle for [Bir] Hacheim could now be brought to a conclusion without serious enemy interference.

Victory in this armoured action of the 'Cauldron' was the turning point in the Gazala battle. The British units involved lost heavily, and although German supplies were again running low, the tactical superiority of the Afrika Korps was now manifest. Rommel was now able to press on with his siege of Bir Hacheim, while further north his panzer forces steadily improved their position.

7th June 1942

DAK continued to achieve victories against the enemy in the crossroads area north of Bir el Harmat. An assault by the 1st Armoured Division from the southeast at 18.15hrs was quickly thwarted. As night fell, the enemy turned his guns northeastwards. The captured support positions were occupied by the Afrika Korps, while 15th Panzer was withdrawn to an area north of El Aslagh. Lively artillery and reconnaissance activity continued around 21st Panzer Division.

Battle Group Wolz occupied Bir el Harmat, and was marched off in the evening towards Bir Hacheim.

The 90th Light Division battled on towards the Bir Hacheim positions heroically. The fortifications were being subjected to a barrage of effective artillery fire and Luftwaffe attacks. Battle Group Hecker, deployed in the north, had broken through the minefields north of Bir Hacheim.

MALTA

Malta was critical to the Mediterranean theatre. It lay across communications with North Africa, and the aircraft and submarines based there, supplied by Enigma intercepts, were able to wreak havoc on Axis supplies.

The Axis plan to take Malta in spring 1942 (Operation Hercules) had been put back when it was decided that Rommel was to be allowed to attack the Gazala Line defences first. The intention was that Rommel should stop at the Egyptian frontier, Malta would be reduced, and the Axis offensive could resume into Egypt. In fact, the momentum that Rommel built up after Gazala was such that Operation Hercules was abandoned, and all resources were put into the advance into Egypt.

Rommel has often been blamed for the Axis decision not to invade Malta. However, as his diaries show, he himself was somewhat puzzled by the decision. In fact, it is very likely that Hitler himself had little intention of attacking Malta. He had been shocked by German losses during the attack on Crete, and although he had sanctioned Operation Hercules, he was only too glad to use Rommel's successes of May-June 1942 as an excuse to abandon the plan.

A number of enemy tanks and supply vehicles managed to slip through a gap in the line and got away to the west, despite the Afrika Korps having units in the area. Between 07.00hrs and 09.00hrs an enemy armoured attack was launched against the Afrika Korps, but this was repulsed.

Review: this day brought the Panzer Army further victories. In the north, the enemy had been dealt a heavy blow, and to the south battle groups were fighting their way ever closer to Bir Hacheim, thereby bettering the chances of taking it.

8th June 1942

The enemy had obviously been forced through defeat and attrition to go on the retreat in the last few days. Their armour had been withdrawn behind artillery and reconnaissance lines. Around 18.00hrs a detachment of the 4th Armoured Brigade launched a reconnaissance in force against the Italian support position at Bir el Harmat. The 15th Panzer Division immediately moved up to counter-attack, and the enemy was forced back.

BELOW: Rommel's May 1942 offensive, which saw the Afrika Korps punch a hole through the Gazala Line.

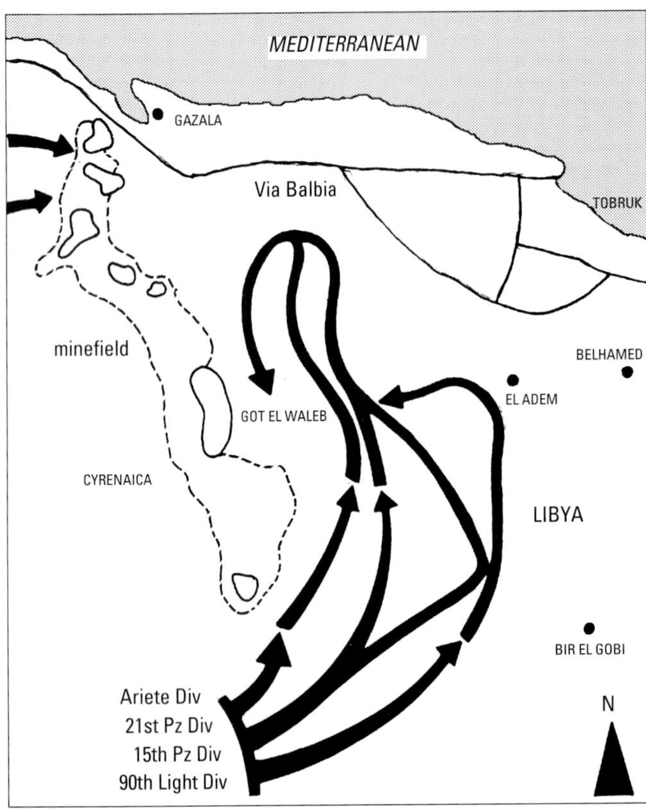

In the fighting for [Bir] Hacheim, further ground was being won. Enemy positions had been destroyed by heavy barrages from the artillery. The Luftwaffe repeatedly attacked the fortress with large forces, and destroyed many armoured vehicles among the reconnaissance units based south of the Mteifel Rotunda.

An enemy battle group had been deployed to cover the supply-route crossroads in the area near Mteifel Rotunda, which for the time being was paralysing supply traffic.

Reconnaissance Detachment 33 was ordered to go in against this enemy formation. It succeeded in pushing the enemy back to the south.

The Afrika Korps overran another battalion support position of 15-20 tanks, and the occupiers were taken prisoner.

Review: the enemy had above all sought to disrupt the supplies. The front had been thinly manned in some sectors, so the enemy had been able to escape with a a number of armoured vehicles to the west in the supply traffic area with relative ease.

In the battle for [Bir] Hacheim, the encirclement was complete and more fortified positions were being destroyed by artillery barrage and bombing raids.

9th June 1942

The DAK sent a detachment under command of Colonel Baade for the attack against Bir Hacheim.

The 90th Light Division provided support via artillery fire and heavy weapons to the forces in the north advancing south on [Bir] Hacheim. At midday, the division itself moved off to the attack. A breach was made in the first line, and by 20.00hrs our stormtroops had penetrated to within 200m (660ft) south of fort Hacheim Ridotta. While the division was pressing home its victory in the north, it had to defend against a strong attack to the south from a detachment of the 4th Armoured Brigade. By evening this armoured unit was holding out to the south of the division with elements of the 7th Motorised Brigade.

The bulk of that brigade – at least two heavy battalions and one reconnaissance section – was positioned to the west and southwest of Mteifel Rotunda, tasked with blocking the supply route. Reconnaissance Battalion 33, which had been deployed against this formation, put up a stubborn defence and pushed the enemy back towards the south and southwest, so as to free the supply traffic from further indirect threat.

The Luftwaffe continued its battle against Bir Hacheim with repeated attacks in force. From 2nd to 9th June 1030 aircraft were deployed against the fortress.

Review: The British command had withdrawn the bulk of their forces, and the fort at [Bir] Hacheim was allocated the vestigial support of just one armoured detachment. They clearly considered the securing of their own supply lines more important than the relief of the Free French forces. Not waiting for any strengthened enemy attack on the encircling lines, the commander-in-chief ordered a concerted attack by the 90th Light Division, Trieste Division, and Battle Group Baade against the fortifications.

10th June 1942

In the morning, the Ariete suffered an attack by some 40 tanks at its strongpoint southwest of the supply-route crossroads. The attack was fought off by the Ariete and the 15th Light Division with the destruction without loss of 25 enemy tanks.

90th Light Division fought off an enemy attack in the southwestern sector of the blockade lines. Battle Group Baade, attacking the fort from the north, achieved a major breakthrough in the main battlefield. Then troops worked their way through heavily mined ground to take the dominating position on Hill 186 (2km (1.2 miles) northwest of Bir Hacheim). Thus one of the most important points of the fortified battleground had fallen into our hands. The attack was undertaken with heavy artillery and Luftwaffe support. The enemy defended at every point of resistance. As a result, their losses were exceptionally high.

Review: following the deep penetration of the main battleground at [Bir] Hacheim, defence of the fortress was no longer possible. The possibility had to be considered that the enemy would at this point try to bring up relief forces from outside to help the garrison attempt a breakout. Sections of the 7th Motorised Brigade, until now occupying positions south and southwest of Mteifel Rotunda, were already advancing towards Hacheim. To guard against all eventualities, the 15th Panzer Division was ordered to [Bir] Hacheim. The attack was ordered to be resumed on the 11th.

11th June 1942

In the night of 10th/11th June the British command pulled back battle groups of the 7th Armoured Division south of [Bir] Hacheim. This measure was clearly undertaken with the view that the continued defence of [Bir] Hacheim was no longer possible. The [Bir] Hacheim garrison managed a breakout in the night to the west, in which the commander and a section of the Free French forces were able to escape under cover of darkness. They managed to join up with the 7th Motorised Brigade south of [Bir] Hacheim, and

Below: A thin smile from Rommel as he poses for a propaganda photograph with the Italian seamen vital for the re-supply of his desert troops. None of them realised that, thanks to Enigma code-breaking successes in England, the Allies knew exactly what was sailing where and when. Rommel secretly blamed Italian treachery at higher levels for losses at sea.

withdrew to the areas around El Gubi and El Adem.

The attack on [Bir] Hacheim from the south began at 06.45hrs, with the 90th Light Division blocking the route to Ridotta Hacheim. The high point to the north was then occupied and 500 prisoners taken. From the north, Battle Group Baade advanced yet further into the main battle area. Only now was a show of resistance put up, so that by early mid-morning the entire fortress was in our hands. Thus the southern cornerstone of the enemy's line had crumbled and any threat to our forces in the south had been removed. The majority of the Free French forces were destroyed. The brigade was withdrawn to the Nile Delta and never showed its face again that summer.

Above: The British cruiser HMS York in Egypt at the beginning of the North African campaign, with freshly unloaded cruiser tanks and assorted armoured vehicles in the foreground. Although faced with similar logistic problems, the British generally fared better than Rommel in terms of re-equipment and supplies.

Immediately after the fall of Bir Hacheim, the commander-in-chief ordered the 15th Panzer Division, 90th Light Division, plus Reconnaissance Detachments 3 and 33, to advance towards El Adem. These units rapidly overcame weak enemy resistance to reach a point some 10-15km (6-8 miles) south to southwest of El Adem by evening. To counter this threat, the enemy moved the 2nd Armoured Brigade from south of Acroma up to the Bir Lefa sector. The 15th Panzer Division engaged the 4th Armoured Brigade southeast of Naduret el Ghesceuasc. On the remaining fronts no action of significance took place.

Review: with the fall of Bir Hacheim, the position of our southern flank was secured. At the same time, the enemy was no longer in a position to disrupt the supply route. With the blockade of Bir Hacheim lifted, the forces were now freed, and mobile warfare was again possible.

There has been criticism of Rommel for his concentration on the siege of Bir Hacheim, which had become of minor importance by the time it fell. The Luftwaffe, and in particular the supporting Stuka units that were used as aerial artillery, suffered heavily, and were never as effective again in the desert war. But Rommel wanted freedom of action and an unthreatened supply line: he gained these advantages when the fortress fell, and could now begin the last phase of the Gazala battle – the move north to the sea, hoping to cut off the enemy forces. British armoured formations were able to offer little resistance to this push, although German resources were at a low ebb.

12th June 1942

The 90th Light Division began its attack in the early hours and had secured El Adem by 10.00hrs. By 11.30 leading elements had already secured El Adem.

The DAK with the 15th Panzer Division was proceeding north and encountered some 100 enemy tanks. By 11.00hrs, contact was finally established between 15th Panzer and the Trieste Division to its left. In the rapid advance that followed Trigh Capuzzo was overtaken by 15.30hrs, and the enemy – 4th Armoured Brigade – was in full retreat towards the highlands north of Trigh Capuzzo. The heights east of Hagiag el Raml were taken. The 21st Panzer Division sent units east at 13.45hrs in support of the 15th Panzer Division, which shot up 45 enemy tanks.

Reconnaissance Battalions 3 and 33 were sent to secure the flanks on the 15th Panzer's right wing, and an enemy tank assault near Gabr el Abidi was beaten off.

Review: The attack by the 15th Panzer Division from south to northeast forced the enemy armoured units into a confined space. They then found themselves between two German panzer divisions without room to manoeuvre. Into this narrow area the British command decided in the course of the day to deploy the 32nd Tank Brigade from the Gazala Line. The continuation of the 15th Panzer Division's attack in a northwesterly direction held out good hopes of success.

13th June 1942
In the course of the afternoon the DAK with the 15th Panzer Division took the dominating ridge of Hagiag el Raml, and forced the 32nd Tank Brigade back from there to the north. Reconnaissance Detachments 3 and 33 were engaged in fighting the 22nd Armoured Brigade. This brigade was also forced by heavy fighting back to an area some 10km (six miles) southeast of Acroma. At 14.35hrs, the 21st Panzer Division moved out against the 4th Armoured Brigade. This formation was also sent reeling east with severe tank losses. Counter-attacks were desultory and had no effect.

The Afrika Korps and the Trieste and Ariete Divisions were putting pressure on the enemy line north of Trigh Capuzzo.

The 90th Light Division was fighting a defensive battle southeast of El Adem against enemy forces on all sides. The division was unable to disengage and join the 15th Panzer as ordered by 13.00hrs. Not until afternoon could it disengage, avoiding heavy British forces to the south. It arrived on the morning of 24th June in the area north of Bir Lefa, and took up the fight to the north.

Review: Successful fighting by the motorised and armoured units of the Panzer Army had forced the enemy armour into an even tighter spot south of Acroma. The enemy clearly had the intention of holding the Acroma position at all costs to prevent their divisions being cut off from Gazala. The British command was clearly committed to use its armoured units to the last.

There was clearly no prospect of the British doing more than managing a controlled withdrawal now, and the abandonment of the 'Knightsbridge' 'box' on 13th July was firm evidence of this. Rommel gave an assessment of his beaten opponents in discussing the Guards who retreated from 'Knightsbridge'.

THE BRITISH SOLDIER
That day the Guards brigade had evacuated 'Knightsbridge', after the area had been subjected all the morning to all the artillery fire we could bring to bear. This brigade was a living embodiment of the positive and negative qualities of the British soldier. An extraordinary bravery and toughness was combined with a rigid inability to move quickly.

The battles along the Gazala Line were perhaps the high spot of Rommel's generalship. He used tactical superiority to offset an enemy that was superior in numbers and to offset a situation that was very weak for several days. Criticisms of his conduct of the battle have centred on his initial over-optimism, the fact that a unified British counter could have exposed the dispersal of his forces and that he spent much time and effort reducing Bir Hacheim. Yet even when criticisms are taken into account, the battle was a triumph of an individual able to impose himself on the modern battlefield. His only dissatisfaction can have been that his German armoured units had suffered too heavily to be able to effect a total envelopment of the Eighth Army, which pulled back into Egypt.

WAR AND CHIVALRY

The war in the desert was one fought according to the rules. Partly, this was because the open terrain and lack of large civilian populations gave the campaigns the atmosphere of a game. To a large extent, however, the relatively good nature of war in the desert lay in the chivalrous tone that Rommel himself gave it. He was always polite to prisoners, and insisted on official conventions being observed – which was one of the reasons he reacted strongly when the British order about 'softening up' German prisoners was discovered during the Battle of Gazala.

Rommel carried this attitude to his enemies with him through to northern Europe. In May 1944, for example, he personally interrogated a captured commando (Lieutenant Lane), and afterwards made sure that Lane, who could have been shot because Hitler had personally ordered commandos to be executed, was escorted to a POW camp.

Chapter VII

Triumph and Attrition

1942 was the watershed for Rommel's Afrika Korps in the Western Desert. Sweeping victoriously along the Mediterranean coast, Rommel eventually exhausted both his men and his supplies before coming up against a well-defended and determined enemy.

Victory at Gazala allowed Rommel to indulge his dream of pushing on to the Nile Delta and throwing the British forces out of the Middle East – perhaps even of linking up with German units pushing down through the Caucasus from the southern Soviet Union. At its most ambitious, this plan included not only taking Egypt and the all-important Suez Canal, but also the eventual acquisition of the oilfields in Persia and Iraq. However, this could only succeed following the occupation of the Soviet Union, in itself an overwhelming objective.

Rommel's troops had shown themselves once again to be masters of mobile warfare, and they were now advancing on the prize that had eluded him the year before: the port of Tobruk. The potential strategic importance of this small harbour town meant that it was sure to be heavily defended.

June 1942

Tobruk was one of the strongest fortifications in North Africa. The excellent troops manning it had caused us considerable difficulties during 1941. Many assaults had collapsed around it. Much of its outer perimeter was literally soaked in blood, battles having raged over a very small area. We knew Tobruk well.

This time, we intended to follow the 1941 plan, forestalled by the Cunningham offensive [Operation Crusader], to attack and storm the fortress. A feint attack on the southwest side of the position was intended to cover our main objective, and hold the defenders there. The attacking sections, who were to undertake the main assault, had to come up unexpectedly. Accordingly, they were to continue on past Tobruk to the east, to give the impression that we were encircling it as in 1941. Then they were to suddenly turn back on the southeast flank of the fortress, taking up positions in the night, and then fall on the enemy positions after a Stuka and artillery bombardment beginning at first light, and overrun them.

For all of us this fortress had become something of a symbol of the British will to resist. The time had come to get rid of it.

The Afrika Korps marched into its new positions in the afternoon of 19th June, while the 90th Light Division advanced east to take the British supply dumps between Bardia and Tobruk. The movement of this division was especially important to maintain British ignorance about our true intentions. As well as the 90th Division, the Pavia and the newly arrived units of the Littorio Armoured Division were to shield the attack to the west and south.

In fact by that evening we had the impression that our movements had only been observed in part by the enemy. All indications were that our assault would come as a surprise. British armour had virtually ceased to exist outside the fortress of Tobruk. We could indeed look forward with great hope to our battle against Tobruk.

Tobruk, hemmed in to east and west by rocky and roadless terrain, extends south into sandy lowlands. The Italians under Balbo had built excellent fortifications there. Full consideration had been given to the kind of weapons available today for the destruction of fortified positions. The numerous defence works, which encircled Tobruk like a belt, were dug into the ground so as to be visible to the enemy only from the air. These positions consisted of a series of underground trenches, each leading to an anti-tank or machine-gun emplacement. The latter remained silent until the very last moment, when they would open up on the attackers with a storm of annihilating fire, while the artillery, under such heavy fire, couldn't find apertures through which to fire at them. Each post was protected by an anti-tank ditch and barbed wire. Also, the entire fortification was surrounded at vulnerable points by a deep anti-tank ditch. Behind the defence system of the outer perimeter, which was mostly several lines deep, were further heavy artillery emplacements, field posts and more forts. Most of the area was protected by extensive minefields.

Rommel's plan for the attack on Tobruk involved preliminary air attacks, which took place early in the morning of 20th June. Unknown to Rommel, the British commanders were themselves already in disarray. Ritchie and his superior, Auchinleck, were pursuing different tactics to one another, and the resultant confusion left an open door for Rommel's divisions. Nevertheless, the extent and quality of the defences around this important strategic fortress remained a formidable obstacle.

20th June 1942

Directly after the Luftwaffe attack, the Afrika Korps infantry 15th Rifle Brigade and the Italian XX Corps moved out into the attack. Paths had been cleared through the minefields the night before. After two

BELOW: Rommel photographed after the fall of Tobruk – a new field marshal in his sparse desert home.

RIGHT: A British 25-pounder night-firing in the desert during the defence of Tobruk, June 1942.

hours the German stormtroops had succeeded in breaching the British defences. Position after position was taken by my 'Africans', following fierce close-quarter fighting.

By 08.00hrs the pioneers had bridged the anti-tank ditches. The work of the pioneers that day deserves particular praise. It is hard to imagine what it meant undertaking such work under the heaviest British fire. The way was clear, and the tanks rolled through.

At 08.00hrs I drove with my staff through the Ariete area, on into the sector of the 15th Panzer Division. I went in an APC as far as the minefields, which were coming under heavy British artillery fire. As a result, traffic was piling up. I immediately despatched my ordnance officer, Lieutenant Brendt, forward to supervise the traffic flow. Half an hour later, I crossed the anti-tank ditches with Bayerlein and inspected two of the positions. Meanwhile the Afrika Korps were coming under tank attack from British forces outside the fortress. A ferocious battle ensued, with artillery on both sides engaged. I gave orders for the Ariete and the Trieste Divisions, which had advanced over the anti-tank ditches and were caught in the British defence zone, to follow up behind the Afrika Korps and support their advance. The German assault carried on. As I could see myself, the Afrika Korps had reached the Sidi Mahmud crossroads about midday. Tobruk all but lay in our hands.

On we went. Soon we reached the slope down to the town. A British strongpoint held on here with outstanding tenacity. I sent Second Lieutenant von Schlippenbach to call on the defenders to surrender. The Tommies' response was to pour fire on our staff vehicles. Our outrider, Lance-Corporal Huber, after a time managed to storm the position with six anti-aircraft gunners and succeeded in silencing it with hand grenades.

Pilastrino capitulated that evening. A Stuka attack on this fort was cancelled. The Fort of Solaro was taken out by my men. In the harbour another gunboat was sunk. By nightfall, two-thirds of the fortifications were in our hands. Town and harbour were taken by the Afrika Korps before midday.

On 21st June at 05.00hrs I drove into the town of Tobruk. Nearly every building in this wretched place was either flattened or reduced to rubble, largely as a result of our siege in 1941. I then drove off westwards on to Via Balbia, where the staff of the British 32nd Tank Corps surrendered. Thirty serviceable British tanks fell into our hands. Numerous vehicles burned to our right and left. The overall picture was of destruction and chaos.

About 6km (3.6 miles) west of the town, at 09.40hrs, I met General Klopper, commander of the 2nd South African Infantry Division, and commander of the fortress. He offered the surrender of the fortress at Tobruk. He had been unable to hold out any longer, although he had done everything he could to keep the troops in hand.

With the fall of this fortification, the fighting in Marmarica had come to an end. For all the 'Africans' [Rommel's name for his Afrika Korps troops] 21st June was the highpoint of the war in North Africa. The Panzer Army issued the following Order of the Day:

'Soldiers!
The great battle in Marmarica has been crowned with the rapid capture of Tobruk. Over 45,000 prisoners of war have been taken, and over 1000 tanks and nearly 400 guns captured or destroyed. Through your matchless courage and determination, you have landed blow upon blow against the enemy during the long, hard struggle of the last four weeks. Through your fighting spirit, the enemy has lost the nucleus of his standing army which was poised to spring back at us, and above all his powerful armoured force. My special congratulations to officers and men for this outstanding achievement.

'Soldiers of Panzerarmee Afrika! Now is the time for the outright annihilation of the enemy. We must not rest easy, until the last elements of the British Eighth Army have been shattered. In the following days, I shall once again call on your greatest effort, to bring this goal about.
Rommel'

It is clear from the tone of this Order of the Day that Rommel intended to press on further, in spite of any preconceived plans for a limited offensive to which Rome or Berlin might still wish to cling. He felt confident that he was able to master events, and in June dictated the first draft of his analysis of the way to wage war in the desert.

Rommel the field commander still retained the discipline of Rommel the college lecturer, noting his observations and lessons for future use in a manual of tactics or training programme. Famed for his exploits on the field of battle, Rommel was after all a career soldier. During his 34 years of military service, only six were spent at war.

June 1942
One of my first lessons in motorised warfare was that speed of operations and reaction time of command were decisive factors. The troops must be able to carry out their tasks with the greatest speed and without delay. One cannot in this situation be satisfied with the norm, but must constantly reach for and demand the best, for whoever makes the most effort is quickest – and the battle always goes to the quickest. Time and again officers and NCOs must drum this into their men. To my mind the obligations of a commander are not limited to staff duties. As well as concerning himself with the details of

TOBRUK AS A SYMBOL

The fall of the port of Tobruk to Rommel's Axis forces on 21st June 1942 was perhaps the supreme personal moment for the German commander. This fortress had caused him such agonies the previous year and it had become a symbol of Allied resistance; but now it was his, along with 5000 tonnes of captured provisions and over 2000 vehicles.

The effect on public opinion in both the Allied and Axis camps was dramatic. The German propagandists created newsreels that showed Rommel entering Tobruk in triumph in an armoured car; Hitler created Rommel a field marshal.

In the Allied camp, the fall of Tobruk caused despondency. There had been optimism about the fortress: the day before it fell, *The Times* had proclaimed 'Tobruk's defences are now stronger than ever before'. Prime Minister Winston Churchill faced a vote of censure in the House of Commons, and survived by refusing to mitigate the extent of the disaster: 'If there are any would-be profiteers who feel able to paint the picture in darker colours, they are certainly at liberty to do so.' Churchill personally had been shocked by Tobruk's fall. As he himself recalled: 'This was one of the heaviest blows I can recall during the war.'

command, he should often go up to the front line, and for the following reasons:

a) Proper execution of the commander's plan by his colleagues is of great importance. It is a mistake to assume that every unit commander will realise all the implications of his situation, and act for the best on his own initiative. Most of them soon give in to the easy way out. It is then only too easy to find an excuse, why this or that cannot be achieved. For them an awareness of the authority of the commander is necessary to force them out of such apathy. The commander must be the driving force on the battlefield. The men should have to reckon with his control.

b) The commander must always strive to make his troops aware of the latest in tactical theory and developments, with a view to learning and applying the practical experience on the battlefield, and ensure that his junior officers are trained to respond to the immediate situation. The best care of the troops is founded in good training, as this reduces casualties.

c) Also it is important for the commander himself to have a knowledge of conditions at the front, and the problems facing his subordinate officers. Only thus can he keep his view up to date and adapted to the conditions in the field, otherwise he becomes rigid through theory, and suffused with his own insight, conducts battles like playing a game of chess. So the best leader of troops is one who allows his ideas to develop freely according to his circumstances, rather than being conditioned by a particular structural imperative.

d) The commander must have contact with his men. He must feel and think like them. The soldier must be confident in him. Here is an absolute ground rule: one must never try to display a feeling in front of one's men that one does not have. The trooper has a remarkably good nose for what is genuine and what is fake.

BELOW: Standing in his Mercedes-Benz 340 staff car, Rommel surveys his new port, Tobruk. Scuppered merchant ships lie in the harbour, which he hopes will be the new supply point for his long-stretched Afrika Korps on its advance towards Cairo.

Feeling confident in his abilities and convinced he had the British on the run, Rommel was also optimistic about his perennial logistic problem. Although only a small harbour town, the tactical significance of Tobruk lay mainly in the fact that it was one of the few ports along the North African coast capable of handling supply ships of any size. In the event, it was to prove almost impossible to supply Tobruk from the mainland, and the Italian Navy came to regard such operations as suicidal since the British seemed poised to strike every time they sailed.

22nd June 1942

Our victory at Tobruk had been at the cost of the last of our strength, since fighting an enemy who had superior numbers of men and equipment had taken its toll on my units. But now that we had amassed enormous booty in the shape of munitions, petrol, rations and supplies of all kinds, the preparation of another offensive strike was possible.

I had been assured several times by Rome that supplies to Africa could only be guaranteed in necessary quantity once the ports of Tobruk and Mersa Matruh were in Axis hands. This increased my determination to exploit the British weakness after the Battle of Tobruk by pushing on as far as possible into the Egyptian desert.

The main reason for this decision was different, however: I wished at all costs to prevent the British establishing another new front, and manning it with fresh troops from the Far East. The Eighth Army was now greatly weakened. Its main strength was two fresh infantry divisions. Its armoured elements, which had been hurriedly brought up from the desert hinterland, were in no position to fight. All in all the balance of power between us and the British compared with earlier days was more acceptable. The British Eighth Army divisions had to be quickly overtaken and brought to battle before they had a chance to join up with other forces from the Middle East. Were we able to annihilate the remnants of the British forces from the Marmarica fight plus the two new divisions – which was perhaps possible – then the British would no longer have sufficient forces in Egypt to obstruct our advance on Alexandria itself, or our capture of the Suez Canal.

This was the plan, with a chance of success, a try-out. The existence of my army would not be threatened in this game. We had sufficient resources to handle any situation that was likely to arise.

An additional important target for Rommel was the port of Mersa Matruh, which had been extensively fortified. The capture of this port, along with Tobruk, meant that not only could Rommel apply further pressure on his superiors in Rome and Berlin to deliver promised supplies for his advance east, but it also weakened the British forces, who could no longer expect re-supplies themselves from these ports. The British were, however, closer to Cairo and Alexandria than were the Germans and Italians to Tripoli, so the threat was less.

27th June 1942

It seemed unlikely that the British command, after their experience with us at Tobruk, would let us destroy the rest of their infantry in western Egypt. This would have opened the road for us to Alexandria. Therefore we had to suppose that the fully mobilised units of the British infantry would try to break out of the encirclement around Mersa Matruh, which was not firmly established on 27th June, make for the open desert, and flee to the west.

BELOW: A crewman poses on his MB 340 ambulance for a snapshot in Tobruk's shell-battered town centre, 30th June 1942. Evidence of the previous occupants is scrawled on a wall behind.

Shortly after the siege against the fortress had been laid, many of their vehicles did try to break out through the open south.

In fact the New Zealand Division under General Freyberg, an old friend from past campaigns, gathered its forces in the night and broke out to the south. A wild shoot-out ensued, in which my headquarters, positioned south of the fortifications, was caught up. Battle Group Kiehl and sections of the Littorio joined in the fray. The firefight between my units and the New Zealanders grew extraordinarily fierce. My headquarters was soon surrounded by burning vehicles and became the target of persistent British fire. One could barely conceive of the confusion which reigned that dreadful night. One could not see one's hand before one's eyes. While the Royal Air Force bombed its own troops, German soldiers shot at each other, and the sky was filled with multiple streaks of tracer fire.

During the early hours of the morning, several hundred more New Zealand vehicles managed to break out of great gaps to the south. Only with difficulty can one improvise an extended front in the desert, one that is capable of standing up against a force which is well commanded and can use motorised forces to concentrate its strength immediately.

28th June 1942

On 28th June at 17.00hrs, the 90th Light Division, 580th Reconnaissance, and Battle Group Kiehl, plus elements of the X and XXI Italian Corps, moved into battle. Despite stiff British resistance, the 90th Light Division made good progress. The fierce fighting continued throughout the night while sometimes large, sometimes small, groups of British vehicles constantly tried to get away. Most of them were taken out. Sometimes, the British set light to their vehicles with the bodies of their comrades still inside, and attempted to flee on foot. But for the most part they were easily rounded up in the moonlit night. Great fires raged in the fortified area of Mersa Matruh.

29th June 1942

In the early hours of 29th June, the 90th

RIGHT: His soldiers watch admiringly as the Italian Colonial Star is bestowed on Rommel after the capture of Tobruk, June 1942. Their combative commander rarely fought shy of medals and honours, wherever they came from.

Light Division in the east, and Battle Group Kiehl and the 580th Reconnaissance in the south forged a way into the fortress. Soon the Bersaglieri were also brought in. Shortly the firing inside died down. Our booty included huge quantities of supplies and materiel of all kinds – effectively an entire division's worth. Forty tanks had been destroyed in the fighting for the fortifications, and some 6000 British were marching to our prison camps. Our troops had yet again fought with tremendous courage.

The last fortified harbour on the Egyptian coast had now fallen into our hands, and once again the British had suffered severe casualties. Despite all this, they had nonetheless been able to recover a major part of their infantry back to the El Alamein position, where new troops were already stationed and where fortification work on the defences had been under way for some time. Straight after the fall of Mersa Matruh, therefore, I set my troops on the march again. The El Alamein position should be reached and overrun before the works were complete and before the fleeing remnants of the Eighth Army had had a chance to prepare its defence. This bastion was the last obstacle to our advance on Alexandria. Once through, our road to the Nile was clear.

There are always times when a commander's place is not with his staff, but at the front with his men. It is incorrect to say that the morale of the troops is the sole responsibility of the battalion commander. The greater the rank, the greater the example. The troops have as a rule no rapport with a commander whom they know to be sitting back at headquarters. They need some kind of physical presence from him. At times of panic, fatigue, disorganisation, or when some extra effort is to be required from them, the personal example of the commander can work wonders, especially if he has the ability to generate some myth about himself.

The physical demands on the troops during these days reached the limit of endurance. This placed a special responsibility on the officers to set an example and be a model for them.

SUPPLY PROBLEMS

The question of supply was one of critical importance in the desert war. It was a war of mobility, where movement essentially depended upon how far a tank could move before running out of petrol. In his first offensive of spring 1941, Rommel's boldness had enraged subordinates who feared they would be stranded without fuel by pushing on as he demanded.

The basic supply conundrum the Axis forces faced was that the sea route across the Mediterranean from Italy was hazardous because the island of Malta lay as a submarine base in the way. In addition, the island's fighter squadrons inflicted great losses on Rommel's supply ships. Malta's influence was magnified by the fact that through their Enigma intercepts the Allies were able to identify the key Axis convoys carrying fuel. Even after his success in mid-1942, Rommel's logistical situation worsened, as Allied naval and air strength in the Mediterranean increased.

Rommel accused the Italians of treachery, and of not fulfilling their tasks of keeping his forces supplied; but in reality, there was a supply problem that, try as he might, not even the genius of a Rommel could circumvent.

Rommel was still confident about his progress, and felt that he could push his men through the last British defensive lines. Once again, speed was perceived as the absolute essential. Rommel knew that Alamein and the Nile Delta would be heavily defended, and that a push east while the enemy was still reeling under its losses in the desert was imperative. It was important to destroy the enemy before he could withdraw with his forces to bolster the defences further east and to strike at the heart of Egypt before fresh defenders could be shipped in from the Far East, as Rommel anticipated.

29. Jun. 42
Dearest Lu!
Now the battle for M(ersa) M(atruh) has been won, and our leading troops are about 200km (120 miles) from Alexandria. Several more battles will have to be fought before we reach our goal. At least the worst is largely behind us.

I am well. Some battle actions are physically exhausting, although a few peaceful hours come along when one can recover. Now we are a good 460km (285 miles) east of Tobruk. Enemy railway and road network in first-class order.

30. Jun. 942
Dearest Lu!
Many thanks for letter of 9th June. Yesterday M(ersa) M(atruh) fell. The army marched on afterwards late into the night. We are now 100km (60 miles) eastwards. Just 150km (80 miles) to Alexandria.

30th June 1942

On the morning of 30th June, I discovered that leading units of the 15th Panzer Division had already reached well beyond El Daba. Much materiel had been captured, among it a 150mm battery, that was immediately re-deployed. The Italians unfortunately were having a difficult time, and didn't arrive in the west of El Alamein until nearly 24.00hrs.

On 1st July, Rommel began his attacks on the Alamein Line, where Auchinleck had decided to make a stand. Rommel's exhausted army – in which the soldiers were at their physical limit, the vehicles had suffered enormous attrition and material supplies were at a low ebb – found it could make little or no progress. While seeking to deny a period of recovery and re-supply to the enemy in retreat, Rommel had omitted to

Below: Italian troops storm a British position during the fighting for El Alamein, October 1942.

recognise the same needs among his own extended, advancing forces. In addition, the further east he pushed, the more extended his supply routes became, while the opposite applied to his opponents, who were being pushed nearer to their home bases.

July 1942

When one comes to consider that supplies and materiel are the decisive factor in modern warfare, it was already becoming clear that a catastrophe was looming on the distant horizon for my army.

The British were doing all they possibly could to gain control of the situation. With wondrous speed, they organised the shipment of fresh troops into the Alamein position. Their higher commanders clearly recognised that the next battle would probably be decisive, and were preparing the ground with considerable foresight. The peril of the hour pushed the British towards ever greater exertions, for when the hour is at hand it is always possible to achieve things that might otherwise seem impossible. Eventually even our suppliers in Rome were suddenly able to ship quantities of materiel that we had not previously seen in Africa, despite the fact that by that time most of the vessels we had had in summer 1942 had been sunk, and the British control of the Mediterranean was much sounder than in the days of our push to Alamein. By then it was altogether too late, for the enemy's ever-increasing supply line outstripped ours several times over.

My colleagues and I had up until this time managed for better or worse by pressing much of the captured materiel into service. Up to 85 per cent of our transport pool continued to be made up of captured enemy vehicles. The troops under me had at all times given of their best. Time and again in our favour was the fact that some German weapons were superior to their British counterparts, especially with regard to armoured vehicles. In the new British tanks and anti-tank weapons, however, it was already becoming apparent that a qualitative superiority was developing in some of the British hardware. It was clear that if this came about it would be the downfall of the Afrika Korps.

Not least, therefore, everything possible had to be done to bring about the end of the British presence in North Africa quickly, before any significant supplies of materiel could be shipped to Egypt from Britain or the United States. Therefore in July there followed a series of costly and bitter battles in front of the Alamein position, during which continuous day and night bombing raids by the RAF played a major role. In due course, we succeeded in taking several defence works in the Alamein Line, and pushing several kilometres eastwards from there. Here alone, our attack came to grief, and our strength failed us. Overwhelming British tank forces rose up before us and slammed against our front. Our one and only chance to overrun the remains of the British Eighth Army and occupy the east Egyptian desert at a stroke was irretrievably lost.

ABOVE: A quartet of diminutive Italians merrily escort their British prisoners-of-war away from the fighting. The capture of El Alamein seemed just a matter of time.

1st July 1942

On 1st July, as the previous evening's events had suggested, the Afrika Korps was late beginning its attack on the Alamein position. At first the assault progressed well. At 02.30hrs I drove from my field HQ to the front south of El Daba to

BELOW: Both sides tried to deny supplies to the enemy: Malta comes under Luftwaffe attack, April 1942 (top), and an Italian oil tanker is hit by Allied bombs (bottom).

observe the operation. The coast road was being heavily shelled by British artillery. In the course of the morning two bomber squadrons dropped their presents next to the field HQ and our staff vehicles. I went at once to the Afrika Korps command post and deployed the artillery there against the British guns. At 13.00hrs that morning I had already requested the Luftwaffe to give its full support. British artillery firing dwindled. We set up a field command post

under continuous bombing and strafing attacks at Hill 31 on the 'Alarm' path. Batteries nearby got special attention from British aircraft. At 09.00hrs, the 21st Panzer Division came up against the Deir el Shein stronghold, defended by the Eighth Indian Division, newly sent from Iraq.

Also, the 90th Light Division reported that its attack had also gone ahead at 03.20hrs, and had advanced successfully at first before coming up against the strongly fortified front of Alamein about 07.30hrs.

Not before the division had repositioned further to the south did the attack advance smoothly again at about midday. Slowly, the division pushed into a position to the southeast of Alamein. It formed a defensive line here running north and south, and re-joined the attack about 16.00hrs, intending to break through to the coast road to isolate the Alamein stronghold and wipe out or force out its defenders. For the British this was a life or death situation, and they brought to bear every gun they could lay hands on, raining a hail of shells on our spearhead. The impetus of the attack slowed and faltered as our troops were pinned down by murderous British artillery fire. An SOS arrived from the 90th Light Division requesting artillery support, because the division's own batteries were out of action. I immediately despatched Battle Group Kiehl to their south and drove in an armoured car forward to recce the situation for myself, and decide what action to take. But we were soon forced to retreat by British artillery fire.

Late that afternoon, I decided to throw our whole weight into supporting the southern flank of the 90th Light Division in their attempt to break through. With my field staff, I joined Battle Group Kiehl. Frenzied artillery fire fell amongst our troops again. British shells whistled in from north, east and south while aircraft tracer blazed through our units. Under such an overwhelming weight of firepower, our attack ground to a halt. We hastily spread out our vehicles and took cover as shell upon shell hurtled into our position. Bayerlein and I had to lie in the open for two hours. To make things worse, a squadron of bombers suddenly appeared flying towards us. Luckily, it was turned back by some German dive-bomber escort fighters. Despite heavy British anti-aircraft fire, our dive-bombers attacked over and over again, and fires soon lit up the battle area. When the British fire began to slow down towards evening, I ordered my field staff to retreat to our old HQ as fast as possible, and the battle group to hold on in the area we had reached.

At 21.30hrs that evening I ordered the 90th Light Division to press home its advance to the coast road by moonlight. I wanted to clear the road to Alexandria as quickly as possible. The British defence of the threatened position was getting stronger by the hour. The Luftwaffe commander advised me during the night that the British fleet had sailed from Alexandria. I was determined to force a decision in the coming few days. The British no longer trusted to luck and were preparing a withdrawal. I was sure that all my forces breaking through across a wide front would cause outright panic.

But the 90th Light Division's night attack was also brought up short, with heavy artillery and machine-gun fire raking its remaining 1300 troops. To the north, the division faced substantial concrete fortifications, and to the east strong defence works. It was impossible to advance more than a little in the face of these, despite the attack resuming the following day.

Rommel may have hoped that the 90th Light Division would break through and cause panic in British units, but, in fact, this crack formation was itself close to panic as it was brought to a standstill on 1st July. Nevertheless, Rommel still flogged his exhausted troops on.

Rommel was also becoming acutely aware that, in order to husband his dwindling resources, he would have to avoid fuel-burning and mechanically wearing mobile warfare – his ace card in desert combat, and the one aspect in which he enjoyed the advantage over his enemy.

2nd July 1942

The Afrika Korps resumed its attack with a push to the northeast on 2nd July, with the intention of breaking through to the coast about 10km (six miles) east of El Alamein and storming the fortress. At first the British retreated to the south, but soon after launched a powerful assault on our unprotected south flank. 15th Panzer was pulled out to counter this attack and it was soon embroiled in a fierce battle with the British. Elements of the 21st Panzer were also increasingly put on the defensive in this sand and scrub terrain, until by the evening the whole Afrika Korps was caught up in a violent defensive struggle against over 100 British tanks and some 10 gun batteries.

The 90th Light Division had blundered into British positions during a sandstorm, which so panicked the unit that reserve elements cut and fled to the rear.

Rommel recognised that the enemy forces were being directed effectively, far more so than before in this summer campaign. It was typical of Rommel's sensitivity to the actions and motives of his opponents in the field that he could easily recognise a change in the style of tactical command.

3rd July 1942

More and more British tanks and guns arrived at the front. Meanwhile, General Auchinleck had taken command at El

THE ITALIAN QUESTION

When Rommel arrived in North Africa, he had been put under the command of the Italian General Gariboldi. Rommel managed to pull the wool over Gariboldi's eyes easily. At one stage, early in April 1941, at a meeting during which Gariboldi demanded that no offensive action be taken, a radio signal from Germany arrived ordering Rommel not to advance. But Rommel told Gariboldi that the signal was from Hitler, giving him 'complete freedom of action'.

Gariboldi was replaced by General Bastico, a personal friend of Mussolini, in July 1941, and Rommel found relations more difficult. He was officially under Italian control, but in effect he did as he wished and managed to get the Italians to go along with his wishes most of the time.

Rommel had little or no respect for the Italian High Command, but the greatest respect for the Italian soldiery, whom he believed were perfectly good material, but badly equipped and poorly led. At Gazala, the Ariete Division had fought very well. Rommel firmly believed that if Rome had taken the war more seriously the Italian units could have acquitted themselves much better.

RIGHT: Constantly on the lookout for enemy activity on the horizon, Rommel was famed for his ability to navigate in the featureless terrain and for his uncanny sense of the enemy's whereabouts.

Alamein himself, and was deploying his forces with considerable skill, more so than had Ritchie. He seemed to view the situation with notable detachment, and was not letting himself accept a second-best solution as a result of any actions on our part. This became especially clear in the events which followed.

After battering vainly at the Alamein position for three days, I decided for the moment to call off the offensive following the next day's attack. Grounds for this decision lay in the fact that the enemy's strength was growing, the reduced fighting capacity of my divisions – amounting to no more than 1200 to 1500 troops – and most of all the severely pressed supply lines.

About midday on 3rd July, after hours of British artillery pounding around my HQ, which was positioned near the thrust of the attack, I ordered the Afrika Korps up to the front again. After some initial success, the assault became pinned down and couldn't move. On the same day, the Italian troops started to show signs of breaking down. An attack by the New Zealanders on the Ariete, which was guarding our southern flank, was successful. Twenty-eight out of 30 guns and 400 men were taken, and the remainder fled in panic.

This setback came as a surprise since the Ariete had fought well against the British onslaught during the weeks of fighting around 'Knightsbridge', although it had to be admitted they were then covered by German guns and tanks. But their casualties had been heavy, and they seemed no longer up to the task required of them.

This occurrence meant a threat to our southern flank, so that the decisive attack planned by the Afrika Korps would now have to be undertaken by the 21st Panzer Division alone, with the result that the attack force lacked weight. The 90th Light Division joined up with them later but it was not able to help push home the advantage. The attack ground to a halt.

Continuing the attack next day under these circumstances would simply have led to more losses. Despite giving the advantage of a breathing space to the British, we had to give our troops some rest and overhaul our equipment. We intended to resume the attack as soon as possible. It was very likely that the next few days would see a British counter-attack, and so our units were deployed to defend the position we had reached.

3. Jul. 42
Dearest Lu!
One loses all sense of time here. The battles for the last positions before Alexandria are hard. Was several days in

the front line and lived in the car or hole in ground. Enemy air force gave us trouble. Nonetheless I hope to succeed.

4. Jul. 42
Dearest Lu!
Unfortunately things are not going to plan here. The resistance is too great, and our own strength exhausted. Hopefully, some way will yet be found to reach our objective. Am always tired and overstressed.

Rommel had to pause, but he intended to resume his attacks on 10th July. He was forestalled, however, by a British attack on the Italian Trieste and Sabratha Divisions. At the end of an extremely long supply line (Tobruk had proved too dangerous for the Italian Navy) and faced with stiff resistance, Rommel had at last run out of impetus. Rommel's string of successes, however, had had a powerful influence on his enemies. In the House of Commons, even fellow Conservatives had tabled a 'motion of censure' against Churchill and pressure was mounting to launch some sort of counter-offensive.

10th July 1942

At 05.00hrs the next morning, 10th July, we were woken up by the distant thunder of artillery fire in the north. I sensed at once that it augured ill. Soon the disturbing news came that the enemy had attacked from the Alamein Line and had overrun the Sabratha Division, which had been holding positions on each side of the coast road. The enemy were now pursuing the fleeing Italians westwards and were in danger of breaking through and getting our supplies. I then drove north with the battle staff and a combat unit from the 15th Panzer Division and positioned them on the battlefield. The advance from Qaret el Abd had to be called off, since the elements of our original strike force remaining to the south were too reduced to carry out the push eastwards.

Meanwhile the battle on the coast quickly took its course. The Sabratha Division had been totally wiped out and many of the batteries seconded to it were lost. It appeared to be the case that the gun commanders had not fired on the advancing enemy because they had no orders. The Italians abandoned the line mostly in panic, and fled for the open desert without putting up any defence and discarding weapons and equipment as they ran. It was largely thanks to Lieutenant-Colonel von Mellenthin of the Panzer Army staff that the British assault was halted. Machine guns and anti-aircraft weapons were quickly collected, and with a part of 328th Infantry of the 164th Light Division which was going up to the front, an improvised defence line was established some 3000m (9900ft) to the southwest of army HQ.

The British push along the coast caused the destruction of the main part of the Sabratha and much of the Ariete and important territories had fallen into enemy hands. We had to recognise that the Italians were no longer able to hold their positions. They had been overstretched by Italian standards and the strain had become too much.

There were outstanding Italian officers who spared no effort to keep their troops' morale high, for example Navarrini (XXI Italian Army Corps) whom I held in the highest esteem, and who did all he could.

Any possibility of launching a full-scale attack in the foreseeable future was out of

ABOVE: Rommel and his staff consult their maps, trying to guess the enemy's next move. In goggles is Alfred Gause, Rommel's valued chief of staff, still suffering intermittent headaches and pain following injuries sustained in an artillery bombardment three weeks previously.

the question. I was forced to order every last German soldier out of his bivouac or billet to go to the front because, with the virtual loss of the bulk of the Italian fighting strength, the situation was becoming one of crisis.

Reinforcements and fresh troops were daily being shipped to the British Eighth Army, and the troops were once again under firm control. Now that the situation had forced us to abandon all offensive plans we also had to give up any hope of being able to take on the British forces at El Alamein while their elements were still suffering from their losses during the summer fighting. The British commander could now press ahead with the re-supply and re-fitting of his once-defeated army. It had not been possible for us to convert our successes in Marmarica into victory.

The front was by now static, and this gave the British their main advantage since static warfare and modern infantry tactics were their strong point. Localised attacks supported with tanks and artillery were a British speciality. The El Alamein position reached from the sea in the north to the Qattara Depression in the south, a flat plain of soft sand interspersed with numerous marshes which was impassable to vehicles. The line could not be turned, so the war assumed a form very familiar to both sides, each having so much experience and theoretical knowledge that it could not surprise the other with any new development. In static warfare, the side that fires the most wins.

I had tried at El Alamein to get away from this immobile, static warfare, at which the British excelled and for which their infantry and tank crews were trained, and take to the open desert before Alexandria, where I could have exploited our superiority in open desert warfare, but I had failed. The British had brought my armies to a halt. Over the preceding few days the British commanders had displayed considerable enterprise and courage. They had found out that the Italians were suffering from the inertia of exhaustion and were sitting targets. They would probably therefore continue their assault.

To make good the mess caused by the defeat of the Sabratha and to eliminate the threat posed by British positions west of El Alamein, I decided to send the 21st Panzer Division against the fortress itself. The attack was to be supported by every gun and aircraft we had. The division was to encircle the fortifications from the east in a lightning attack, and then break through to it.

The attack misfired and did not even reach the line of the 9th Australian Division, which had recently taken over the garrison area from the 1st South African. The grounds for this failure, apart from the heavy artillery fire and the very well-built defences including dug-in tanks, was probably due to the 21st Panzer Division's failing to assemble in the Italian line, but assembling instead in an area some way behind. The British gunners were able to pinpoint their targets early in the operation, and brought them to a halt while still behind our own lines.

I decided to call off the attack that evening. It put me in a particularly bad mood that a sandstorm had then blown all

ROMMEL'S BIG MISTAKE?

Rommel's decision to press on towards Cairo and Alexandria after the triumph of Gazala and the fall of Tobruk has been a great cause of debate. Against Rommel are those who take the view that he was hopelessly optimistic about the logistics of the situation: that the only long-term hope for victory lay in the taking of Malta – and that this should have been given precedence, especially as losses of Axis supply ships were increasing dramatically. Pressing further on towards the Nile Delta merely extended supply lines and gave the RAF more targets.

The opposite view is the one that Rommel sold to Hitler and Mussolini when they gave him permission to attempt his dash into Egypt on 24th June 1942. There were three aspects to this: firstly that the retiring Eighth Army should in no way be allowed to recoup itself; secondly that sufficient supplies had been captured in the aftermath of Gazala and especially in Tobruk to underpin the advance; and finally that the British in Cairo and Alexandria were panicking and one good push might finish them off.

Electrified by Rommel's victories, Hitler agreed and persuaded Mussolini that Egypt was within Axis grasp.

day, blinding the British. This would have been our saving! We missed a unique opportunity.

13th July 1942

Next day I again ordered the 21st Panzer Division forward. Their objective was the position lost by the Sabratha and now being heavily reinforced by the Australians. The attack was launched following heavy air attacks, but again the infantry were too late to take advantage of the preliminary bombing. Heavy British air attacks battered our transport columns and British artillery opened up with every gun. Our units fought their way forward from south to north, with the sun behind them, to a point between the road and the railway, where the attack faltered. The Australians put up a fierce fight, as we had learnt to expect after the siege of Tobruk, lasting most of that night.

The initiative was now sliding slowly but surely towards Auchinleck's forces, which made calculated moves to break the fighting spirit of the Italian formations in Rommel's army. Having thus pinpointed the weak spot in his forces, the British hoped to wear down the more resistant Afrika Korps, which would now have to bear the brunt of the battle. It was a good plan. Auchinleck, however, remained unhappy with the progress of events, feeling that he had been pressured by Churchill to act for political reasons when the military situation was unstable.

Above: Mobile anti-tank warfare: a truck-mounted Rhodesian 6-pounder in action against Panzer IVs, July 1942.

14th July 1942

The British launched an attack that night, 14/15th July, on the Ruweisat Ridge and their 1st Armoured Division succeeded in breaching X Italian Corps positions. Shortly after, they broke through the Brescia Division and penetrated as far as German armour and artillery positions, where the leading elements were brought up against fierce close-quarter fighting. They resumed their attack early the following morning and took Ruweisat Ridge, from where the assault force headed off to the west. Sections of this force then turned back east behind the Pavia and Brescia Divisions, resulting in the British taking the bulk of these two forces as prisoners of war.

14. Jul. 42

Dearest Lu!

My expectations for yesterday's battle were bitterly disappointed. It achieved nothing at all. The blow must be borne, further operations undertaken with renewed spirit. Three letters arrived from you: 1st, 4th, 5th and 7th. Heartfelt thanks. Healthwise I am well. Today I am wearing 'shorts' for the first time this year. It's mighty hot. The battle in the east [the Eastern Front – in the Soviet Union] is going well. That gives us the courage to hang on here as well.

Auchinleck's tactics were now paying off, and Rommel's thinly spread forces could hardly hold the line, as a despondent Rommel recognised. Stretched out, desperate for replacement vehicles, running out of fuel, the troops physically exhausted, the Panzerarmee Afrika was in mortal danger. In the course of a few weeks, the flush of victory had come full circle, and Rommel now knew his ambitions in North Africa would never be realised. Nevertheless, his opponents were also nearing their point of exhaustion, and the situation remained more flexible than was apparent.

17. Jul. 42
Dearest Lu!
It is going pretty badly for me. The enemy's superior infantry is taking out one Italian unit after another. German units much too weak to halt them alone. It makes one cry!

17th July 1942

That day every last German reserve was thrown into battle to fend off the British assaults. Compared with the constantly growing strength of the British our force was so small that only by luck could we expect to continue to hold our line. At about 16.00hrs that afternoon, Field Marshal Kesselring and Count Cavallero arrived at my HQ. Cavallero typically tried to make light of our supply problems again, while I was trying to make clear how serious they were. Following a lengthy argument, Kesselring and I at last demanded firm decisions. This discussion showed how low our fortunes had sunk and also how little reliance we could place on the Italian authorities. Cavallero promised they would now use barges to bolster supplies to the army, and that the railway to the front would be running again. After our past experiences we remained sceptical, correctly as events were to show.

18. Jul. 42
Dearest Lu!
The past, crucial, day was particularly bad for us. Once again we got away. It cannot go on much longer, or the front is lost. Militarily, these are the worst days I have lived through.

RIGHT: A British armoured column moves out to engage the enemy at El Alamein. The newly arrived American Lee-Grant M3 medium tank, with the cumbersome but powerful side-mounted 75mm gun, was to prove a decisive factor in the British defence of Alam Halfa.

ROMMEL

IN HIS OWN WORDS

Left: For them the war is over. Italian prisoners in an impromptu POW cage during the fighting for El Alamein sample the delights of British 'bully' beef, July 1942. It was a genuine improvement on their own equivalent, 'AM', known to their German allies as Alter Mann (Old Man).

Over the next four days the front remained quiet. The British launched no further attacks. It was the calm before the storm. We spotted British assembly areas near the central section of the line on 19th and 20th July, where Auchinleck was amassing armour and artillery.

The storm finally broke on the night of the 21st. Wave after wave of British infantry pounded the 15th Panzer Division sector, and broke into their line. However, the spearhead forces were cut off and some 500 British taken prisoner. Because of the recent huge losses suffered by the Italians, our line was now sparsely manned despite our having shortened it by withdrawing to the line of our captured fortifications at Deir el Shein and Qaret el Abd. We were out of reserves.

Vulnerable though the Afrika Korps was, its fighting skills did not desert it. The German forces fought off the British assaults, and discovered that the Eighth Army, too, was tired: in near-constant combat since May, Auchinleck's units were unable to summon up the energy to land a decisive blow. Allied to this was the somewhat unimaginative leadership displayed by the British commanders.

Something of the static, blow-for-blow 'position' warfare Rommel was so anxious to avoid was beginning to assert itself in North Africa. With better supplies, the British were in a stronger position to hold out in such circumstances. Meanwhile, however, Rommel's severely depleted forces were being gradually reinforced with both Italian and German troops, and this injection of new blood did much to restore confidence.

23rd July 1942

Following the fighting on 22nd July, I sent a signal to all troops:

'I send all tank crews special congratulations on their courageous actions during our victorious defence of 22nd July. I am sure further enemy attacks will be met with the same resistance.'

Meanwhile, replacement infantry troops had been slowly arriving in the line over several weeks and the large gaps in our ranks were gradually filling. Some elements of the 164th Infantry Division were flown in from Crete but they brought neither heavy guns nor transport. Some Italian paratroops also arrived at the front.

Meanwhile the army continued apace on work to strengthen the defence line. Despite all these improvements, however, the danger will not be over until an operational reserve has been created behind the lines.

ABOVE: Dust in the desert as a British column moves out at El Alamein – a sure sign of enemy activity was the sight of dust clouds billowing on the horizon, though a sandstorm could also raise false alarms.

26. Jul. 42
Dearest Lu!
A relatively quiet day has passed. Went down to the great Depression [the Qattara Depression of soft sand, impassable to vehicles, that gave the Alamein position its unturnable southern flank]. It was a fantastic sight. It lies well below sea level. Slowly our desert is filling up again. The worst troubles are dwindling.

As the fighting died down, Rommel analysed events of recent months. He believed that he had been right to follow the retreating Eighth Army to deliver a knock-out blow; what he did not know was that his criticisms of Italian High Command treachery and inefficiency were misplaced. Unbeknown to them, the Italian Navy was sailing its supply ships across the Mediterranean at a distinct disadvantage. Enigma intercepts gave the British a clear view of what was happening on the Axis side – what moves Rommel would make and which were the most important supply sailings, for example. The debate over Rommel's advance into Egypt – whether he culpably ignored logistic realities or whether he was correct to seize the moment – will probably never be resolved. It is probably a failing that Rommel tended to assume the provision of supplies to be a matter of course, whereas the reality of the situation meant that he was fortunate to receive what he did.

30th July 1942

I had made great demands of myself, my officers and my men. I realised that the fall of Tobruk and the collapse of the British Eighth Army was the key point in the war in North Africa when the way to Alexandria lay open and almost undefended. My staff and I would have been foolish not to seize this unique opportunity at all costs. If, as often in the past, victory had depended on the courage and willpower of my officers and men, we would have taken El Alamein. However, our supply lines had run dry, thanks to the laziness and inefficiency of those in charge on the continent.

Also, many of the Italian forces had lost their will to resist. As their overall commander, I feel obliged, through comradeship, to set out clearly that the ordinary Italian soldier was in no way responsible for the defeats borne by the Italian units at El Alamein in early July. In view of their conditions of service, the Italians were willing, unselfish and good comrades in the front line. There can be no disputing that the achievement of all the Italian units, especially the motorised elements, far outstripped any action of the Italian Army for 100 years. Many Italian generals and officers earned our respect as men as well as soldiers.

Rommel's view of his Italian allies and counterparts seems to have varied almost according to whim. Generally scathing about their effete, self-important commanders, he was more forgiving of the troops on the ground. Nevertheless, as new troops began arriving to strengthen the defensive line, Rommel concluded that the Italian contribution was 'useless', and was quick to say so when his bombastic Bologna Infantry Division commander, General Gloria, proudly boasted that no Italian soldier would desert his post. The truth, Rommel tersely pointed out, was somewhat different. He went on to complain that what he needed was not more Italians, but combat-hardened German soldiers and equipment.

The cause of the Italian defeat sprang from the entire Italian military and state system, from the poor Italian equipment, and from the small interest shown in this war by many high-up Italian leaders and statesmen. This failure often prevented me from carrying out my plans.

In a document written shortly after the Alamein battles, entitled 'The struggle in North Africa in retrospect', Rommel reflected on the essential differences between the British and German approach to mechanised warfare, characterised by the British failure to recognise the importance of mobility. This, Rommel believed, was in large part responsible for the successes his Afrika Korps achieved between its arrival in North Africa and the high point of its campaign in the summer of 1942. He also paid tribute to some of his opposing commanders.

Victories – apart from those won by great numerical superiority in men or materiel – are not simply the result of excellent leadership or prior planning. They also originate from the mistakes of the loser. It was errors by the British, for example, certainly originating in part from before the war in North Africa, that made our victories possible. The reasons for the defeats of the British Eighth Army are briefly summarised below.

While, as mentioned above, most in Germany can thank the fact that shortly before the war General Guderian crystallised the modern theory of tank tactics into practice, combined with the fact that the will of the Fuehrer resulted in the equipping and organisation of our tank forces, the British remained conservative with regard to armoured warfare. At the beginning of the war, the British emerged with almost no infantry or reconnaissance tanks. The value of mobile warfare was recognised by only a few in England before the war, with the result that little consideration was given to speed, flexibility and the relationship between leaders and their troops. One exception to this were the British reconnaissance units, which proved to be excellent.

The commander of the Eighth Army was about to become the biggest thorn in the Afrika Korps' side. In his battlefield caravan HQ, Lieutenant-General Bernard Montgomery kept a portrait of Rommel pinned to the wall, plus a quotation from Shakespeare's Henry V*: 'O God of battles! steel my soldiers' hearts'. The picture served as a constant reminder of Rommel, the man Montgomery referred to as 'the field marshal', and whom he was determined to defeat. In his aim Montgomery was aided greatly by the large amount of war materiel reaching him, which was commented upon in envious terms by Rommel himself:*

Montgomery had the opportunity to make his evaluation based on the experiences of his predecessors...While our supply shortage grew ever graver, British and American merchant fleets were delivering materiel to North Africa in quantities that had not been at the disposal of Auchinleck or Wavell.

FIRST ALAMEIN

The Alamein Line was one of the few positions in the desert war that could not be outflanked from the south. The Qattara Depression was a great inland 'sea' of soft sand impassable to vehicles, and blocked off the southern flank. On this line, the last readily defensible position before the Nile Delta, Auchinleck, who had taken personal command of the Eighth Army in June 1942, halted his retreat, and turned to face the advancing Germans.

The initial German thrusts at British positions were blocked, and when momentum ran out, it became clear that the Afrika Korps was almost exhausted. Auchinleck made the best use of his strengths – especially his Commonwealth infantry of the New Zealand and Australian divisions – and kept the Axis forces off balance with attacks on the Italian infantry formations. But although the German offensive collapsed, Auchinleck could not destroy the Axis army. His attacks on Italian formations were successful, but the Afrika Korps responded successfully to attacks. By the end of July 1942, both sides were exhausted. The Eighth Army by this time had suffered 13,000 casualties.

Chapter VIII

The Fox at Bay

The period from high summer until the end of November 1942 saw a parallel decline in Rommel's fortunes, from the summer of his successes at Bir Hacheim and Tobruk to the autumn of his ambitions in Egypt after the defeat at El Alamein. The sun of the Afrika Korps was beginning to set, and with it hopes of a Nazi victory in North Africa.

The July stalemate along the Alamein Line was, in retrospect, probably fatal for Rommel. But at the time, the pause in the fighting did not appear to mean this. The general world situation was still one of steady advance by Italy, Germany and Japan: the British Army had been forced to retreat from Burma and Libya; Malta was under siege; the German summer offensive in southern Russia was chalking up impressive advances; and submarine sinkings had hit a new monthly high in June.

Despite some reverses on the battlefield, Rommel was fast gaining a reputation for invincibility not only at home, where such sentiments were carefully nurtured by Goebbels' news and propaganda machine, but also among British troops fighting him in the desert – a source of alarm, and some pique, among the senior British commanders. A famous directive to his chiefs of staff from Auchinleck sounds a plaintive note, and a captured copy was in due course translated for Rommel, who proudly added it to his documentary collection:

There is a real danger that our friend Rommel is becoming a kind of magician or bogeyman to our troops, who are talking far too much about him and I am therefore begging you to dispel by all possible means the idea that Rommel represents something more than an ordinary German general, and a pretty unpleasant one at that, as we know from the mouths of his own officers...PS, I am *not* jealous of Rommel. Signed, Auchinleck.

The picture in retrospect is rather different. With hindsight, we can see that the US entry into the war was the vital factor leading to Japanese and Axis defeat; that the sea battle of Midway in June had decisively altered the naval balance in the Pacific; that Hitler's decision not to invade Malta was a strategic error of great magnitude; that the drive into southern Russia was to lead to the catastrophe of Stalingrad; and that the crisis of the Battle of the Atlantic would pass. But this must not lead us to underestimate the real trepidation felt by ordinary British soldiers who were waiting for Rommel's next offensive against their lines of defence. For the German commander had decided he must attack before British logistic superiority became overwhelming, even though he recognised that the Alamein position, unlike that at Gazala, tended to favour his enemy's strengths.

From the point of view of command the British were here in their element, for their strong quality was a form of tactics which expressed itself in the modern kind of infantry fighting and static warfare.

Their speciality lay in local attacks, carried out under the protection of infantry, tanks and artillery. The El Alamein position adjoined the sea to the north, and to the south it sank away into the Qattara Depression, a level area of moving sand with many salt-marshes, and therefore impassable for heavy vehicles. As the El Alamein position could not, therefore, be outflanked, the war became one in which both sides disposed of great experience and knowledge, but neither could make use of revolutionary methods which would come as a complete surprise to the other. The outcome of this static war depended on who had more ammunition.

Rommel's health was flagging during August as he planned an offensive for the full moon at the end of the month. The morale of his troops was high, and the successes of the offensive on the Eastern Front were comforting.

24. Aug. 42
Dearest Lu!
Yesterday I was again unable to write. Healthwise I'm well enough now to feel myself from time to time. Nevertheless, I won't be able to get out of the six-week treatment in Germany. My blood pressure will have to be restored to order. A doctor from the Fuehrer should be on his way. I shall definitely stay at my post until I can hand over to my replacement without worry. Who's coming, I don't know.

There's another examination today. It is some consolation to know that it can probably all be cleared up. Given our turnover of five generals per division in Africa over one and a half years, it is small wonder that I need refreshing occasionally.

26. Aug. 42
Dearest Lu!
A disturbed, bright moonlit night...The English are probably shooting out of frustration. The land bridges north of Stalingrad between the Don and the Volga have apparently been taken by us. That is a great achievement.

Healthwise, things are now good enough that I can carry out my duties. The worst of the fever is now past and recovery

Left: Reinforcing the Eighth Army, Suez, July 1942. An M-4 Sherman tank being lowered from a supply vessel onto a special 'Z Craft' for onward shipment into the harbour. The Sherman was to prove a worthy opponent for the robust and mobile German armour.

on the way. Nonetheless I shall be away mid-September, if all is quiet on the front...

In spite of the good news from Russia, there was less good news on Panzerarmee Afrika's logistics. Rommel complained bitterly about the failure of the Italians to give him the support he wanted. In fact, the fault was hardly theirs. They sent what they could, but British Enigma intercepts identified the crucial vessels. Nor was Rommel's complaint that his allies broke their promises totally justified: other witnesses to the meetings recall Cavallero saying he would do what he could – and not promising Rommel precisely what he wanted. Rommel often seemed conveniently blind to the fact that scarce resources were needed by Germany's forces on their more important Russian front, and that the Italians were being decimated in their attempts to deliver what supplies could be released for the North African campaign. Nevertheless, supply was clearly the German field marshal's biggest problem.

By the end of August the urgently needed supplies of ammunition and petrol, promised by the Supreme Command, had still not arrived. The full moon, absolutely vital to our operation, was already on the wane. Further delay would have meant finally giving up our offensive. Marshal Cavallero, however, informed me that the petrol ships, heavily escorted, would arrive in a matter of hours, or the next day at the latest. Hoping for the fulfilment of this promise; trusting to the assurance of Marshal Kesselring that he would fly up to 500 tons over to North Africa in case of need; but above all certain that if we let the full moon go by we were losing our last chance of taking the offensive – I gave the order for the attack to be carried out on the night of 30th/31st August as planned.

Rommel's plan for this offensive followed that of Gazala: a demonstration in the north, but a drive through the south of the position by the German armoured units, aiming to defeat the tank formations of the Eighth Army in a sweep north. The British, however, were not going to be caught again by Rommel's manoeuvre. They now had a new commander: Auchinleck (who had been Ritchie's superior, but had then replaced him in direct command of Eighth Army) had been sacked by Churchill, and a new team, with Alexander in overall command and Bernard Montgomery taking over Eighth Army, had been installed.

Montgomery had strong views on the state of affairs he found in his new command. Whether he was right or wrong in his condemnation of the way things were done, he certainly got one thing right. All the forces that were to meet Rommel's expected assault were given precise instructions as to what they should do. Even more importantly, the way that the British intended to fight the battle would maximise their strengths. They expected Rommel to attack through the south, and would meet him by digging in their armour around the Ruweisat and Alam Halfa Ridges. There was to be no attempt to fight a mobile battle: Rommel would be stopped and then artillery and aircraft would destroy his materiel wherever it was concentrated. By nullifying any scope for genius or manoeuvre, Montgomery would crush the German armoured forces. And so it turned out. Indeed, Rommel, with his instinct for the battlefield, recognised what was happening to him almost at once.

ALAM HALFA – END OF THE BLITZKRIEG?

After the fighting on the Alamein Line had died down in July, both sides began to build up their strength. Rommel's plan for the attack on the Allied position was similar to that he had used at Gazala earlier in the year (see text). He hoped he would achieve a fluid breakthrough which would end with his armoured formations engaging Allied elements in a mobile battle.

Unfortunately for Rommel, Enigma intercepts gave Montgomery a very accurate picture of his plans. The British formations were ordered to fight defensively, and not to engage in a mobile battle.

Rommel's attack began during the night of 30th August. It hit troubles from the start, when the armour took longer than expected to clear the first set of minefields. Heavy air attacks took their toll, and when the German armour swung north towards the Alam Halfa Ridge it made no progress at all in the face of intense defensive fire. Rommel broke off the offensive on the morning of 2nd September.

In the early stages of the battle, the British defended their strong positions with extraordinary toughness and so hindered our advance.

My plan, to go forward with the motorised forces another 50 kilometres by moonlight, and from there to proceed to a further attack northwards in the early morning light, did not succeed. The tanks were held up by unsuspected ground obstacles and we lost the element of surprise, on which the whole plan finally rested. In view of this we now considered whether we should break off the battle.

Had there been a quick breakthrough in the south by the motorised forces, the British would have needed time for reconnaissance, for making decisions and for putting them into effect. During this time our movements need not have met with any serious counter-measures. But we had now lost the advantage of this breathing-space. The British knew where we were. I resolved that my decision, whether or not to break off the battle, should depend on how things stood with the Afrika Korps.

I learned soon afterwards that the Afrika Korps, under the outstanding leadership of the Chief of the General Staff, General Bayerlein, had in the meantime overcome the British mines, and was about to push further eastwards. I discussed the situation with Bayerlein and we decided to carry on with the attack.

Owing to the fact that the British tank forces were again assembled ready for immediate action, a wide outflanking drive to the east could not be carried out, in view of the constant menace to our own flank which would be presented by the 7th Division to the south and by the 10th and 1st British Armoured Divisions in the north. We had to decide on an earlier turn

Above: Strewn with debris, an abandoned Afrika Korps Panzer III is gingerly inspected by its prospective new owner near Tel el Eissa in August 1942.

northwards. In the event, the offensive failed because:

(a) The British positions in the south, contrary to what our reconnaissance had led us to believe, had been completed in great strength.

(b) The continuous and very heavy attacks of the RAF, who were practically masters of the air, absolutely pinned my troops to

Above: On the lookout for the enemy. An observer scans the horizon through fieldglasses from the turret side-hatch of this Panzer IV with its long-barrelled 75mm KL/43 main gun.

the ground and made impossible any safe deployment or any advance.

(c) The petrol, which was a necessary condition for the implementation of our plans, did not arrive. The ships which Cavallero had promised us were some of them sunk, some of them delayed, and some of them not even dispatched. Kesselring had unfortunately not been able to fulfil his promise to fly over 500 tons a day to the vicinity of the front in case of need.

The criticism of Kesselring and the Luftwaffe was justified to a certain extent: there was no doubt that the Italian and German squadrons were less effective than they had been earlier in the year. As the Luftwaffe commander in Africa, von Waldau, pointed out, however, his units had suffered greatly in the late spring and early summer – partly in the close support they had given to the ground troops during the offensive, especially in the attack on Bir Hacheim – and they were badly off for aviation fuel. Allied air superiority was never to be seriously challenged for the rest of the war in North Africa.

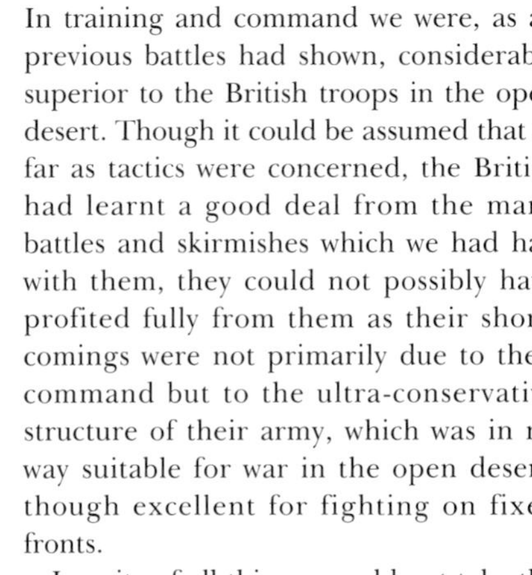

Having failed in his offensive, it was imperative that Rommel take the sick leave that he needed. It was now clear that an Allied attack could be expected, and before he returned to Europe, he made an assessment of the state of relative strengths of the opposing forces in the Alamein position.

In training and command we were, as all previous battles had shown, considerably superior to the British troops in the open desert. Though it could be assumed that as far as tactics were concerned, the British had learnt a good deal from the many battles and skirmishes which we had had with them, they could not possibly have profited fully from them as their shortcomings were not primarily due to their command but to the ultra-conservative structure of their army, which was in no way suitable for war in the open desert, though excellent for fighting on fixed fronts.

In spite of all this, we could not take the risk of shifting the main weight of the defensive action on to operations in the open desert for the following reasons:

(a) The relative strengths of the motorised divisions had become too unequal. While our adversary was constantly being reinforced by motorised units, we received only non-motorised forces, which, in the open desert, were as good as useless. We were obviously forced, therefore, to choose a form of warfare in which they too could play their part.

(b) The British air superiority, the new air tactics of the RAF, and the resultant tactical limitations on the use of motorised forces.

(c) Our permanent shortage of petrol. I did not want to get myself again into the awkward situation of having to break off a battle because my armoured vehicles were immobilised by a shortage of petrol. In a

mobile defensive action, shortage of petrol means disaster.

Before he left for Germany late in September, replaced by General Stumme, Rommel had begun the construction of a considerable defensive position, based on his analysis that mobile warfare was now very difficult because of British material superiority. He recognised that extensive minefields would be necessary, and also instructed his staff to be prepared to deal with seaborne landings (he did not know, of course, that the crucial seaborne landings would take place on the Atlantic seaboard, in November, as Operation Torch).

Rommel's arrival back in Germany was the signal for some public celebrations of his achievements, and Rommel himself gave a speech in which he made confident noises about the situation in Egypt. For his recuperation, he went to the Austrian Alps. It was unclear at this point whether he would actually return to Africa: Hitler had dangled the possibility of a major command in Russia. Stumme wrote confidently about the progress of the defensive line he was constructing. Then, on 24th October, news came through that the offensive had begun, and Hitler asked him to return to the front.

24th October 1942
The Fuehrer's call came through. The situation at El Alamein had developed in such a way that he had to ask me to fly to Africa to take over command. I set off next morning. I knew that there were no more laurels to be earned in Africa, for I had learnt from the reports of my officers that supplies there had fallen far short of the minimum demands which I had made. It very soon became clear, however, that I had not had any idea of just how bad the supply situation really was.

25th October 1942
When I arrived in Rome towards 11.00hrs, I was met at the airport by General von Rintelen, Military Attaché and German

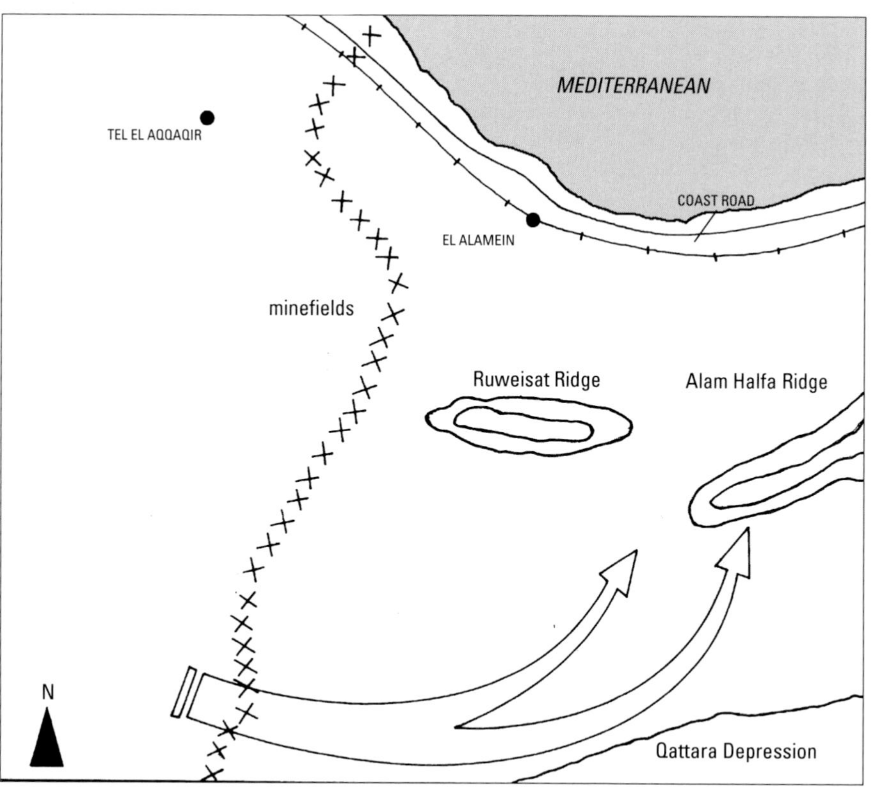

LEFT: The Battle of Alam Halfa (31st August-2nd September 1942). Rommel tries to break through the British line but is repulsed.

general attached to the Italian forces. The British attack was still in progress and General Stumme was still missing. General von Rintelen further reported to me that only three issues of petrol remained for the army in the African theatre, for it had not been possible in recent weeks to send more across, partly on account of the sinkings by the British, partly because the Italian Navy did not provide the transport. This situation was disastrous, since our petrol supplies meant each vehicle had a range of only 300km (180 miles). Thus a prolonged resistance on our part was not to be expected. Shortage of petrol would completely prevent our taking the correct tactical decisions and would impose tremendous limitations upon our planning. I was extremely angry, for at my departure there had been at least eight issues left for the army in Egypt and Libya and, in comparison with the minimum essential 30 issues, even that had been ridiculously little. Experience had shown that one needed one issue of petrol for each day of battle. Without it one was crippled and the enemy could operate without one being able to take practical counter-measures. General von Rintelen regretted this situation and said that he had unfortunately been on leave and had thus been unable to give sufficient attention to the supply question!

Above: A sun-blackened Italian soldier shovelling sand from the entrance to his dugout, July 1942.

Feeling that we would fight this battle with but small hope of even a defensive success, I flew across the Mediterranean in my Storch and reached my battle headquarters at dusk.

October/November 1942

The El Alamein position lay between the Mediterranean Sea and the Qattara Depression, which our reconnaissance units had finally established to be impassable by heavy columns. It was therefore the only North African front apart from the Akarit Line which could not be approached from the south. All other positions could be frontally bound up, outflanked to the south, and in this way brought to capitulation. All other positions could be by-passed to the south using mobile forces, forcing a decision in the enemy's rear. The existence of this open flank had led time and again to novel situations in our theatre of war.

On the El Alamein front it was different. The line, if strongly held by infantry all along, afforded no opportunity for the enemy to launch a surprise attack in the rear. The enemy first had to achieve a breakthrough, which gave the defender the opportunity to hold the line long enough to await the arrival of reserve formations to join the battle. Here we faced a completely different set of tactical considerations. Here the defenders had a certain tactical advantage, since they could dig in behind their mines, while the attacker had to contend with being fired at from these dug-in positions. The positions would have to be directly assaulted in any event.

The positions were well defended with the installation of many mines. Including the captured British minefields, we had something in the region of 500,000 mines. In deploying these mines, care was taken to ensure that the holding units would also be able to defend themselves on the flanks and to the rear. Large quantities of captured British mortar and artillery munitions were re-used. Built into the defences, these materials were in some cases wired to detonate by remote control.

The Italians were mixed in with their German comrades at the front, so that an Italian position was always next to a German one. So badly were the Italians armed that their weapons had to be evenly distributed across the whole front, ensuring that German weapons were available to every sector.

The outposts were provided with dogs, that would give warning of any British approaching the minefields. We wanted to ensure that the British could clear these minefields but slowly, and only after taking out these pickets. Unfortunately, most of the mines available in the North African theatre were anti-tank, which the infantry could walk over without harm and could be relatively easily avoided.

With these points in mind, the troops were prepared for the defence during my absence. As events showed, all our efforts came to nothing against the greatly superior British forces, not because we had made mistakes, but because the conditions under which we entered the battle made it impossible to win.

23rd October 1942

The battle at El Alamein which began on 23rd October turned the tide of war against us in North Africa. The conditions under which my courageous units entered battle were so utterly hopeless it remained quite impossible to imagine coming out of this fight victorious.

Something over 200 German and 300 Italian tanks stood against British armour of a strength equivalent to over 1000 armoured vehicles. Although we had a fair number of guns, these were for the most part obsolete Italian models; many others were captured, and in both cases sufficient ammunition of the right type was lacking. Also, the British had meanwhile succeeded in establishing complete air superiority over the Mediterranean, and through intensive bombing of our ports and close aerial observation over the sea, combined with unceasing enemy naval activity on the water, were in the position to render our supply traffic as good as immobile. Our supplies were so bad, that severe shortages in all materiel were evident even early on in the battle, as will become clear from the following account.

23rd October 1942 was just another day like all the rest on the El Alamein front at this time, until about 20.40hrs when the entire front erupted under an immense artillery barrage which in time began to concentrate on the northern sector. Never before had we experienced such rolling-fire in North Africa, and it continued throughout the entire course of the battle

BELOW: A British tank crew in a Grant approach to view their victim, a 'brewed-up' Panzer I reconnaissance tank.

ROMMEL AND AIR POWER

In the open spaces of the desert and with the long supply lines of the North African campaign, air power was extremely important. Rommel was always demanding more support from the Luftwaffe, while resenting the demands for aviation fuel. The air war in the desert had been more or less even up to August 1942, and German aircraft had often played a crucial role.

During August 1942, however, the British Desert Air Force asserted a decisive air superiority. Rommel had often had to take shelter from air attack in the past, but he personally had never been under such pressure as on 1st September during Alam Halfa. Some of his own staff were killed, and he could have been badly injured.

The experience affected the German commander profoundly, and he felt that both the mobility of his armoured units and his own movements round the battlefield were seriously restricted by Allied air power. All his future planning had to take full account of this change.

at El Alamein. With extraordinary accuracy, British gunners shelled our positions, resulting in very heavy casualties.

Soon the rolling-fire had destroyed our communications network, so virtually no further reports came from the front. The forward outposts fought to the last round before they surrendered or fell.

Under the weight of the horrendous British artillery fire, like those experienced in World War I, sections of the Italian 62nd Infantry Regiment deserted their posts and fled. Their nerve failed in these partially completed defences. After an hour the British had overtaken our forward positions and stood 10km (six miles) across in front of our main defence line. Our infantry resisted fiercely, despite the destruction of most of their heavy weapons by the British artillery. On and on the British tanks came. Soon they had overrun the positions abandoned by the 62nd Italian Infantry Regiment, and were eventually brought to a halt only by an artillery barrage. A further two battalions of the 164th Infantry Division were taken out by British artillery fire in the morning.

Above: An Afrika Korps gun crew with a 105mm Light Field Howitzer in action during El Alamein, a battle of relentless artillery bombardments. Rommel was particularly irate at the failure of his deputy, Stumme, to order the return of fire early enough.

24th October 1942

General Stumme, my deputy, heard this tornado of British fire back in the HQ, but still did not order the artillery to open fire on the British positions on account of the scarcity of ammunition in North Africa. This was an error, since it might at least have taken some force out of the British assault. Later our artillery was not able to respond with much power, since the British were by then established in positions they had captured from us during the night. As 24th October dawned, very few reports were coming in, and the situation remained very unclear. General Stumme decided therefore to drive up to the front himself.

Stumme drove to the front – just what Rommel would have done himself – and died, probably of a heart attack under British air attack. On 25th October, Rommel was back with his army. He directed the defence of the northern sector, into which Montgomery's forces were making inroads, and was able temporarily to restore the situation. His problem was that the British pressure was reducing his reserves, and making him commit more forces than he wanted. The situation worsened over the next two days.

The following day I had to commit to bringing further units north, at the risk of leaving the southern flank completely bereft of heavy weapons and German forces. They were replaced by the third section of the Ariete which had previously been deployed on the northern front. In the course of the morning, the British made three further assaults on our northern front, but were pushed back to their positions by our tank units. We lost many tanks during these days.

As on previous days, uninterrupted British bombing raids were directed against the German-Italian troops. Our Luftwaffe did all in its power to help us, but could not succeed against their overwhelming numerical superiority.

The supply situation remained perilous. In Italy, auxiliary vessels and destroyers were being mobilised on our behalf to bring munitions and petrol. Unfortunately the bulk of promised shipping was bound for Benghazi, with only the residue to Tobruk. Transport from these ports we knew from experience would take several days, so there could be little hope that these supplies would arrive in time.

From about midday on the 28th, a powerful force of British armour was observed concentrating in Minefield 1. We took it that the British were poised to begin what they saw as the decisive breakthrough, and so got ourselves ready to fight off the attack with dwindling resources. The whole Afrika Korps had to be put into position as a result of the heavy losses suffered by the German-Italian infantry divisions. I once again informed all commanders that this was a battle for life and death, and that every officer and man had to give of his best.

Around 21.00hrs, a tremendous British rolling-fire hammered the area west of Hill 28. Soon the hundreds of British guns began to concentrate their fire in the area of the II/125 north of Hill 28. At about 22.00hrs the British assault began. The force of the British attack was of unabated ferocity. By concentrating every gun in the area, we managed to halt the British attacks which were coming from the Minefield 1 area. In the sector between Minefields 1 and 2, farther north, British tanks and infantry made a successful breakthrough. For six hours a furious battle raged here. Finally, the II/125th and the XI Bersaglieri Battalion were overrun by the enemy. The British had until now used only a few divisions in the front line and still had a complement of over 800 tanks, which were now preparing in the northern area of our front line for the decisive assault. For our part, we had just 90 German and 140 Italian tanks. But how the situation was perceived in Rome is most clearly shown in the following signal from Cavallero which arrived on the evening of 1st November:

'The Duce has instructed me to pass on to you his profound appreciation of the successful counter-offensive led by you personally. The Duce also affirms his complete confidence that the battle now taking place will be brought to a successful conclusion under your command.'

1st November 1942

It was soon to be shown that the Fuehrer's HQ was no better informed of the situation in North Africa either. Sometimes it is disadvantageous to have a military reputation. One is aware of one's limits, but others go on expecting miracles and put defeat down to deliberate obstinacy.

Meanwhile, the reconnaissance reports on the Fuka position had arrived. In the southern positions, the steep ground was impassable by tank, so we could hope that in an emergency we could hold on there while the British brought up their artillery, possibly giving time for reinforcements of some kind to arrive.

Possibly some inkling of our doings filtered through to Fuehrer HQ. It was already known, as I was to discover later, that we had devised a timetable for the operation.

Rommel's defence against the new British offensive of 28th October had been very successful. Montgomery, however, held all the best cards, and could claim (with some truth) that the battle was still going according to plan: that his operations were 'crumbling' the Axis positions. And he was certainly maintaining the initiative. He was able to plan a further push, Operation Supercharge, against which the weakened Axis army had faint hopes of success.

Below: US-built RAF Martin Baltimore bombers unloading over a German supply column. Rommel complained of the pounding he received at the hands of Allied aircraft, against which the Luftwaffe was at a numerical disadvantage.

RIGHT: 'Kiwi's last flight'. Luftwaffe personnel pick at the carcass of this Mk IIA Hurricane, probably brought down by Axis anti-aircraft fire in the desert near El Alamein.

The anticipated British main attack came on the night of 1st November. For three hours hundreds of British guns rained shells on our positions, while rolling British night air raids on our German-Italian troops followed. Then massed British infantry and tanks advanced westwards through a curtain of fire and behind a screen of smoke. First came a powerful push against the 200th Infantry Regiment either side of Hill 28. Quickly the British established a breakthrough. With tanks and armoured cars they continued the thrust westwards. We were able to bring the enemy to a halt only after heavy fighting by bringing in the divisional reserves of the 90th Light. But he continued to force ever more troops through the gap in our defences.

Shortly afterwards, massed British units broke through the 15th Panzer Division's front southwest of Hill 28. New Zealand infantry and heavy British tank units – from captured documents, some 500 armoured vehicles – rolled west, overran a regiment of the Trieste Division and a German grenadier battalion, despite courageous resistance, to find themselves by daybreak at a point west of Telegraph Road. According to reports from my artillery observers, another 400 British tanks stood east of the minefields. Single British tanks and armoured cars successfully broke out in the west, hunting out our supply units.

At first light, the Afrika Korps mounted a counter-offensive, achieving some success, but at the cost of heavy losses in armour, since our tanks were simply not robust enough against the English heavies. The breakthrough, in which the enemy had positioned (besides the tanks referred to) 15 artillery regiments with limitless ammunition, was now closed off. It was only desperate efforts by our artillery and anti-aircraft guns on all enemy positions, regardless of the munitions shortage, that further British advances were arrested.

2nd November 1942

Those elements of the 21st Panzer and 15th Light that were not already at the front were put in north and south to squeeze the British out of their position. Uninterrupted British air attacks and artillery fire hammered our troops. In the space of one hour at about midday, seven flights of 18 bombers hit my troops. More and more of our 88mm anti-aircraft guns, our only effective weapons against heavy

British tanks, were going out of action. Although every available anti-aircraft gun had been brought up, we still had no more than 24 88mms on that day. Before long, all available units were positioned in the front line. Our battle strength was only a third of what it had been at the beginning of the struggle.

That day I drove time and again to the front, and watched the battle from a hill.

By evening I was receiving reports from the Panzer Army that its supply situation was totally desperate. We had already let loose 450 tons of ammunition that day, while three destroyers had brought only 190 tons into Tobruk. The British had as good as complete control over the air and sea to Tobruk and beyond, and were constantly bombing the town and port. A number of ships had been sunk in the harbour over the last few days. Also, the fuel situation was becoming critical and the worst of the fighting was yet to come.

By evening it was clear to me that the British were concentrating their second-line armour at the point of penetration. Thus we faced total annihilation. The Afrika Korps had barely 35 serviceable tanks remaining.

Here was the moment to slip away to the Fuka Line. Already in the preceding days some of our materiel had been transported to the west. During the night, the southern front reoccupied the old positions held before the offensive of August and September. The 125th Regiment was redeployed to the area south of Sidi Abd al Rahman. The 90th Light Division, the Afrika Korps and the XX Italian Motorised Corps now had to slip back slowly enough to allow the foot divisions to march or be transported off. Since the British had only reluctantly followed up, and their operations were often incomprehensibly over-cautious, I hoped to get away with at least some part of my infantry.

The army's strength was so sapped after the protracted battle that it was no longer in the position to offer resistance to the anticipated enemy breakthrough next day. Given our dire shortage of vehicles, an orderly retreat of our non-motorised forces seemed impossible. Also, the mobile forces were engaged in battle, and we could not wait for them to be freed up. From this position we had to reckon on the gradual destruction of the army. In those terms I reported to the Fuehrer's HQ that same day.

On 2nd November we had to withdraw our forces south under British pressure to a position 15km (eight miles) east of El Daba. Our abandonment of the central and southern sectors went unnoticed. Unfortunately this operation progressed very slowly, since no vehicles were available and the heavy weapons had for the most part to be manhandled away. Despite these difficulties, the next morning saw the southern divisions in their new positions.

Rommel was defeated, and he knew it. He had, however, held the British offensive, and his forces were still intact, though battered. He could expect to pull back, and to restore his front. The normal course of events in the North African theatre usually involved deep penetration, followed by withdrawal at speed, with a

ROMMEL'S HEALTH

The climate of North Africa took a heavy toll on all who fought there. Sandstorms and wind combined with the sun to make life difficult. Water was often in short supply, and frequently dangerous to drink. Add to this the strain of battle and the hard physical regime Rommel inflicted on himself, and it should be no surprise that his health suffered badly.

After he arrived in Africa, Rommel soon began having problems with blood pressure and digestion. In addition, Rommel became jaundiced as 1941 wore on, with a first attack in August of that year. In 1942 he sent Berlin the findings of a medical report: 'Field Marshal Rommel suffers from symptoms of low blood pressure, with a tendency to fainting fits. His present condition is due to stomach and intestinal complaints he has had for a long time, aggravated by the great physical and psychological strain of recent weeks, particularly aggravated by the unfavourable climate.'

Rommel left Africa for a period of sick leave on 23rd September. He arrived at Semmering in Austria for some well-earned rest – soon interrupted by news of Montgomery's attack on Axis positions.

Below: All smiles for the camera as Rommel greets Goebbels at an international press conference at the Propaganda Ministry in Berlin, October 1942. 'We are only 80 kilometres from Alexandria and Cairo, and we have the door to Egypt in our hands...' he crowed, before leaving for his rest cure in Wiener Neustadt.

period to re-supply and regroup after that, prior to launching a new attempt. Now, however, Hitler himself intervened.

3rd November 1942

3rd November will remain a memorable day in history. Not only was it becoming clear that the fortunes of war had deserted us, but also from this point on the freedom of the Panzer Army to make its own decisions was to be eroded by the interference of high command in its operations.

I had already that morning felt uncomfortable that in spite of our frank and factual situation reports, the true scale of the problem was still lost on our higher command, and decided therefore to send my adjutant, Captain Berndt, to explain the situation in person to Fuehrer HQ. Berndt had to make our situation absolutely clear to Fuehrer HQ, and explain that the North African war was all but lost already. Furthermore he was to demand

complete freedom of action for the Afrika Korps. I was not willing to play into British hands by letting them surround us, but instead intended to fight rearguard actions, forcing the opposition to bring up his artillery time and again, while avoiding any decisive battle until we either had sufficient strength to do so, or until the bulk of the Afrika Korps had been transported to Europe, leaving the rest to cover the retreat.

Around midday I got back to my command post. We had only just escaped, through some wild driving, a carpet of bombs dropped by 18 British planes. 13.30hrs brought an order from the Fuehrer, containing in effect the following:

To GFM Rommel
In the situation in which you find yourself, there can be no consideration other than to stand firm and throw every gun and every man into the fight. Everything possible is being done to help you. Notwithstanding his superior numbers, the enemy must also be worn out. It will not be for the first time in history that strength of will shall have triumphed over larger forces. As for your men, you can offer them no path but to victory or death.
Adolf Hitler

In this order, the impossible was required. Even the most committed soldier can be killed in a bombing raid.

Hitler's order enraged the Afrika Korps' staff, who knew exactly what they should be doing in the circumstances in which they found themselves. Rommel himself was confused – it was against his nature to go against Hitler, and yet he knew that the order amounted to suicide. The most conspicuous protest was made by von Thoma, commanding the Afrika Korps. It is very likely that he had decided that the game was up, and his gesture of going to the front seeking death or capture was a signal that he had lost all faith in the political direction of the German forces. After his capture, von Thoma was taken to see Montgomery, and the two professional soldiers had a friendly meal with each other, the Afrika Korps commander reportedly unguarded in his comments about the conduct of the campaign, and even about German plans for the immediate future.

4th November 1942

Colonel Bayerlein returned to Afrika Korps HQ from the front at around 13.00hrs. He reported on the positions of the panzer units. The Gefechtstaffel was situated in the centre at Tel el Mampsra.

To the north was the 21st Panzer Division and to the south the 15th Panzer Division. The two divisions were well dug in. The battle staff had been annihilated, reported Bayerlein, and General Ritter von Thoma had not been persuaded to leave the front line, where he presumably sought death. Since the British tanks were getting ready to overrun Tel el Mampsra hill, where the burnt-out vehicles and equipment of the Kampfstaffel lay, and break through, Bayerlein was just able to get away at the last moment on foot.

South and southeast of the HQ, huge clouds of dust were to be seen. Here the desperate battle was being played out between the small and inadequate Italian tanks of XX Corps and about 100 British heavy tanks, which had overtaken the Italians on their open right flank. As Major von Luck later reported to me, the Italians, who at that time represented our strongest mobile force, fought with unsurpassed courage. Tank after tank blew apart or burnt out, while continuous British heavy artillery pounded Italian infantry and artillery positions. Around 15.30hrs the last radio message came from the Ariete:

'Enemy tanks penetrated south of Ariete, with Ariete now surrounded. Located about 5km (three miles) northwest of Bir el Abd. Ariete tanks fighting on.'

By evening the Italian XX Corps was annihilated after fighting against armour with outstanding courage. In the Ariete, we had lost our oldest Italian comrades, of whom we had probably demanded more than their poor equipment allowed them.

Right of the Afrika Korps, the enemy's destruction of the XX Italian Corps had smashed a 20km (12 miles) breach along the front, through which large British tank formations were pouring into the west. This meant that our forces to the north were threatened with encirclement by enemy forces 20 times their number. The 90th Light Division had defended their front fiercely against British attacks, but had eventually given way. There were no reserves left, as every available gun and man had had to be put in the front line.

So it had come about, the thing we had been trying with all our might to prevent: the front was broken through, with fully motorised enemy streaming through into our hinterland. At this point in time, no orders from on high could help. After consulting with Colonel Bayerlein, who had now resumed command of the Afrika Korps, I immediately gave the order to begin the retreat forthwith, and to save what could be saved. The Afrika Korps commander, General Ritter von Thoma, had tried, with the Kampfstaffel, to prevent the British breakthrough. As we later heard over the British news service, he had been taken prisoner after the destruction of his unit.

This decision could at least mean the saving of the motorised section of the army from destruction. Nevertheless so much had already been lost as a result of postponing the retreat by 24 hours, including virtually all its infantry and a large number of tanks, that it was no longer in any position to offer effective resistance to the British advance anywhere. The orders to retreat were issued at 15.30hrs, and the operation began forthwith.

It was now no longer possible to organise our columns, as nothing other than rapid retreat could save us from British air attacks, which reached a highpoint that day. Anything that didn't immediately make it onto the road and flee was lost, as the enemy swept on across a wide front, and overtook everything in its path.

At 21.00hrs that evening, far too late, radio signals arrived from the Fuehrer and also from Commando Supremo, which authorised the withdrawal of the army to the Fuka position.

The orders from Hitler that countermanded the initial withdrawal had come as a great shock to Rommel, who was not used to being treated in this fashion. He realised later that obeying orders he knew were wrong had been an error.

5th November 1942

With all my experience, I can confess to

only one mistake – that I did not circumvent or even disregard altogether the 'Victory or Death' order 24 hours earlier. Then the army, together with all its infantry, would in all probability have been saved in a battleworthy condition.

In order to leave no doubt for future historians about the conditions and circumstances under which the command and troops were labouring at the Battle of El Alamein, I include the following summary:

(a) An adequate supply system and stocks of weapons, petrol and ammunition are essential conditions for any army to be able successfully to stand the strain of battle. Before the fighting proper, the battle is fought and decided by the quartermasters. The bravest man can do nothing without guns and plenty of ammunition – and guns and ammunition are of little use in mobile warfare unless they can be transported by vehicles supplied with enough petrol. Supply must be equal in quantity to that which is available to the enemy and not only in quantity but also in quality.

(b) In future the battle on the ground will be preceded by the battle in the air. This will decide who will have to suffer under the operational and tactical disadvantages detailed above and who will, therefore, from the start be forced into tactical compromises.

None of the conditions to which I have referred were in any way fulfilled and we had to suffer the consequences.

The British command of the air was complete. There were days when the British flew 800 bomber sorties and 2500 sorties of fighters, fighter-bombers and low-flying aircraft. We, on the other hand, could at the most fly 60 dive-bomber and 100 fighter sorties. This number moreover became continually smaller.

Generally speaking the principles of the British command had not altered. Now, as ever, their tactics were methodical and cast to a pattern. On this occasion the British principles did in fact help the Eighth Army achieve success, for the following reasons:

(a) It did not come to a battle in the open desert, since our motorised forces were forced to form a front for the sake of the frontally engaged infantry divisions, who were without transport. The war took on the form of a battle of materiel.

(b) The British had such superiority in weapons, both quantitative and qualitative, that they were able to force through any kind of operation.

As always, the British command showed a marked slowness in reaction. When, on the night of 2nd/3rd November, we started on the retreat, it was a long time before the enemy was ready to follow up in pursuit. But for the intervention of Hitler's unfortunate order, it is highly probable that we would have escaped to Fuka with the bulk of our infantry. As always the British High Command showed its customary caution and little forceful decision. For instance, they attacked time and again with separate tank formations

PREPARATIONS FOR EL ALAMEIN

Montgomery's preparations for his attack at El Alamein were thorough, and involved a complex deception plan to persuade the Axis that the main attack was likely to come in the south rather than the north. Construction of a pipeline to the front was even synchronised to suggest that no attack would take place before mid-November.

British material superiority was recognised to be great – the key factor was that 1200 Allied tanks faced 530. The High Command of the Axis forces was surprisingly optimistic, however. Rommel had supervised the establishment of thick defensive minefields, and had 'twinned' Italian divisions with German ones.

After a big public reception on 30th September in Berlin, Rommel gave a press conference declaring that German soldiers would not be driven out of Egypt.

In October, the Afrika Korps' staff wrote an assessment of the situation in Africa. This report explained that over 400,000 mines had been laid, and the army would be ready to repulse the expected Allied assault. Once that had been defeated, a further Axis offensive could then be planned.

and did not, as might have been expected, throw into the battle the 900 tanks which they could, without risk to themselves, have employed in the northern front, thereby using their vast superiority to gain a rapid decision with the minimum of effort and casualties. Actually, under cover of their artillery and air force, only a half of that number would have been sufficient to wipe out my forces, which were frequently standing immobilised on the battlefield. Moreover, the British themselves suffered tremendous losses for this reason. Probably their command wanted to hold its tanks in the second line so as to use them for the pursuit, as apparently their assault forces could not be re-formed fast enough for the follow-up.

In the training of their tanks and infantry formations, the British command had put to excellent use the experience which they had gained from their previous battles with the Axis troops, but it is true to say the new methods which were now being applied were only made possible by the vast quantity of ammunition and new war material they had.

The British methods were possible here through the deployment of new tanks, which were more heavily armed and better armoured than our own – including the Grant, Lee and Sherman; the heavy Churchill was also reported as having been seen – and their limitless supplies of ammunition.

The light tanks would be sent out in the spearhead, with the more heavily armed tanks being kept more and more to the rear. The light armoured vehicles would be tasked to draw our anti-tank and anti-aircraft guns and armour. Once our weapons had opened up and thus given away their positions, the British heavy armour would unleash their destructive firepower from a range of up to 2.5km (1.5 miles), if possible from behind cover. The fire was apparently always targeted by the squadron commander. The huge

BELOW: Guest of honour. Newly promoted Field Marshal Rommel, baton in hand, joins Goebbels at the head of a Nazi rally at the Sportpalast stadium in Berlin, autumn 1942. A moment of pride before the fall to come at El Alamein.

amounts of ammunition this system needed was continually brought up by Bren carriers. In this way the British heavy tanks were able to take out our armour, machine-gun posts, anti-tank and anti-aircraft weapons from a distance at which our guns could not penetrate their armour; in any case they lacked the ammunition needed to do so.

The British artillery demonstrated once again its well-known excellence. Especially noteworthy was its great mobility and speed of reaction to the requirements of the assault troops.

The British armoured units clearly had artillery observers to relay their requirements from the front back to the gunners as quickly as possible. As well as their ample supplies of ammunition, the British also had the benefit of long-range guns, allowing them to engage the Italian artillery positions at a range over which the Italians couldn't return fire, most having a maximum range of 6000m (19,800ft). As the bulk of our artillery consisted of these obsolete Italian pieces, it was an especially painful position for us.

Once our defence had been shattered by artillery, tanks and air raids, the British infantry attacked. Our forward positions were hemmed in by artillery fire, since their location had been established long before by aerial reconnaissance; well-trained engineers, under cover of a smoke-screen, cleared mines to cut wide paths through our mine fields. The tanks then attacked, closely followed by the infantry. British assault teams, using tanks as mobile artillery, advanced to our forward defence lines, and forced their way into our trenches and positions at bayonet point. It was all conducted methodically and according to training. Each separate action was carried out using a concentration of superior strength. The artillery came up close behind the infantry so as to extinguish the last glimmer of resistance. Victory was not usually exploited to any degree, the conquered positions were simply occupied, and reinforcements and artillery were brought in and deployed for a defensive position. Night assaults continued to be a British speciality, which they conducted well.

Montgomery's victory at El Alamein was a visible turning point of the war in North Africa. There was no disguising the importance of what had happened. And at Alam Halfa and Second Alamein, Rommel came across an enemy who knew how to apply material superiority to squeeze the life out of a more able but logistically weaker opponent. He recognised that this was going to be the warfare of the future: a

RIGHT: Rommel lays down the law to his Italian allies. Nominally answerable to the Italians, on whose behalf Germany had sent forces to North Africa, Rommel short-circuited the Commando Supremo by reporting direct to Berlin and by firmly wresting control from his inexperienced and unpredictable counterparts.

form of warfare to which he and the Afrika Korps could have no long-term answer.

Recognising the inevitability of defeat, Rommel began to look at the methods of retreat he would have to consider, and at how best he could conserve both manpower and materiel for the eventual withdrawal from North Africa.

In the existing conditions of supply, which permitted us neither the replacement tanks, vehicles and weapons that had been overdue for months, nor a stock of petrol such as was necessary to carry through a mobile battle, we could not hope to be able to hold out against a powerful British attack in any position in Tripolitania.

Our problem in this retreat was the non-motorised Italians. The slowest formation, assuming that one does not want to abandon it, always determines the speed of retreat of the whole army. This is a disastrous disadvantage when the attacker is fully motorised. It was thus necessary to move the Italian divisions to the west into new positions before the British attack, and to keep my motorised troops at Mersa el Brega to tie down the British. It was also necessary to mine the roads and to take advantage of every opportunity of inflicting damage on the enemy advanced guard. The British commander had revealed himself as over-cautious. He risked nothing which was in the least doubtful, and any bold action was foreign to him. It was, therefore, the task of our motorised forces to give an impression of constant activity so as to make the British even more cautious and slow up their speed. It was clear to me that Montgomery would never take the risk of striking boldly after us and overrunning us. Indeed, looking at the operations as a whole, such a course would have cost him smaller casualties than his methodical insistence on overwhelming superiority in each tactical action, at the sacrifice of speed.

In any case the retreat to Tunisia was to be carried out in several stages, with the British to be forced into deploying as often as possible. This was a gamble on the caution of the British commander which proved to be very well justified.

Rommel was later to gather his observations together in a passage he called 'The Rules of Desert Warfare'.

THE RULES OF DESERT WARFARE

Of all the theatres of operations, North Africa was probably the one where the war took on its most modern, and purest, form. Here were opposed fully motorised formations for whose employment the flat desert, free of obstructions, offered hitherto unforeseen possibilities. Here alone could the principles of motorised and tank warfare, as they had been taught before 1939, be fully applied and, more importantly, further developed. Here only did the pure tank battle between large armoured formations actually occur. Even though the struggle may have occasionally hardened into static warfare, in its more important stages, in 1941-42 during the Cunningham-Ritchie Offensive and in the summer of 1942 up to the capture of Tobruk, it remained based on the principle of complete mobility.

Militarily, this was entirely new ground, for our offensive in Poland and the West had been against opponents who, in their operations, had constantly to consider their non-motorised infantry divisions, and whose freedom of decision was thus disastrously limited, particularly in retreat. They were, indeed, often obliged by this preoccupation to adopt measures which were quite unsuitable for holding up our advance. After our breakthrough in France in 1940, the enemy infantry divisions were quickly overrun and outflanked by our motorised forces. When this happened, the enemy operational reserves had to allow themselves to be ground to pieces by our attacking forces, often in tactically unfavourable positions, in an endeavour to gain time for the retreat of the infantry.

Against a motorised and armoured enemy, non-motorised infantry divisions are of value only in prepared positions. Once such positions have been pierced or outflanked and they are forced to retreat from them, they become helpless victims of the motorised enemy. In extreme cases they can do no more than hold on in their positions to the last round. In retreat they cause tremendous embarrassment since, as mentioned above, motorised formations have to be employed to gain time (to extricate them). I myself had to submit to

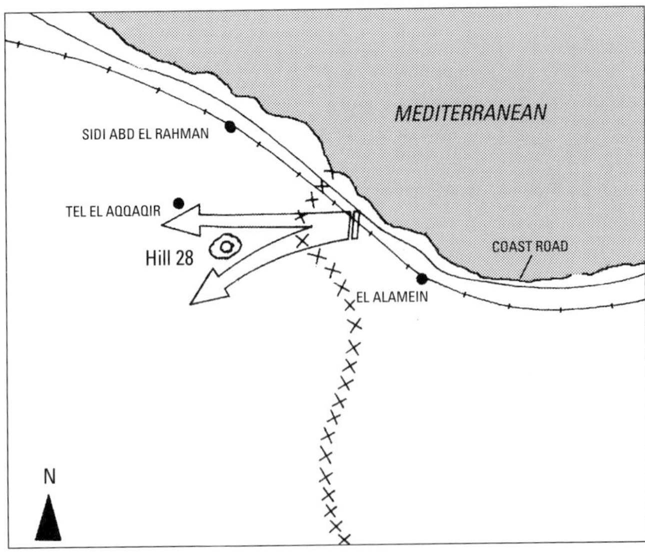

ABOVE: Rommel is defeated at El Alamein.

this experience during the retreat of the Axis forces from Cyrenaica in the winter of 1941-42 because the whole of the Italian and a large part of the German infantry, including the majority of what was to become the 90th Light Division, had no vehicles. Parts of them had to be carried by a shuttle service of supply columns, parts had to march. It was only thanks to the prowess of my armoured formations that the retreat of the German and Italian infantry could be covered, for the fully motorised British were in hot pursuit. Similarly, Graziani's failure can be attributed mainly to the fact that the Italian army, the greater part of it not motorised, was helpless in the open desert against the weak but nevertheless fully motorised British forces, and the Italian armour, although too weak to oppose the British with any hope of success, was compelled to accept battle and allow itself to be destroyed in defence of the infantry.

Out of the purely motorised form of warfare which developed in Libya and Egypt there arose certain laws, fundamentally different from those that are applicable in other theatres. They will be the standard rules of engagement for future conflicts, which will apply to fully motorised formations.

In the flat desert country, so well suited to motor transport, the encirclement of a fully motorised enemy produces the following results:

(a) The enemy is placed in the worst tactical situation imaginable, since fire can be brought to bear on him from all sides. Even when he is enveloped only on three sides his position is tactically untenable.

(b) When the envelopment is completed, he is tactically compelled to evacuate the area which he occupies.

The encirclement of the enemy and his subsequent destruction in the pocket can, however, seldom be the primary aim of an operation but is usually only an indirect object, for a fully motorised force whose organisational structure is intact will normally and in suitable country be able to break out at any time through an improvised defensive ring. Thanks to motorisation, the commander of the encircled force will be in a position to concentrate his main effort unexpectedly against a favourable point and force his way through. Time and time again this was demonstrated in the desert.

Tactically, the battle of attrition is fought with high mobility. The following points require particular attention:

(a) One should endeavour to concentrate one's own forces both in space and time, while at the same time seeking to split the opposing forces and destroy them at different times.

(b) Supply lines are particularly vulnerable as all petrol and ammunition must pass along them. Hence, one should protect one's own by all possible means and seek to confuse, or better still, sever, the enemy's. Operations in the opposing supply area will cause the enemy immediately to break off the battle elsewhere, since supplies are the basis of the battle and thus must be given a high priority of protection.

(c) The tank force is the backbone of the motorised army. Everything turns on the tanks, the other formations are mere ancillaries. A war of attrition against the enemy tank units must, therefore, be carried on as far as possible by one's own tank destruction units. One's own tank forces must deal the last blow.

(d) Results of reconnaissance must reach the commander in the shortest possible time, and he must then take immediate decisions and put them into effect as quickly as possible. Speed of reaction in taking command decisions decides battles. It is, therefore, essential that commanders of motorised forces should be as near as possible to their troops and in the closest signal communication with them.

(e) Speed of one's own movement and organisational cohesion of the forces are decisive factors and require particular attention. Any sign of confusion must be dealt with quickly.

(f) Concealment of intentions is supremely important so as to provide surprise for one's own operations and so make it possible to exploit the time taken by enemy commanders to react.

(g) Once the enemy has been thoroughly softened up, victory can be exploited by attempting to overrun and destroy major elements of his disrupted forces.

Regarding the technical and organisational aspects of desert warfare, particular attention should be paid to the following:

(a) The prime requirements in a tank are manoeuvrability, speed, and a long-range gun – because the side with the bigger gun has the longer reach and can be first to engage his enemy. Armour cannot be a substitute for lack of fire-power.

(b) The infantry's role is to occupy and hold positions in order to deny the enemy certain operations, or to force him into undertaking others.

I myself hold the view that bold decisions are the best way to succeed. Strategic and tactical boldness must be distinguished from a military gamble. Bold is that operation which, while having the possibility of success, also leaves one with sufficient forces in hand to cope with circumstances which might arise in the event of failure. A gamble, on the other hand, is an operation which can bring either victory or the total annihilation of one's forces. There are situations in which a gamble is justified, such as when defeat is only a matter of time, so that gaining more time is pointless, and the only chance lies in a risky operation.

The only time a commander can be sure of the outcome of a battle is when he has forces so superior to those of his enemy that a victory is self-evident. Then it is not so much how but when. But even in a situation like that, I believe it is better to pursue operations boldly.

THE SECOND BATTLE OF EL ALAMEIN

The battle began with an immense artillery barrage on the evening of 23rd October. Rommel had been alerted to the beginning of the Allied offensive on the 24th, and arrived back in Africa on the 25th. That evening he sent out a message to the army that he was back. The Axis forces had suffered severely, but the front had not been broken.

The Germans might be winning tactical victories, but the effort was draining them of men, machines and fuel. An Allied thrust along the coast road was halted on 31st October, but the German commander knew that his line was being stretched dangerously thin.

In the early hours of 2nd November, Montgomery launched Operation Supercharge, a final big attempt to shatter the Axis front just north of Hill 28. An Axis counter later that morning failed, and Rommel recognised that the game was up. He signalled to Rome that he was disengaging, and could not guarantee to save the non-motorised Italian elements, and also signalled to OKW that a proper defensive front could not be maintained. The battle for the Alamein Line was lost.

Chapter IX

Afrika Korps in Retreat

The early months of 1943 saw the end of Rommel's ambitions in North Africa. Weary of the battle, the climate and above all the stubbornness of his superior commanders, his main aim was how to spare his troops further losses. The Desert Fox was about to experience the bitterness of continual withdrawal in the face of the enemy.

BELOW: Alongside his camouflage-painted M3 Lee-Grant command tank, Montgomery gazes towards the west, to where Rommel and the Afrika Korps are rapidly retreating in some disarray.

Having made the decision to retreat from El Alamein, in spite of initial orders to the contrary from Hitler and Mussolini, Rommel showed his usual drive and ability in the race to save his troops from the encroaching Allied forces, who (fortunately for the Axis soldiers) did not follow up with the ruthlessness that the situation required.

4th November 1942

My headquarters left during the night for Fuka. Time and again we got stuck in the sand. Everyone had to climb down and help dig the vehicles out. It reminded me of the desperate time we had of it trying to reach Alexandria, following our victory at Tobruk, when my troops were exhausted but elated after the long battle, crossing the same stretch of ground that we were crossing now, in order to grasp the one chance of seizing the initiative in North Africa. Our supply route had failed, and we were finally seeing the consequences. Bitter thoughts in this night of defeat.

By morning, the coast road on our immediate right was lit up by flares, and British bombs continued to fall on our columns. Authorisation for the retreat from El Alamein to Fuka came – as did the authorisation from the Fuehrer – much too late in the day, requiring us to extricate all German-Italian troops, in particular the non-motorised units.

Rommel's hopes of establishing a defensive position at Fuka were soon dashed, as British armoured units followed hard on the heels of the fleeing Axis units.

5th November 1942

Around midday, heavy fighting broke out between our motorised units and the British forward column near Fuka. Time and again sandstorms blew up and deprived us of visibility. Soon a strong British flying column came up behind our unprotected southern flank. It was therefore clear – we had to sound the retreat, or all would be lost.

Now that the Afrika Korps had been breached between the 15th and 21st Panzer Divisions and we had no more reserves, I ordered – with a heavy heart on account of the German and Italian units still on the march – the withdrawal to Mersa Matruh.

The only formations retaining any fighting strength were the remnants of the 90th Light Division, under Count von Sponeck, small combat groups from the two panzer divisions of the Afrika Korps, the Panzergrenadier Regiment Afrika, and a quickly assembled body of German troops drawn from the last of the 164th Light Division.

On the morning of 6th November, as we tried to gather ourselves together, we came across a coloured British soldier who had hidden near our vehicles. In the course of the morning we were able with difficulty to gather our vehicles and filter them through the mined zone seven kilometres east of Mersa Matruh.

During the retreat we suffered an acute shortage of fuel, since the withdrawal of the armies had increased our rate of consumption.

Meanwhile, our columns were rolling westwards and approaching Sollum. In the afternoon, the Italian General Gandin appeared on behalf of Marshal Cavallero to enquire after our situation and intentions. I was pleased at this. I delivered a detailed account of the fighting, in particular underlining the supply problems, the Fuehrer's and the Duce's orders, and especially those from the Commando Supremo. I told him directly that given the existing balance of forces, we could under no circumstances hold the enemy, and that the British, if they wished, could advance unopposed to Tripoli. We could not engage in battle, but would have to hold off the British as best we could while our troops, in chaotic disorder, were pulled back over the Libyan-Egyptian border. They could not be set in order until Libya was reached, for fear of being completely cut off. Therefore, speed was essential.

No operation could be undertaken with our remaining tanks and motorised units because of the complete lack of fuel. Whatever fuel we received, had to be reserved for the withdrawal of the men.

Gandin was clearly disturbed as he left my battleground.

Clearly, war was a simple affair to the Commando Supremo: when during the El Alamein crisis in July, I had advised Marshal Cavallero that in the event of a British breakthrough we would be faced with two possible situations either to stay in the positions and be forced into surrender after two to three days for lack of water, or to retreat fighting to the west, Count Cavallero said he could not advise on what to do: the prospect was simply not to be considered. Easy enough to say.

Above: End of the road. Victim of an Allied strafing attack, this Axis supply column lies motionless in the desert. Easy prey to marauding fighter-bombers, supply trucks were the slender lifeline on which the much-extended forces on both sides relied to wage war in the barren desert.

The fuel situation was desperate, even though ships had unloaded nearly 5000 tons of fuel at Benghazi on 4th November – a record achievement – since news of our predicament had apparently stirred even Rome into action. But fuel on the dockside was no use to us. We needed petrol here, at the front, where our columns were waiting. Meanwhile, some 2000 of the 5000 tons had been destroyed in British bombing raids over Benghazi. We tried hard to persuade the Italians and Kesselring to transport the fuel on. Torrential rains were falling at this time; many tracks were too hopelessly waterlogged for vehicles and we mostly had to use the coast road. However, the British also faced problems since they also couldn't move their columns through the desert fast enough. The result was a major slowing down of operations on both sides.

In view of the bad transport situation, we could not expect any reinforcements from Europe in the foreseeable future. It was unavoidable, then, that in the event of a further British onslaught we would have to evacuate Cyrenaica, and we couldn't contemplate making another stand before Mersa el Brega. Perhaps, I hoped, by the time we arrived, more materiel would have been sent from Tripolitania so that we could meet the British strike force much better equipped, and have the chance of attacking enemy elements.

Since it was becoming apparent that the British were moving with an armoured division to the south of Mersa Matruh, I ordered 90th Light Division to act as rearguard while the remaining forces all evacuated the area during the night and withdrew to Sidi el Barrani. The British correctly turned north during the night of the 7th, to try to cut us off. But the trap was already empty, and the British found only the wreckage of various vehicles we had destroyed for lack of fuel. It is pointless to try outflanking an enemy without having first engaged his front, because the defender can always use his motorised elements, when he has fuel and vehicles, to hold out against the flanking column while evacuating the trap.

Throughout the night, the enemy carried out uninterrupted bombing attacks on the Sollum-Halfaya passes. The two glaring problems were getting the columns through in time, and the fuel situation. So long as the large columns were jammed at the entrance to the passes, the motorised units would have to hold off the enemy at all costs. By morning there was still a 40-kilometre-long queue of vehicles waiting to get through the passes. Very little progress had been made during the night due to the continuous RAF attacks.

Around 08.00hrs I met Colonel Bayerlein to inform him that a convoy of 104 ships was approaching North Africa, and that the British and Americans were possibly about to strike from the west. This supposition was confirmed at about 11.00hrs. The British and Americans had landed during the night in northwest

Africa, I was soon informed by Army Chief, Colonel Westphal. This meant the end of the army in Africa.

Operation Torch, the Allied landings in French North Africa from the Atlantic, drove Rommel into a deeply pessimistic mood. He now believed that there was no point in holding on – that the evacuation of German troops from the desert theatre back to Europe was the only sane course of action. This pessimism did not affect his military skills on the ground in November: he conducted the withdrawal with great verve, and with great understanding of the factors involved in managing such a retreat.

8th November 1942

As I observed for myself that evening, progress of the traffic over the passes was comparatively smooth, numerous officers and traffic squads manning the control posts and organising the flow. It now looked hopeful that we might have all the supply columns across by midday on 9th November, allowing the Afrika Korps to use the road to the west. With fuel in short supply, and a large number of vehicles under tow, this would make things much easier. In such a situation, it is a big mistake to try and restore order to supply troops who are in a state of panic and completely disorganised, until you have got them to a place of comparative safety. One should leave them to run away and in time try to direct them into organised routes. After a few days the inherent discipline and self-confidence returns, and then reorganisation can be undertaken without further hindrance.

The Sollum Line was to be held on orders from the Duce. The patent impossibility of this was self-evident from the fact that we no longer had battle-worthy armour or anti-tank units powerful enough to bring a British assault in the open desert to a halt. Thus it could not even come into question. The casualties – dead, wounded and captured – suffered by the German motorised units had been severe, but not excessive in terms of overall manpower, and were less than those sustained by the fully-motorised Eighth Army in the summer. Most important was to get as many German-Italian troops and as much materiel as possible away to the west, either to make another stand, or for transportation to the European armies. Meanwhile, the Italians had moved elements of the Pistoia Division and other units up to the Libyan-Egyptian border, wishing to place them under my command. I had to turn them down, for I could not meet their communications, transport or supply needs.

Having pulled much of his army back into Libya, Rommel had to decide whether to make a stand near the frontier or to abandon Cyrenaica. He had strong feelings on the matter.

10th November 1942

The administrative staff, scattered troops and fractured units were now flowing into Cyrenaica. The few combat-strength units formed up to present a delaying defence. We could not even hold the Gazala Line, since that also required mobile support we could not provide. We still did not know how many troops there were in the rear administrative section.

THE FIGHTING WITHDRAWAL

It was not until the afternoon of 4th November that Rommel had decided that he had to disobey the Fuehrer and order a retreat. Having made up his mind, Rommel reacted swiftly. His retreat along the Egyptian coast and through Cyrenaica to Tripoli was masterly. Typically, he ignored Italian orders that he considered wrong: he refused to try to hold on at the Egyptian frontier, which Mussolini insisted had to be defended, and abandoned Tobruk and Benghazi.

The Axis forces were helped by British insistence on taking no risks – partly because of Rommel's own reputation – and by expert laying of real and dummy minefields. It is often considered that Montgomery missed a crucial opportunity by failing to drive straight across the Cyrenaican 'bulge' to cut off the retreating Axis columns, but the British commander was determined to retain his 'balance'. He did not want to give his German adversary the slightest chance to demonstrate his mastery of a fluid battlefield; after all, the last British move across Cyrenaica had been followed by a sudden German counter that had pushed the British back to the Egyptian frontier again!

Because of the situation, I invited Marshal Cavallero and Field Marshal Albert Kesselring to come to North Africa. I hoped to get from them a decisive view on the possibilities of holding Tunisia and getting some reinforcements for my army in the Mersa el Brega Line. The situation required a strategic decision and, while tactical decisions should be made with boldness, strategic moves must be made with due consideration of all possibilities, for they must by definition be 100 per cent safe at all times.

However, neither Cavallero nor Kesselring deemed it necessary to come to Africa, so I decided to send Second Lieutenant Brendt to the Fuehrer's headquarters next day to report on our situation. When he returned a few days later, he said he had met little understanding there. The Fuehrer instructed him to tell me to leave Tunis out of my plans and proceed on the assumption that the bridgehead would hold. This attitude was typical of our top command. It characterised and influenced the series of defeats which lay ahead. Although our tactical achievements in all theatres of the war were considerable, the strategic decisions which would properly exploit them were lacking. In other ways the 'Boss' had been distinctly unfriendly, reported Brendt. Although he sent me an assurance of his special confidence, he had been in a noticeably bad temper. On the question of supplies, he promised immediate action and demanded that we pass on our requirements straightaway, and promised that nothing would be withheld. The Mersa el Brega position was to be held at all costs, as it was to be the springboard for a new offensive.

We hoped to stay near Tobruk for as long as possible to transport away as much as possible of the 10,000 tons of materiel sitting there. Despite our request that nothing other than petrol be flown over, our transport aircraft had brought in another 1100 men by 11th November. These men were wholly unfit for battle, being ill-equipped and lacking their own vehicles, so that they were entirely dependent on our column for transport.

Throughout the whole withdrawal we used all our imagination to provide the enemy with new booby-traps to instil ever greater caution into the British. The achievements of our Pioneer leader, General Buelowius, one of the army's finest engineers, was outstanding.

Had Rommel been leading the British pursuit, there is no doubt that he would have sent mobile units through the 'bulge' of Cyrenaica to cut off the retreating column that was moving round

Below: The Yanks are coming. Smiling American GIs wade ashore during the unopposed Torch landings in French North Africa, 8th November 1942.

LEFT: Well equipped, well motivated and well led, the freshly arrived GIs lacked only the battle experience they were shortly to receive from Rommel's troops to prove the decisive factor in the final outcome in North Africa.

the coast. So he was particularly anxious about this possibility.

12th November 1942
After the British had overtaken the Gazala Line we were left in a particularly difficult situation, since they now had ample opportunity to outflank us, with a view to securing the whole of Cyrenaica. It was of paramount importance, therefore, to keep close watch on the tracks around Mechili, so that our motorised units could be promptly dispatched to meet the British assault forces. Also, the evacuation of Cyrenaica had to proceed with the greatest swiftness to avoid being surrounded. Time and again in various North African engagements the Gazala Line had proved to be the critical point in any retreat westwards. Though in 1941 and 1942 [after the Crusader battles] we had, through skilful manoeuvres, been fortunate enough to escape without serious loss, Bergonzoli's less mobile troops [in 1940-41] had been trapped there.

Fortunately for Rommel, the British made no attempt to cut through Cyrenaica via Mechili, and he was able to bring his army to relative safety, although he was pessimistic about the whole situation.

13. Nov. 42
Dearest Lu!
The battle in North Africa (west) is coming to its end. But that does not improve our position. Soon the end will come here too, because, inevitably, superior strength is crushing us. The army is not to blame. It has made an excellent showing.

17. Nov. 42
Dearest Lu!
It's raining and blowing up a storm. Situation nearly hopeless due to lack of supplies. Despite it all we must not give up the struggle. Maybe we will make it through. How I am feeling defies description.

November 1942
When we arrived in Agedabia, we had virtually no fuel left. Five hundred tons lay at Tripoli, 10 tons in Buerat, but even the latter was 400km (240 miles) from Agedabia. The main cause of this crisis lay in the fact that the front line was beyond reach of our transport aircraft which now

had to come from Italy. That day an Italian tanker carrying 4000 tons of fuel was sunk off Misurata, though a smaller tanker with 1200 tons was successful in reaching Tripoli. Every vehicle that could be made to work was sent off to Tripoli at once. It was an uncomfortable position to sit for any length of time immobilised in the desert. Marshal Bastico promised to help all he could, and to bring the 500 tons, already unloaded in Tripoli, up to El Agheila as quickly as possible.

RIGHT: Urgent Axis supplies are flown in to Tunisia, to reinforce the beleaguered forces now facing a combination of battle-hardened Commonwealth troops plus their well-supplied US allies.

Meanwhile work on the Mersa el Brega positions under the command of Marshal Bastico was progressing at all speed, so far as our resources allowed. The Mersa el Brega Line was very well sited. A few kilometres south from the coast it joined a salt-marsh some 15km (nine miles) across. Then followed a long stretch of very rough terrain. Thus an approaching enemy from the east would have to divert a long way to the south in order to complete a flanking operation and strike the defence from behind. The further one has to withdraw south in North Africa, the greater is the operational risk.

Nevertheless, even the Mersa Line could only be defended using motorised elements, of sufficient strength to face the enemy's outflanking force. In an action between opposing forces of equal number in such a situation, the tactical position of the attacker would be that much harder since his extended supply route to the south would be open to harassment by the defender's mobile elements. The key actions would be to block the defile at Mersa el Brega, secure the Sebcha crossing, and have a mobile force on standby behind the front with ample supplies of fuel and ammunition. Without the latter, or without fuel, the Mersa el Brega position could not be held.

Rommel had already decided, by mid-November 1942, that in the face of British material superiority, there was little point in trying to save Tripoli. He preferred to move back to Tunisia, to more defensible terrain, and so pulled his forces back against the wishes of his Italian superiors.

November 1942

Recalling 1941-42, we discussed the possibility this time of surprising the British at Agedabia and knocking out the limited force they had there. This was something that could naturally only remain a theoretical discussion, since not only had we no petrol, we didn't even have the anti-tank units necessary for such a plan. The central point for supply was no longer Tripoli as at the end of 1941, but had to be Tunisia, making it yet more impossible to assemble the stores and equipment needed for such an operation.

If I were attacking from the east and intended taking Agedabia, I would never face a counter-attack there, but would withdraw and await reinforcements before joining battle, as Wavell did in the spring of 1941.

For these reasons given above, in January 1942 we had succeeded in breaking up the British leading elements with superior forces before their main columns could come to their aid. The Ritchie Offensive thus came to grief. However, all these musings had to remain theoretical, and could not be put into practice [in 1942] because the necessary pre-conditions, that had existed in 1941-42, were now lacking. The bitterest pill, though, was that the British deployment made such an operation ideal.

The mass withdrawal followed our defeat. German and Italian troops had behaved impeccably, once the initial disorganisation had been overcome. Our losses during the retreat, with the exception of the El Alamein campaign, had not been great. Of the 90,000 German soldiers, including air force and navy, that we had before El Alamein, 70,000 had survived, not including thousands sick and wounded that had been flown back to Europe.

In spite of the wishes of Mussolini and the Italian High Command, Rommel got his way in abandoning all of Libya, including Tripoli.

22. Jan. 43
Dearest Lu!
Yesterday I didn't get the chance to write. From morning till night there was too much going on. Severe reprimands from Rome because we aren't managing to withstand enemy pressure. We are going to do what we can...Will it be possible to continue the fight in the face of the present difficulties with supplies? We want to fight and shall fight as long as possible. You can imagine that I have my fair share of problems with that ally. That they are now getting angry [at Rommel's proposed abandonment of Tripoli] was predictable, I guess.

24. Jan. 43
Dearest Lu!
From the OKW report you will have gathered that we had to withdraw from T[ripoli]. You can fathom how difficult that was for all of us. Now we only hope that we manage to reunite with the army in the west.

25. Jan. 43
Dearest Lu!
Yesterday [the withdrawal to Tunisia] went according to plan. I can't tell you how hard it is for me to experience this retreat and all that goes with it. Day and night I am tortured by the thought that all could be lost here in Africa now. I am so depressed that I can hardly do my work. Maybe someone else can see this situation

ROMMEL AND HIS ADVERSARIES

Rommel had been an admirer of Wavell, whose essays he had carried with him to North Africa, and he also recognised the skills of Auchinleck, whose determination during Operation Crusader and tactical skills during First Alamein had threatened to wreck the Afrika Korps.

His attitude to Montgomery demonstrated no such respect. He believed the new man in the desert to be unable to comprehend the rules of fluid warfare; after Alam Halfa in September 1942, he told his staff 'If I were Montgomery we wouldn't still be here!' He also ridiculed Montgomery's pedestrian approach to assaulting the Mersa el Brega and Buerat positions late in 1942, positions which he (Rommel) was planning to evacuate at the first British bombardment.

But although he ridiculed Montgomery, Rommel feared him and allowed his adversary to capture Tripoli without a fight in spite of overstretched logistics. For he recognised in Montgomery a man who knew how to utilise Allied material advantages to the full.

in a more favourable light and make something of it even now. K[esselring], for example, is full of optimism and maybe sees in me the reason why the army didn't persevere for longer. But he just cannot imagine the relative strength of my hard-pressed troops, particularly the poorly equipped Italians, and how we are especially at a disadvantage considering the enemy's excellent motorisation, his tanks and armoured cars and his favourable supply situation.

ABOVE: Self-appointed aesthete and art-lover, Reichsmarschall Hermann Goering was uninterested in Rommel's pleas for more supplies in North Africa during their visit to Mussolini in November 1942, and later telegraphed Hitler to observe that Rommel had lost his nerve.

Rommel may have exaggerated the 'favourable supply situation' of the Eighth Army, which was actually giving Montgomery cause for concern, but he realised that fighting in the open desert was not now possible for his battered Afrika Korps. He set up a new defensive line in Tunisia – the Mareth Line – and then turned his attention to the Anglo-American forces advancing from the west following the Torch landings. General von Arnim was in command of Axis forces, 5th Panzer Army, in northern Tunisia, reporting directly to Field Marshal Kesselring, and there was some friction between himself and Rommel. Nevertheless, the two combined in a counter-offensive in February. The first move was the capture of an important pass in the mountains.

14th February 1943

On 14th February, the 21st Panzer Division advanced from its bridgehead at the Faid Pass to surround the 2nd US Armored Division positioned in the desert near Sidi Bouzid. Having held the enemy to the front, one armoured section advanced to the north and penetrated deep into the American southern flank, while another pushed on to the south of Sidi Bouzid and attacked the enemy's rear.

The enemy found himself in a tactically untenable position. There followed a violent tank battle in which my battle-hardened tank crews steadily wore down the inexperienced Americans. Soon large numbers of Grants, Lees and Shermans lay blazing on the battlefield. Most of the American forces were destroyed, while the remainder fled west.

Accordingly, I urged [von Arnim's] 5th Army, which had been in charge of the operation, to continue the offensive during the night, keep the enemy moving and take Sbeitla. The tactical advantage must be seized. The fleeing enemy who cannot be destroyed today, may return to the battlefield with his power restored tomorrow.

The Americans lacked practical battle experience, and it was up to us to give them a severe inferiority complex from the beginning.

After the 21st Panzer Division's success at Sbeitla, the Americans in the south had withdrawn their garrison at Gafsa during the night of 14th/15th February, before my battle group could mount their attack. Sections of the Afrika Korps and the Centauro Division were able to occupy Gafsa the following afternoon without a fight.

Rommel recognised that possession of the pass at Gafsa gave him a great opportunity to slice into the inexperienced US troops. He wished to move to Tebessa, but his plan for driving deep into rear areas was amended by his superiors to something less penetrative, to an attack via the Kasserine Pass through Thala to Le Kef. The advance lay through difficult country, and the first attacks on US positions, on 19th February, were unsuccessful.

20th February 1943

At both points what I most feared had now happened. The enemy had the opportunity to deploy his reserve troops in the unassailable hill positions. He had thereby won himself time to bring up further reinforcements. Had we attacked Tebessa, we would probably have been well advanced before coming up against serious opposition, whereas now we had come face to face with an enemy who was not disorganised after a hurried march to the front, and who had been able to make himself ready at his ease.

By my reckoning, the Allies' weakest point was at Kasserine, so I decided to concentrate the attack there and ordered the 10th Panzer Division to move up.

At about 07.00hrs on 20th February, I drove up to the Afrika Korps Field HQ at Kasserine. I met with General von Broich (10th Division commander), who unfortunately only had half his complement with him, since von Arnim had retained a section of it in the north. The motorcycle battalion was already en route, and I passed it on the way.

Finally, by about 17.00hrs, the pass was in our hands. The American soldiers had fought exceptionally well. Menton's [the commander of the panzergrenadier regiment] losses were heavy. In the course of the evening we discovered an enemy armoured unit on the other side of the pass, which was partly deployed in a side valley and apparently due to aid the defenders. I immediately dispatched an armoured column through the pass.

This assault over the quickly repaired Hatab-Bach bridge caught the enemy totally unawares, and they were pushed back to the mountain and swiftly annihilated by the experienced tank crews of the 8th Panzer Regiment. This fight was at extremely close quarters. The enemy quickly abandoned their tanks and vehicles and fled on foot back over the mountain. We captured about 20 tanks and 30 APCs, for the most part having 75mm anti-tank guns attached. The Americans were remarkably well-equipped. Also, we had much to learn from them organisationally. Particularly impressive was the standardisation of parts for their armoured equipment. Experience gained by the British had subsequently been put to good use by the Americans.

Apparently, the enemy intended to fight a rearguard action from new positions, and to remain on the defensive. I decided, on this basis, to attack the rear immediately. At about 12.00hrs [on 21st February], the 10th Panzer Division advanced towards Kalaet Jerda, where they were to cut off the road and rail junction, and make it impassable. The Afrika Korps battle group was to push the enemy back at El Hamra, and take the top of the pass on the road to Tebessa. The 21st Panzer Division was to hold its positions. By placing our troops at various trouble spots I hoped to break up the enemy's troops more than our own. The 5th Panzer Army [von Arnim's command] was to hold down the enemy meanwhile by frontal attacks and prevent him sending reinforcements to the southern sector.

By about 13.00hrs, the 10th Panzer Division was in full swing towards Thala.

BELOW: The Battle of Kasserine Pass. Rommel mauls the Americans in a superbly planned and executed action.

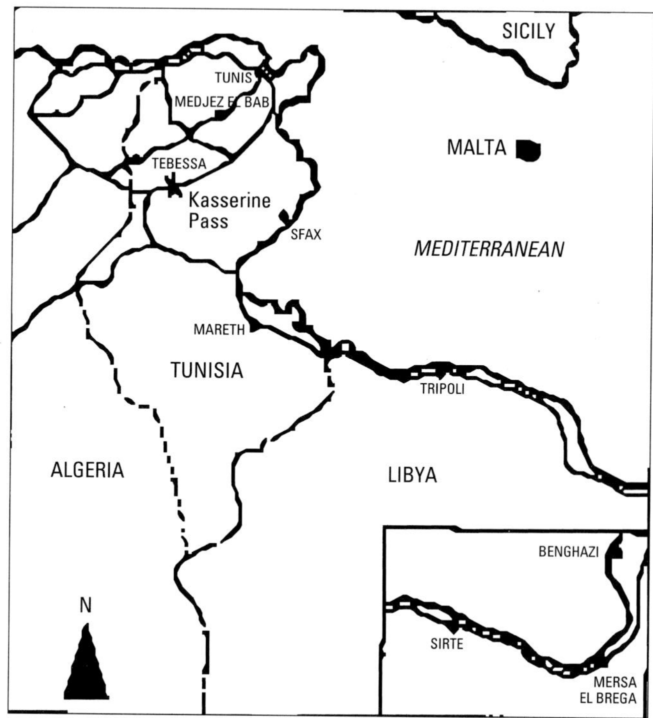

On the way it overtook a British tank company, the advance element of an approaching force. At midday I went with Bayerlein and Horster to 10th Panzer. On the way a reconnaissance vehicle in front skidded and crashed, causing the commander serious injury. The division was not making sufficient progress forwards. Constantly I had to keep on at them. They failed to understand that we were in a race against the Allied reserve forces. To get a better picture of what the enemy were up to, and to fully understand the situation, I went ahead to the leading reconnaissance section who were taking cover in a cactus plantation by an Arab village. As the British artillery were pounding the village, we positioned ourselves by a hillock 400m (1320ft) away and observed the results from there.

On the morning of 22nd February, I went up to Thala again where I was forced to the conclusion that the enemy had become too strong, and that our attack could no longer be sustained.

At around 13.00hrs I met Field Marshal Kesselring, who had come to my HQ with Westphal and Seidemann. We were in agreement that continuation of the attack towards Le Kef would not succeed, and came to the conclusion that the offensive should be reduced bit by bit.

Rommel's description of this meeting with Kesselring hardly accords with other descriptions. The decision to call off the Kasserine offensive was first opposed by Kesselring, who urged Rommel to be optimistic. But Rommel believed that US strength opposite him was growing, and he insisted that he wished to return to the Mareth Line to meet a possible British attack.

22nd February 1943

During the night, the 10th Panzer Division was withdrawn to Kasserine. The 21st Panzer Division was to remain at Sbiba, but to be ready for orders to mine the road and move back.

Kesselring asked me if I wished to take command of Army Group. Apparently, I was no longer persona non grata after the offensive, despite my assumed defeatism. After my recent experiences, however, and knowing that the Fuehrer had already chosen Colonel-General von Arnim as Army Group commander-in-chief, I declined. Also, I didn't want to lead a formation subordinate to Commando Supremo and the Luftwaffe, and lay myself open to tactical interference from both.

Despite his undoubtable qualities, Field Marshal Kesselring had no understanding of the tactical or operational requirements of the North African theatre. He saw everything through rose-tinted spectacles, and following our victory over the Americans he was strengthened in his illusion that, so he believed, more opportunities of the kind would arise, and that American fighting skills were weak. Although they did not have the battle-hardened experience of the British Eighth Army, the Americans were better equipped and had more flexible tactical command. So great were the American supplies of anti-tank weapons and armoured vehicles that we could anticipate the running battles ahead with but faint hope. The tactical foresight of the enemy's intelligence operation had

ROMMEL FLIES TO HITLER'S HQ

On 28th November 1942, Rommel flew to Hitler's HQ at Rastenburg in East Prussia. He wished to explain in person his strategy: abandoning Tripoli and setting up a defensive line in Tunisia. For the first time, Rommel encountered one of Hitler's rages. He was accused of having abandoned his army. But Hitler then calmed down and promised that Rommel should have all the materiel he required. The Fuehrer suggested that Goering accompany Rommel to Rome, to arrange material support with Mussolini.

During the trip to Rome, Rommel managed several long conversations with his wife, and it seems likely that he expressed his belief that the war was lost. He had been shocked by Hitler's outburst, and his state of mind was not improved by travelling with Goering, whose main topic of conversation was his collection of looted art treasures.

Rommel managed to get the Duce to agree that rather than allow his Italian infantry to be cut off, he could move back from Mersa el Brega to the Buerat Line. But that was the main concession to a reality that Rommel was finding it very difficult to get across to his political masters.

shown itself to be outstanding. After the initial shock, the enemy had quickly recovered and were soon blocking our advance by deploying their reserves along the passes and at other strategic points. However, not all their troops had been able to move up so fast, and I firmly believed that if we had continued the assault on Tebessa, we should have pushed further north without serious enemy opposition.

On the evening of 23rd February, an order arrived from the Commando Supremo stating that I was to become commander of Army Group Afrika, to meet the urgent need for a single command structure in Tunisia. I didn't know whether to laugh or cry. On the one hand I was happy, in that I would have a greater influence over the fate of my own men, General Messe having shortly before taken over command of the Mareth front, but on the other hand, it wasn't good to have to continue playing whipping-boy to the Fuehrer's HQ, Commando Supremo, and the Luftwaffe.

It came as something of a surprise to Rommel in his new command that von Arnim had been planning an offensive in northern Tunisia, towards Beja. This offensive had been planned without any reference to Rommel's attack towards Thala via the Kasserine Pass.

25th February 1943

Typical of the small-mindedness of Commando Supremo was the fact that they lacked sufficient grasp of reality to form a rational view of the military situation. They did not allow in their plans for the real eventualities of a situation, but let the wish be father to the thought. Although those in Rome considered themselves fit to make tactical decisions regarding Tunisia, they had proved incapable of coordinating their attack on Beja with the operation against Thala.

Von Arnim's offensive failed to put pressure on the Allied forces, and was abandoned after five days. The last large-scale action in Africa in which Rommel was engaged directly was the battle of Medenine, Operation Capri, on 6th March 1943. This was an attempt to force Montgomery back from his position opposite the Mareth Line, and was a total failure: the offensive was called off on the first day. On 9th March, Rommel handed over his Army Group command to von Arnim and left Africa on sick leave. He did not return.

ABOVE: Italian minelayers at work in the Tunisian desert, winter 1942. Rommel felt the Italians had little faith in the Axis.

Chapter X
Italian Interlude

At a loose end following his recall from North Africa, and still recuperating from the cumulative effects of two years' harsh desert life, Rommel was a commander without a command. Reluctant to send him to the Eastern Front, Hitler toyed with the idea of giving Rommel overall command in Italy in the event of that country's collapse.

BELOW: Rommel met Mussolini immediately after his last flight from North Africa in March 1943. The field marshal spoke of supplies and the Duce of willpower, but both probably knew that the forces remaining in Africa could not prevail against an overwhelming enemy.

The next eight months were to be among the most frustrating of Rommel's career. For nine weeks he remained inactive, recovering his health and preparing his account of the North African campaign, and it was not until mid-May that he began to resume any military responsibilities. By then, the war in Africa was over – the last Axis troops surrendered to the Allies on 13th May – and Hitler's attention was diverted to the Eastern Front, where he was preparing the doomed counter-attack at Kursk, scheduled for early July. Nevertheless, the threat to Italy once Tunisia had fallen was apparent, and Hitler turned to Rommel for advice. For two months he became a familiar figure at many of the Fuehrer's planning conferences, where he helped to compile plans for German action in the event of an Allied invasion of Italy. As early as 17th May Hitler ordered him to prepare, in secret, a new army group headquarters that would, in the event of a crisis, spearhead an armed occupation of Italy under the codename Alarich. Rommel responded by gathering around him many of the surviving members of his Afrika Korps staff, while consulting as widely as possible with experts who could tell him how best to secure the vital Alpine passes that linked Italy to the Reich. On 15th July, five days after the Allied invasion of Sicily, Hitler confirmed Rommel's appointment as commander of Army Group B, with the job of coordinating resistance to the Allies (and, if necessary, to the Italians) in central Italy.

Rommel interpreted this as meaning that he would become supreme commander in Italy, but he was to be disappointed. Probably as a result of jealousy among members of Hitler's entourage, Rommel suddenly found himself transferred, with his headquarters, to northern Greece, under orders to defend the area against a possible Allied invasion. He arrived in Salonika on 25th July, although within 24 hours he had been recalled to discuss the deteriorating situation in Italy, where an anti-fascist coup had led to the arrest of Mussolini and opened up the distinct possibility of an Italian surrender.

Rommel's headquarters was transferred to Munich and his troops prepared for intervention. Alarich was confirmed on 29th July and put into effect 24 hours later, spearheaded by 26th Panzer Division, under strict orders not to provoke the Italian authorities. It was a successful operation; by the time the Italians reacted, the panzers had taken the Brenner Pass, allowing the 44th Infantry and 1st SS Panzer Divisions to advance across the border. The Italian High Command responded by ordering forces up from the south, away from the battles in Sicily, and this strategic inconsistency led to heated exchanges between General Alfred Jodl, Hitler's chief planning officer, and Italian commanders at Bologna on 15th August. Rommel attended the meeting, but said little. His contempt for the Italians was well known, and the blustering he now observed did nothing to alter his conviction that the Italian High Command was about to give in to the Allies. When he set up his headquarters at Lake Garda in northern Italy two days later, he already had secret orders, codenamed Axis, that would authorise him to disarm Italian troops and seize coastal defences in his area of operations.

Axis was triggered on 8th September, five days after the British Eighth Army had landed at Reggio di Calabria on the extreme southern tip of Italy, and only hours after news of an Italian surrender had broken. Rome was occupied by German troops and Rommel's men

ROMMEL THE DEFEATIST?

There can be no doubt that many of the senior Italian and German officers that Rommel had to deal with late in 1942 and early 1943 felt that he had become a defeatist, who was overly pessimistic. After his return to Germany in November to talk to Hitler about the general situation it seems likely that he decided that the war was lost.

Rommel realised that he appeared a defeatist to those such as Kesselring, who always tried to look at the best side of events, but found he could not deny what he took to be reality. There were two occasions when this pessimism may well have clouded Rommel's military judgment. The first was in January 1943, when he abandoned Tripoli to the British without attempting to fight – to the fury of the Italians and to the relief of Montgomery, who was acting at the end of his own supply lines.

The second occasion was during the Battle of Kasserine. Rommel's decision to stop the offensive was taken partly because he expected a British attack against the Mareth Line; and yet General Messe, in command there, had told him that there were no signs of any offensive preparations.

moved into Milan, Turin and Florence. The next morning, elements of the US Fifth Army landed at Salerno, south of Naples, and although Field Marshal Albert Kesselring, Commander-in-Chief South, managed to contain the beachhead, it was obvious that the situation had deteriorated badly. To make matters worse, Rommel went down with acute appendicitis and was out of action for a week.

By 30th September he was sufficiently recovered to attend a special conference on Italy at Hitler's headquarters in East Prussia, but by then he had lost the initiative in planning terms to Kesselring. Rommel's proposal for an ordered retreat up the Italian peninsula to a defensive line north of Rome was rejected on 6th October in favour of Kesselring's preference for delaying operations south of the city. In the event, Kesselring's strategy was to delay the Allies around Monte Cassino, but to Rommel the incident confirmed that his chances of assuming supreme command in Italy were doomed. The bickering that went on between Kesselring and Rommel did little for the reputation of either commander.

There is some evidence to suggest that Hitler remained convinced that Rommel was the right man to direct the Italian campaign. On 17th October he offered Rommel the job of defending the line currently held by Kesselring, from Gaeta to Ortona, but Rommel made little attempt to disguise his reservations. Two days later, Kesselring was effectively confirmed as supreme commander in Italy, leaving Rommel out on a limb, with a reputation in some circles for uncharacteristic pessimism. In retrospect, the incident suggests that Rommel was beginning to have serious doubts about the conduct of the

BELOW: LCTs unload supplies from offshore Liberty ships after the invasion of Italy brought Allied troops back onto Continental Europe, September 1943.

war, although his high public reputation meant that he could not be allowed to languish unoccupied. On 30th October Jodl solved the problem by suggesting to Hitler that the hero of North Africa, with his experience of fighting both the British and Americans, should be transferred, with his staff, to the West, where an invasion was expected sometime in the near future. On 5th November 1943, Hitler confirmed the transfer, directing Rommel, as commander of Army Group B under the strategic control of Field Marshal Gerd von Rundstedt as Commander-in-Chief West, to carry out a detailed inspection of anti-invasion defences from Denmark through the Low Countries and into France. It was a tough assignment, since fears existed in some quarters that the existing defences were inadequate, and that time was fast running out. Although the Fuehrer had ordered the construction of the Atlantic Wall as early as December 1941, the truth was that there was a lot of work still to do.

LEFT: The Allies reach Rome – Rommel would have abandoned the "Eternal City" in autumn 1943 – believing a defensive line in northern Italy was the correct strategic approach.

Chapter XI
Defence of the West

Rommel's return to Normandy in November 1943 was in marked contrast to his departure over three years earlier. The hero of the Blitzkrieg in France and the Low Countries in 1940 had seen defeat in North Africa, and now sought to fend off the mighty armada gathering across the Channel.

ABOVE: Desert goggles and tartan scarf left behind, a dapper Rommel begins his tour of the Atlantic Wall defences following his appointment to inspect the north European coastline facing England.

After his frustrating period in Italy, Rommel saw a great opportunity when he was given the task of reporting on the defences of western Europe in November 1943 and then given direct command of the sector from Holland to the Loire in January 1944. The task was, he believed, important in that only by defeating an invasion attempt by the Western Powers could Germany hope to negotiate a peace settlement. If the British and American forces established a second front, their material superiority would be too great for the Wehrmacht and SS to resist.

Rommel got to know his new command well. Late in December he toured the area held by the Fifteenth Army – that is, from the Belgian frontier to the mouth of the river Somme. He believed that this was the most likely area for an invasion. Early in January he toured the Dutch and Belgian coasts, and in mid-January he investigated northern Normandy, near the mouth of the Seine. Then he moved farther south to southern Normandy and Brittany, where the crisis of the war in the West was to take place. These regions were under the control of General Dollmann's Seventh Army.

Rommel's strong belief, in which he was backed by Hitler, that the Allies must be thrown back from the beaches as soon as they landed, led him to an intense wave of activity, in which his experiences in North Africa were invaluable.

In the two-year campaign in North Africa, I had a chance to examine the significance of minelaying in the various forms of warfare, and came to know about the enemy's use of mines in very great quantities. Unfortunately, our supplies were comparatively small. After the fortunate outcome of the 1941/2 winter campaign in Marmarica and Cyrenaica, the British made optimum use of mines in the defence of their new line from south of Ain el Gazala to 80km (50 miles) into the desert. Over two months they laid well over one million mines, creating interlinked minefields that were over 1km (0.6

miles) in depth. The motorised infantry divisions and a section of our tank forces had been caught in the middle of these large minefields. Only a few vehicles were able to penetrate these defences...In the fighting around Bir Hacheim, up to the Ain el Gazala position, in the approach to Tobruk and at Tobruk itself, we time and again came up against an enemy who had reinforced his position with numerous anti-tank guns, and sometimes even tanks, in the depths of their mined area. These battles were especially hard, although thanks to the outstanding courage of the German soldier they were eventually brought to a successful conclusion. In all these battles I learnt the value of the enemy's minelaying skills. Had German soldiers been manning the British positions, it is probable they would not have been taken.

Rommel made it clear to his staff in early 1944 that he intended to undertake a linked set of measures to protect the coast, as one of them described to US interrogators after the war:

1. Declaring the beach (high-water line) as 'main fighting line' [HKL – Haupt-Kampf-Linie].

2. Putting all the infantry and artillery (including staffs up to divisions, auxiliary services and reserves) into strongpoints in a belt along the beach. This belt was to be 5-6km (3-3.6 miles) deep.

3. Filling the spaces between the strongpoints with land mines and other obstacles.

4. Putting the armoured divisions immediately behind this belt so that part of their artillery could reach the beach with indirect fire.

5. Making the infantry belt and the area of the armoured divisions unsuitable for the landing of paratroops and gliders.

6. Protecting the coast artillery against bomb attack using armour or concrete, increasing the security of the other batteries by repeated change of positions and by the construction of dummy positions.

7. Making the landing itself as difficult as possible by placing obstacles in the water from just below the high-water line to below the low-water line.

BELOW: Surrounded by camouflage netting, a hefty piece of coastal artillery awaits the invading Allies. Concrete – or the lack of it – had now replaced Italian supply convoys as Rommel's bête noire in France.

8. Making the approach difficult by laying some mines in shallow water and others on the probable routes of approach and the probable bombardment positions.

9. Attacking the points of embarkation and points of concentration with aircraft and rockets before the beginning of the invasion.

10. Increasing the fighting strength of Army, Navy and Air Force.

11. Coordinating the three services.

12. Making use of propaganda.

Rommel threw himself into all the details of beach defence, inventing some obstacles himself and using every method to get hold of mines. As in North Africa, he poured scorn on all other uses for the raw materials – now concrete rather than tank fuel – that he required and pushed his subordinate commanders to their limits. He had strong views on everything, from the demolition of houses near likely landing beaches to the best way of dealing with parachutists, as he described in his report of 22nd April.

My inspection tour of the coastal sectors during the past weeks gives me reasons for the following comments and instructions. Almost without exception unusual progress has been made in all defence group sectors in accordance with the seriousness of the situation. I expressed my satisfaction to the commanders and troops of all available forces, and their clever employment of a great part of the civilian population. However, here and there I have noticed units that do not seem to have recognised the urgency of the situation, and who do not even follow instructions. There are also reports of cases in which my orders have not been followed, for instance that all minefields on the beach should be live at all times. In that instance a commander of a lower unit gave an order to the contrary. In other cases my orders have been postponed to later dates or even changed so that minefields were to be live only at night. Reports from other sectors say that they intended to try to put one of my orders into effect and they would start doing so the following day. Some units did know my orders but did not make any preparations to execute them, forcing me to take immediate action. I do not intend to issue unnecessary orders every day. I give orders only when and if necessary. I expect, however, that my orders will be executed at once and to the letter, and that no unit under my command makes changes, or even gives orders to the contrary, or delays execution through unnecessary red tape. On the contrary I expect that all my orders will be followed immediately and precisely, and that the carrying out of orders will be supervised. I want to call your special attention to the latter point. It has been

BELOW: Rommel and Seventh Army commander in Normandy and Brittany, General Friedrich Dollmann. The many press and propaganda images of these senior officers and their impressive hardware concealed a genuine concern that the Atlantic Wall defences would not be up to scratch on the day.

found that orders were given correctly, but that the work had not been checked. At one place, for instance, a sector several hundred kilometres wide, equipped with beach obstacles, was ordered by me to be made secure through mines and stakes. In this sector where thousands of mines should have been used only a few were installed, and I blame this on faulty supervision. I have come to the following conclusions:

Beach Defences

Again I have to emphasise the purpose of these defences. The enemy most likely will try to land at night and in fog after a tremendous shelling by artillery and bombers. He will employ hundreds of boats and ships in unloading amphibious vehicles, waterproofed and submergible tanks. We must stop him in the water, not only delaying him but destroying all enemy equipment while still afloat. Some units do not seem to have realised the value of this type of defence.

A number of new items will enable us to increase the depth of our defences and make them very effective. I refer to such items as the Nutcracker Mine I-III, the concrete shell for the T-Mine which will reduce the shock of explosions, and the concrete obstacles (Tetrahedra).

A lot has to be done until the defences are complete. Right now, most battalion sectors have sown only a few mines, do not have any depth, poles are much too weak, and they cannot stop even small boats. Commanders down to company level must supervise installations and see to it that all defences are dense and effective.

Factories for Concrete

In each sector factories making concrete structures must liaise with Organisation TODT, in order to produce special mixtures of concrete. The units must work in close cooperation with the Organisation TODT, which has already received the necessary instructions.

Nutcracker Mines

According to all experiments this mine will be very effective against landing craft and amphibious vehicles and also against submergible tanks. They can be made very easily on the beaches. They contain T-Mines and Grenade Mines and should be either tarred, or, even better, they should be covered with concrete. The mine itself should rest in the concrete block and be covered with planks, iron sheets or concrete. This should eliminate the transmission of the shock of the explosion. For that reason mines will be placed in several rows, with a distance of at least 25m (165ft) between rows. In addition, the rows should be staggered to achieve depth. In places where the tide does not recede very far it will be possible to place these mines in the water at low tide. The rail of the support should be long, especially in low-tide waters, to make the mine effective at the various water levels.

Container for T-Mines and Projectiles

The purpose is to protect the mines against penetration by salt water, to centralise the pressure developed by the dashing of waves, which can cause the charge to detonate, and to keep the

ROMMEL AND TANK DEPLOYMENT

After Rommel's initial brief to report on coastal defences along the west coast of Europe, his Army Group B staff took over responsibility for an area that included Holland, Belgium and northern France. The most important area that he had to defend was split between the Fifteenth Army, under General von Salmuth, north of the Seine in eastern Normandy and the Pas-de-Calais, and General Dollmann's Seventh Army, in Normandy and Brittany.

The biggest area of dispute within the German High Command in the months leading up to D-Day lay in how the panzer and panzergrenadier divisions in France should be allocated. Rommel had been shaken by Allied air power in North Africa, and he recognised that movement would be severely restricted when the expected invasion took place. He favoured placing panzer divisions near the most threatened areas of coast so that they could move rapidly into action against the first wave of landings. So far as Rommel was concerned, the invasion had to be defeated on the beaches. If a beachhead was established, the war in the West was lost.

transmission of detonation below water as before. Little by little the density of mines should be brought up to one mine per metre in the K-obstacles. That seems to be very dense, but it has to be remembered that on account of the tides, only around 15-20 per cent of mines will be effective during the first hour of an enemy landing.

Concrete Foundation for Tschechenigel [Czech Obstacles – Concrete Block with Iron Tubes]
In several places units and Organisation TODT have improved the Tschechenigel, of which there are a great many, by installing them on concrete foundations. These foundations raise the Tschechenigel and make them much more effective. Choking up with sand, a major threat to beach defences, is prevented by employment of mats of brushwood. One division had these mats made and delivered by the local civil population. These mats have proved very effective as supports for Tschechenigel and Rollbocke [beach obstacles]. At present it is not possible to build a concrete foundation for every Tschechenigel. However, as more concrete is provided for this purpose it should be possible to provide a foundation for all our Tschechenigel. This valuable material must not be choked up with sand.

Beton Tetrader [Steel Tetrahedra]
The concrete obstacles that have been delivered by the Organisation TODT do not fulfil our requirements at most of the places where they are employed. They are too light, and certainly cannot withstand the shock caused by the push of even a medium-sized boat, let alone that of a landing boat weighing several hundred tons. When subjected to such loads they will collapse. The Tetrader, on the other hand, which are manufactured in Brittany, and which can be seen on photographs and in drawings, suit our purpose adequately, particularly if the courses are well filled with concrete. Tetrader are particularly valuable at those locations

BELOW: Wherever he went on his inspections of the Atlantic Wall defences, Rommel was met by impressive military displays. But would the soldiers be able to throw the Allies back into the sea?

where it is impossible to drive in stakes (such as on cliffs).

Tetrader are particularly valuable for the construction of K-obstacles in shallow water at ebb-tide (they are also used in the Mediterranean). They can be placed on any spot in the water using pulleys, which are mounted on anchored boats or floats and which are operated by horses. As the photos show they represent very strong obstacles in the water. By attaching mines in concrete containers to the front part, they will not only stop a vessel but destroy it as well. The base piece of the mine container needs to be fixed into the top of the Tetrader. It will be possible at many places to fill the corners of these Tetraders from Organisation TODT. In this way they still can be converted into valuable obstacles for the beach area, as shown by the photos.

Hemmbalker [Ram Logs]

The Hemmbalker has proved on several occasions very effective as an obstacle, even against bigger boats. It must have a slope of approx 30-40 degrees so that the boat to runs on to it with its stern, and is held there. It has therefore to be constructed of many strong logs and has to be supported at the sides since it has to be able to withstand the load of the onrushing ship. It is recommended that a mine be placed on the upper end of the log which is not supported, in order to damage the boat without damaging the ram log. The installation of saw-like or chisel-like steel plates or obliquely cut iron bars, which only have to protrude a few centimetres out of the log, is required to cut open the bottom of the ship and prevent it from slipping off to the side. Workshops and forges as well as Organisation TODT can provide these metal pieces.

A mined log approximately 30cm (11in) in diameter with a seaward slope of 45 degrees proved very successful during tests. A landing boat of 500 tons suffered a hole in its bottom of almost two square

BELOW: Another day, another bunker, as Rommel's detailed inspection tour of the Atlantic Wall continued throughout the chilly spring of 1944.

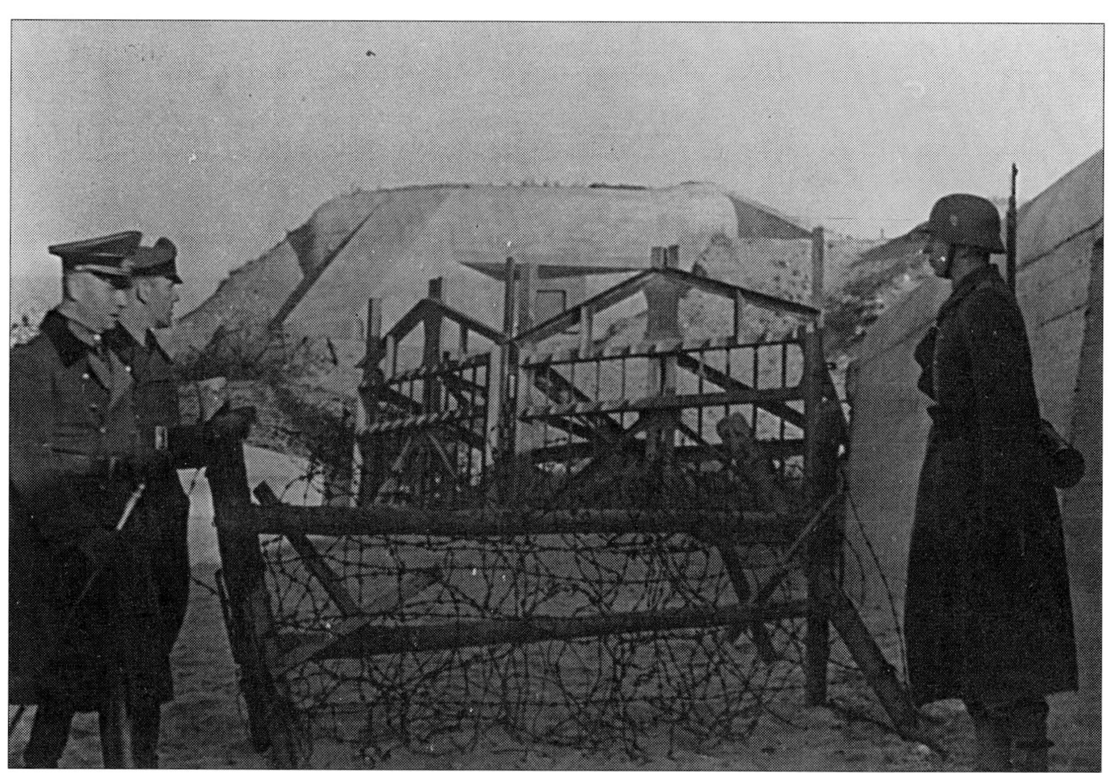

metres (6.6 square feet) in area through by the impact and completely sank within three minutes. Furthermore, the coiling of the boat was penetrated in several places. These mined logs should be carefully systematically placed at wide intervals, at least 20m (66ft), and in great depth. The new concrete container for the T-mine will give protection against transmission of detonations, so that the mined logs can be placed closer together. Some divisions have already started to install these mined logs in the water during ebb tide. It can be done without difficulty, particularly if the logs are notched to prevent them from floating loose.

BELOW: The deployment of German forces prior to D-Day.

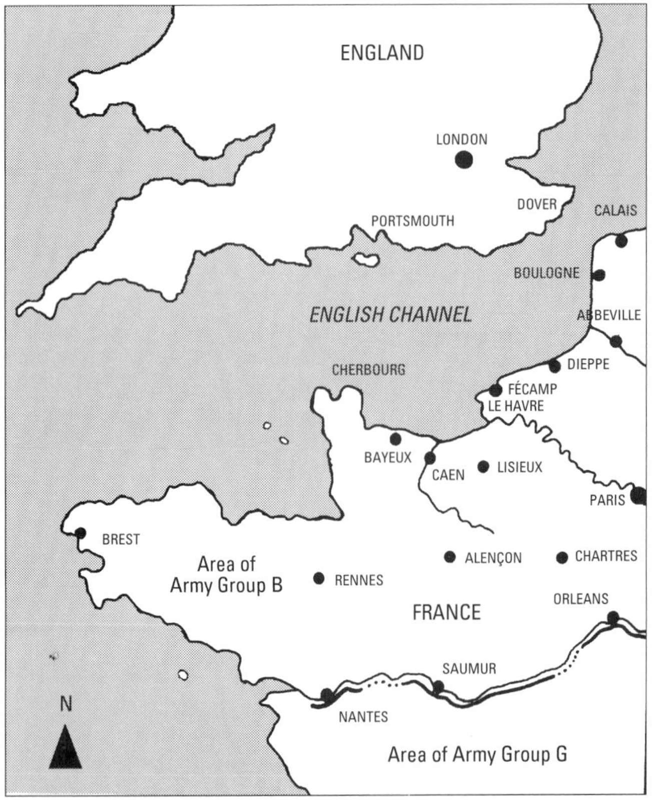

Belgische Rollbocke and Hemmkueen [Beach Defence Obstacles]

These obstacles have proved to be very valuable. They have to be partly emplaced or protected against choking up with sand by placing mats of brushwood. These are especially effective objects, even against bigger boats, and are like the Tschechenigel. Indeed, they are so valuable that no unit can afford to let them choke up with sand by not taking appropriate counter-measures. Some divisions even installed mines on Rollbocke, which I advise strongly. The stopping and destructive capabilities of these obstacles are particularly impressive. The different kinds of K-obstacles in the beach area should be changed as often as possible so as to create a field with a variety of obstacles. Many units, however, have been slack in this respect.

Defence Measures against Airborne Troops

By order of Army Group B, I have been ordered to take charge of defence measures against airborne troops. I express my appreciation to the 348 ID for the way they have already installed, and continue to install, strong obstacles against airborne troops in the sector between land and sea in such a quick and thorough manner. The division succeeded in employing civilians to a large extent for that job. To some extent local women offered themselves for work voluntarily, and concluded their labours singing. The point was that these jobs were immediately paid for in cash. These examples are worth following. The defence measures against airborne troops, such as the placing of logs and the wiring of fields, is of the greatest importance for those divisions concentrated in the coastal areas, as well as for those in reserve located behind that sector. The time seems to be near when the coast cannot be penetrated from the sea by amphibious units on account of the strength of the K-obstacles and the fortress-like defences. Only by using numerous airborne troops as reinforcements will a seaborne assault have any chance of succeeding. The enemy may employ the mass of his airborne troops on the first day, and it may be his plan to crush the units manning the coastal defences in the sector between sea and land by mass drops, with divisions attacking in the direction of the coast, and thus succeeding in breaking open our coastal defences. Currently the enemy is capable of landing three divisions from the air in any chosen area within three minutes, and of forming the units for battle shortly after landing. Airborne troops carry very many light guns and armour-piercing weapons, and during the attack will be supported very effectively by the strong enemy air assets. Cargo gliders can land without sound on every small field, also in hilly terrain with angles of declination up to 30 degrees. It is up to us to prepare the probable landing area in such a manner that the enemy planes and cargo gliders crash while landing, so as to cause heavy losses in men and material to the enemy, over and above those caused by conventional German weapons.

As airborne troops are committed mainly on moonlit nights or at twilight or dawn, it is necessary to be especially watchful at these times. The thorough fencing-in of the area between land and sea is to be accomplished as quickly as possible by all divisions. Fortress commanders are required to guard the interior of the fortress and the field of fire with special care. Furthermore, those divisions committed on both sides of the Somme between Amiens and the land front, and threatened from the air, will be secured in an area 15km (nine miles) wide on both sides of the Somme through fencing-in by the Fifteenth Army.

What is true of these larger areas is also true of the smaller sectors. There can be no strongpoint, no defensive point, no area which has not been secured against airborne troops in its immediate or further surroundings. At many places the mining of the coastal sector in a band of 300-10,000m (990-33,000ft) has not been completed, or even covered with dummy installations with fences and death heads. In many places ploughing and grazing of cattle on the meadows continues close to the defensive points on the coast. Sometimes this is the case at places where there are no mines, for where one ploughs and cattle graze there are no mines. Here there exists the possibility of that cargo gliders and planes may land without danger, and the coast could be penetrated very quickly. I know very well that the supply of mines is being interrupted at many points, partly on account of transport difficulties, and partly on account of smaller supplies from home.

Below left: Field Marshals Rommel and Rundstedt (right) and General Blaskowitz (left) confer during a meeting in Paris before the invasion. Although Blaskowitz was based in Bordeaux, far from the English Channel, Rommel prudently considered all of the coastline to be potentially at risk.

However, the production of mines has proceeded well. Nevertheless, a skilfully laid dummy minefield will in this case accomplish its purpose.

Areas of large minefields will be taken up only by permission of the armies. During combat the commander of the coastal defence sector will decide on how battle installations and their surrounding territory will be secured. At many places prior preparation is not sufficient. Towards the sea the fortress-like installation must be secured strongly by beach obstacles in great depth so that, in the event of an invasion, no flame-throwing tank or boat can put the installations close to the beach out of action.

A broad minefield must be laid all round the installations, and at many points it will be necessary to mine the interior, or at least lay a dummy minefield so that it will be difficult for a landing enemy to attack the installations quickly. Both the English and Americans dislike entering areas recognised as being mined.

Usually the enemy will first get specialists, who have to clear these areas of mines. They will not know if they are dummy minefields. At many points, especially at artillery positions and supply depots, troops lack the understanding of the value of dummy minefields. Engineers are not needed for the construction of them except for planning. Officers must be able to construct dummy minefields.

Mobile commitment of mortars against armoured vehicles has been considered at some places. I consider this as appropriate, especially with regard to the defence of those areas that are only thinly occupied.

Camouflage of Defence Positions

At many places I have seen large, very well constructed battle installations in the middle of green fields. Yet the installations were camouflaged with the old-type black camouflage nets. The contrast will allow the enemy bomber formations will be able to recognise them from great heights, and with today's bomb-sights to bomb with great accuracy. These old camouflage nets must be newly sprayed to fit in with the surroundings, or they have to be used for the construction of dummy installations for which purpose they are excellent.

Use of Smoke Screens

Again and again lately the enemy have bombed important installations and caused the disablement of valuable guns. Fighter planes with rocket guns and flame throwers may attack our emplaced guns. Here and there skilled camouflage may prevent recognition of these usually large emplacements. At other places emplacements can be successfully secured by using steel nets and similar objects. In order to

BELOW: Rommel and the legendary, if unsavoury, SS panzer commander 'Sepp' Dietrich. The SS was to perform doggedly during the Normandy battles.

prevent the enemy from seeing clearly and to make impossible accurate recognition of a valuable target, the use of artificial smoke during enemy attacks is highly recommended. Smoke is very scarce. But even with make-shift smoke (use quickly lit straw or leaves) a certain degree of camouflage of threatened gun positions or emplacements may be achieved: equally the attention of the enemy can be drawn to empty places.

Attacks on dummy artillery and flak installations on the outskirts of villages, on conspicuous houses on the beach, on dummy entrenchments and emplacements among the dunes and on high ground, will attract a great part of the enemy artillery during the battle of the beaches, and thereby relieve our real positions. Infantry and artillery must prepare these installations so that they can be used if necessary. However, there are no reports from any place that these preparations have been made. I therefore ask everyone to give more attention to this point.

Tearing Down and Mining Beach Houses

There has been too much tearing down of houses. Most likely the enemy will shoot at all houses, villages and cities visible from the sea. Only if a field of fire has to be created should houses be taken down. Otherwise they should remain targets for the enemy. The mining of houses has been proved unsatisfactory. Our own troops, despite our orders, will always go into these houses and casualties have occurred quite frequently. Mines can be put to better use on the beach and in minefields.

Dummy machine-gun nests can be made very easily by digging up parts of the green meadow. They are very useful facing the sea. Every bomb dropped and every shell fired by the enemy on these installations will not do us any harm.

Employment of Troops for the Reinforcement of the Defence Areas

In the short time left before the enemy operations are likely to start, it is necessary that all commanders employ every single man at the utmost for the reinforcement of all defence areas, and to use any members of the civilian population who can be used. Most units have acted accordingly, but I still noticed some who did not comply. One company, for instance, is still training its troops two hours in the morning and two in the afternoon, in contrast to the divisional order which allows only one day in the week for this purpose. In this company's beach sector obstacles are very thinly spaced, and there are no obstacles at all against airborne troops in the rear areas. This is against all orders and must be changed. For another company 180 men strong, only 13 are working on beach defences while the remaining 167 are occupied with their bivouac area in which they have been living for over a year. Nothing has been done to protect their front lines in the way of fortifications. This also is not the right attitude to be taken by any company.

Cooperation of Infantry and Artillery

I witnessed a demonstration with live ammunition in which airborne troops cooperated closely with infantry and naval units to direct artillery fire accurately, and

FIGHT THEM ON THE BEACHES

Rommel began his inspection of western coastal defences on 30th November 1943, in Denmark, and from this date until the landings on 6th June 1944 he did not waver in his determination to stop the Allies on the beaches. He firmly believed that the invaders had to be thrown back into the sea at once, since once established, the Anglo-American forces would inevitably triumph because of their material superiority, particularly in air power.

Rommel's basic plan was to have minefields laid to a depth of five miles in areas where invasion was likely, and for there to be a series of belts of obstacles on the beaches where invasion was possible: one layer in six feet of water, one at low tide, one at high tide, and one at mid-tide. These beach obstacles were to be backed up by as many reinforced-concrete strongpoints as possible.

Meanwhile, airborne landings were to be disrupted by sets of poles laid out in open fields. He was not too worried by the prospect of these parachute and glider forces: he believed that successful defence on the beaches would permit the airborne units to be dealt with at leisure later.

without the use of artillery observers. All arms interacted with great speed and professionalism. I was very pleased with the cooperation of the navy batteries and the infantry of the army. I think very highly of this type of cooperation, which should be encouraged on land and on sea.

We must succeed in the short time left till the offensive starts in bringing all defences to such a standard that they will hold up against even the strongest attacks. Our defences, together with the sea, represent one of the strongest defence lines in history. The enemy must be annihilated before he reaches our main battlefield. In our army on this front there are a lot of young National Socialists alongside our experienced soldiers. These boys do not have battle experience, but they have proved on other fronts that they will live up to our expectations.

From week to week, the Atlantic Wall will grow stronger, and the equipment of our troops manning the defences will get better. Considering the strength of our defences and the courage, ability and the determination to fight being displayed by all our soldiers, we can look forward with utmost confidence to the day when the enemy will attack the Atlantic Wall. It will and must lead to the destruction of the attackers and that will be our contribution to the revenge we owe the English and Americans for the inhuman warfare they are raging against our homeland.

(Sgd) Rommel
General Field Marshal

Defences on the beaches were just one aspect of the defence of the West, however. There were severe disagreements within the High Command over the question of how German armour should be deployed to meet the threat posed by those Allied forces that landed. This became almost a philosophic debate, with Rommel accused of heresy in wanting to distribute tanks well forward to support his beach defences (which meant they would be used in small-sized, relatively isolated groups), rather than use them in a concentrated counter-punch, as per German theory. As always, Rommel's refusal to back down when he thought he was right manifested itself. Meetings in January led to disagreement, and the situation was still unresolved after a meeting at which Hitler was present on 21st March – although Rommel clearly believed his views had prevailed at this meeting. He continued to push his point of view, and let the head of OKW, General Jodl, know how he felt late in April:

RIGHT: An RAF low-level reconnaissance aircraft – probably a Spitfire – took this dramatic shot of Rommel's beach obstacles at low tide along the Normandy coast just before the invasion. Sharpened stakes and posts topped with mines were designed to blow up and sink troop landing craft in the final stages of their run-in.

LEFT: Watching and waiting. A 105mm gun emplacement looking out to sea along the threatened coast.

Dear Jodl
Please accept my heartfelt condolences on the loss of your dear wife.

Gause [Rommel's chief of staff] has provided me with the opportunity to drop you this line and to furnish you with my thoughts. Herewith my comments on the remarks and arrangements following my last visit to the front, as well as my proposal to OKW. Please pass on the accompanying photos to the Fuehrer.

Work on completing the Atlantic Wall defences is proceeding with urgency. By the end of May, it is anticipated that the most important coastal positions will be so well defended that enemy forces would suffer such heavy casualties from the beach obstacles and artillery fire that they would be unable to clear the shoreline.

If we are successful in getting many of our mobile units into action in the threatened coastal defence zones in the first few hours of invasion, despite enemy air superiority, I am sure the enemy main attack will be routed on the first day. The heaviest enemy air attacks on our reinforced concrete emplacements have so far done little damage, although our field positions, trenches, and communications have been in places completely destroyed.

This shows the importance of concreting-over all those emplacements, including artillery, anti-aircraft and reserve positions located behind the lines.

My real concern is over the mobile forces. Despite the resolution at the 21st March conference, they have still not been placed under my command. Some of these units are spread about a long way inland, which means they will come up too late to play a decisive part in the battle for the coast. Given the anticipated weight of enemy air superiority, any large-scale movements of mobile units towards the coast will attract prolonged and heavy aerial bombardment. Without speedy assistance from the tank divisions and the motorised units, those in the coastal divisions will be faced with to counter-attacks from the sea and simultaneously from airborne troops on land. The land front for these divisions is too thin for that – the deployment of our combat-ready and reserve forces must be such that, as soon as the invasion begins, be it in the Netherlands, in the actual Channel zone, in Normandy or in Brittany, with the least possible movement or delay, they can be deployed to destroy the greatest number of enemy troops.

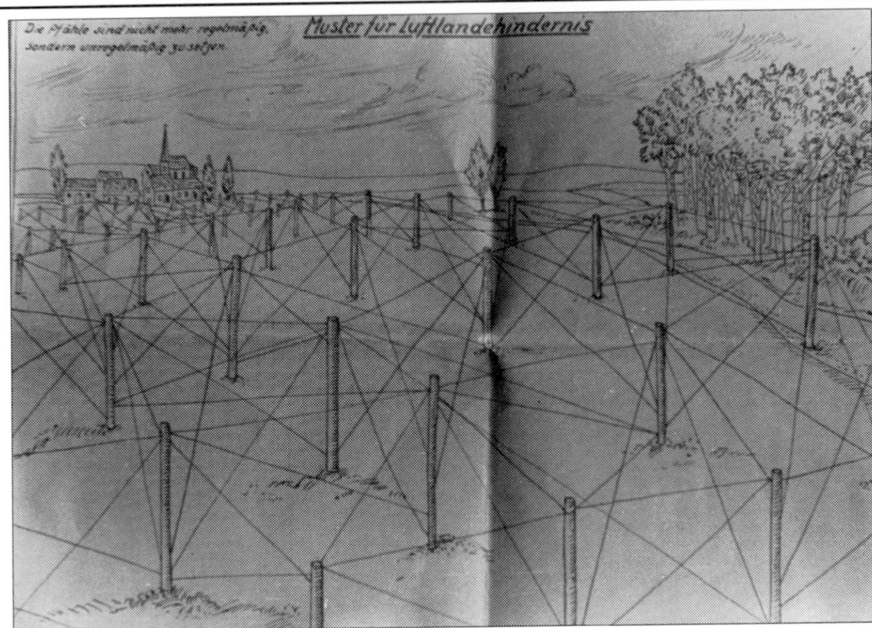

RIGHT: One of Rommel's own meticulous sketches for the ingenious system of obstacles devised to foil enemy airborne landings – in this case a grid of irregularly spaced spikes linked with wire. The greatest losses, however, came from the simple but effective expedient of flooding the low-lying meadows of Normandy and Brittany.

Panzertroop General Geyr von Schweppenburg [ostensibly in command of all armoured forces in France as head of Panzer Group West], who well knows the British in peacetime but has yet to meet them on the battlefield, believes unlike me that the main force of the enemy air assault will take place well within France, and wants to be able to counter them quickly. His units have been deployed above all to that end. Furthermore, he does not wish to come up with his tank divisions to an area behind the coastal defences where the enemy might make airborne landings.

I see the worst outcome in a situation in which the enemy succeeds in breaking through our coastal defences along the widest front using every weapon at his disposal, including airborne forces, to gain a foothold on the continent. If the invasion is to be halted at the coast, an enemy airborne landing must to my mind result sooner or later must be met and destroyed. In my experience, enemy airborne troops landing in an area held by our own troops have always been wiped out. I believe more bloodshed can be avoided this way than by mounting an attack against an already established enemy, who could then deploy anti-armour against us at a few moments notice, supported by bomber formations. I have had fierce differences of opinion with General Geyr von Schweppenburg on this question, and it will only be resolved when he is placed under my command.

This will be the most decisive campaign of this war, and will seal the fate of the German people...

Rommel's immediate staff had originally been based in Fontainebleau, but in March they moved to a comfortable chateau on the river Seine, La Roche Guyon. Although Rommel himself spent much of the spring visiting units (he even travelled far south to examine the Atlantic and Mediterranean coasts from 23rd April to 3rd May) – he enjoyed the periods he spent in the chateau. He also took possession of two young dachshunds. By May, defensive preparations were far advanced, and Rommel had also managed to get some panzer divisions situated near the coast under his control.

8.5.44
Dearest Lu!
With thanks for your dear letters of 2nd May and 4th May, which are now in my hands. You mustn't grieve over Ajax too

long. What is past is past. Meanwhile, the OT [Organisation TODT] has sent me a large, short-haired, brown hunting dog who has quickly settled into his new home and is exceptionally obedient and affectionate. Ebbo made a long face at first, but is now enjoying his playmate. Only at feeding did Ebbo suffer initially. Anyway, the pair of them succeeded in getting me up the hill four times. Either I will send Ebbo back to you, he's a loud barker, if the enemy come, or you should look out for a dog yourself. It is funny what a distraction such creatures can be, and how they can dispel one's problems...

The enemy offensive appears to have been delayed. For us every day is worth a fortune. It is still too cold and windy. The Anglo-American attack on Ploesti [a series of bombing raids on industrial plants in Romania] proves my point, that they have to pander to Stalin's perpetual impatience.

Today there is a large reception at R[undstedt]'s. Clearly this is for propaganda. In practice my ideas have won through. That is also known higher up.

Rommel was confident that his defences would at least make life difficult for the Allied forces trying to land in western Europe. He was less sure of the long-term possibilities. He left for Germany on Sunday 4th June, hoping to be able to see Hitler (and to press his case for more armoured divisions to be put under his control), and hoping to be able to enjoy a day with his wife Lucie on 6th June, her birthday. So he was at his family house when his chief of staff, Speidel, telephoned early in the morning of 6th June, to explain that Allied airborne forces had begun landing in the night, not in the area predicted by Rommel but in Normandy. Unclear as to whether these airborne landings were a feint, Rommel remained at home until a further conversation with Speidel around 10.00hrs confirmed that this was a major assault, with seaborne forces coming ashore. He was back at his staff HQ by 22.00hrs that evening, to receive the news that Allied troops had not been seriously checked by his obstacles: that they were ashore in five different areas.

The one panzer division that was positioned near the landing beaches (21st Panzer Division) was able to do considerable damage, and to reach the sea; but the two other nearest armoured formations (12th SS Panzer 'Hitler Jugend' and Panzer Lehr Divisions) had not been released for action until the afternoon of the 6th, and could not immediately affect the battle on the ground.

Rommel's forces battled to hold the Allies over the next few days. His involvement in the battle was intense; but this was not like the battles of manoeuvre of the North African campaign. The fighting took place in a cramped, restricting countryside that aided the defensive, and in which the dogged fighting qualities of German infantry and armour and the tactical nous of their experienced immediate commanders enabled them to hold their own against Allied units, whose armour was inferior, but who had command of the air and enjoyed intense naval gunfire support. There was no way that Rommel could exert his influence on the course of the fighting here. He could only do his best to hold the line, to support the front-line units.

Even in these first few days, the outcome was clear to those on the ground, even to those fanatical followers of Hitler such as 'Sepp' Dietrich, commander of I SS Panzer Corps, whose men and material were being ground down remorselessly as they battled to defend Caen on the eastern sector of the Allied lines. Rommel made this clear in a report to OKW of 11th June.

Teleprinter
Most Secret
Oberkommando [High Command] of the Army Group B.1a to Herr Generalfeldmarschall [Field Marshal] Keitel
Chef [Chief] OKW [Supreme Command of Armed Forces]
Appreciation of the situation on 11.6.1944

The course of the fighting in Normandy so far shows that enemy objectives are:

(1) To establish a deep bridgehead between the Orne and the Vire as a base for a later attack with strong forces into central France, probably in the direction of Paris.

(2) To cut off the Cotentin Peninsula and take Cherbourg as quickly as possible so as

to have a large and serviceable harbour. It seems possible also, however, as things are developing, that the enemy may abandon the occupation of the Cotentin Peninsula, if the fighting becomes too hard there, and make an early thrust into the interior of France, throwing in all his resources. Through the obstinate fighting of the troops employed in the coastal defence sectors and the counter-attacks immediately undertaken by the major reserves available, the course of the enemy operations has, in spite of the employment of the most powerful array of military hardware, taken longer than I'm sure our adversary hoped. Our adversary also appears to have employed more forces than was originally intended.

The enemy is strengthening himself visibly on land under cover of very strong aircraft formations. Our own air force and navy is, especially by day, not in a position to offer him appreciable opposition. Thus the strength of the enemy on land is increasing more than the number of our reserves being brought up. Owing to the specially strong superiority of the enemy in the air, it was not possible to bring the I Panzer Corps, the 7th Werfer [Mortar] Brigade and the IIIrd Flak Corps, as well as the IInd Fallsch Jg [Parachutist] Corps Meindl, speedily into the area between the Orne and the Vire and to go over to the counter-attack against the enemy who had landed there. The Werfer Brigade, Flak Corps and the Corps Meindl are still on the march up. The I SS Panzer Corps has been forced onto the defensive in hard fighting, and is being attacked on its open west wing by superior Allied armoured formations.

The army group must content itself for the present with forming a connected front between the Orne and Vire and allowing the foe to come on. Unfortunately, it is not possible in these circumstances to relieve the troops still remaining at several places on the coast. The army

Above: H-Hour, 6th June 1944. The waiting is over. Thick smoke fills the sky as heavily laden GIs scramble ashore from a Coast Guard landing craft amidst the roar of artillery and the chatter of German machine guns.

group is endeavouring to replace the Panzer formations thrown in, as soon as possible, with infantry formations, and to reform mobile reserves with them. The army group intends to remove the centre of its own operations in the next few days to the area Carentan-Montebourg to annihilate the enemy there and avert the danger from Cherbourg. Only when this has been successfully done can the enemy between the Orne and Vire be attacked. Unfortunately this operation cannot be supported any longer by our own fighter formations as there are no longer any airfields near the front at our disposal.

Our operations in Normandy are moreover rendered exceptionally difficult, and in part impossible to carry out, by the following:

(a) The exceptionally strong and in some respects overwhelming superiority of the enemy air force. As I and officers of my staff have repeatedly convinced ourselves personally and as the Truppenkommandeure [unit commanders], especially SS-Obergruppenfuehrer [SS Corps Commander] 'Sepp' Dietrich, report, the enemy has complete command of the air over the battle area up to about 100km (60 miles) behind the front and cuts off by day, with powerful fighter-bomber and bomber formations, almost all traffic on roads or by-roads or in open country. Movements of our troops on the field of battle by day are thus almost entirely prevented, while the enemy can operate freely. In the countryside all roads are exposed to constant attacks. It is very difficult to bring the necessary fresh supplies of munitions and fuel to the troops. The movement of smaller formations on the battlefields – artillery batteries moving into position, deployment of armoured cars and the like – is also immediately bombed from the air, with annihilating effect. Troops and staffs have to hide by day in areas with cover to avoid the continuous attacks from the air.

In the battle area of the SS Corps on 9th June the situation was that numerous hostile fighter-bomber formations circled over the battlefield and powerful bomber formations bombed troops, villages, bridges and road junctions most intensively without consideration for the population. Neither our anti-aircraft guns nor the air force seem to be in a position

LEFT: What Rommel feared most: an established Allied beachhead securing a vital toehold on the German-held continent. He realised that the only way to stop the inevitable Allied advance was to throw the invaders back into the sea before they had the opportunity to build up supplies and reinforcements.

to put a stop to this crippling and destructive display of airpower (27,000 engagements in one day). The troops of the Wehrmacht and of the Waffen-SS protect themselves as well as they can, but ammunition is scarce and can be supplied only under the most difficult conditions.

(b) The effect of heavy naval artillery. Heavy calibre guns, up to 640mm, were used. The effect is so strong that an operation either with infantry or with armoured formations is impossible in an area commanded by this quick-firing artillery. In spite of this heavy fire, the garrisons on the coast and the troops assigned to the counter-attack in the Montebourg area have held their positions with the utmost tenacity and courage. However, it is to be expected that the enemy warships will intensify the shelling of land targets with their heaviest-calibre weapons, especially on the Cotentin Peninsula, unless the German Navy and Air Force succeed in destroying them.

(c) The military equipment of the Anglo-Americans, including numerous new weapons and items of war materiel, is greatly superior to the equipment of our own divisions. As SS-Obergruppenfuehrer Sepp Dietrich has informed me, the enemy armoured formations conduct combat at a range of up to 3500m (11,550ft), regardless of expenditure of ammunition and are ably supported by the enemy air force. This was also the case at El Alamein in North Africa. Furthermore, their great artillery superiority and their seemingly unending supply of ammunition are already making themselves evident.

(d) Parachute and air-landing troops are brought in in such numbers and with such effect that it is difficult for the troops

BELOW: Allied troops examine a battered German 105mm gun emplacement on the seafront after the beachhead has been secured.

OFFICIAL REPORT – THE WOUNDING OF ROMMEL

As on previous days, on 17th July Field Marshal Rommel made a journey to the front which then ran along a line: Orne rivermouth-Colombes-southern tip of Caen-Hill 112-Gaumont-St Lô-Lessay. After a six-hour drive, the field marshal had his first meeting at the field command post of the 277nd Infantry Division, in the I SS Panzer Corps sector, followed by a meeting in that of the 276th ID, which had taken over in the 47th Panzer Corps sector. In the previous days, the two divisions had come under a massive enemy attack, which had only been held off by throwing in the last reserves. Subsequently, the field marshal drove to the headquarters of I and II SS Panzer Corps, and spoke with their respective commanders, SS-Gruppenfuehrer Bittrich and SS-Obergruppenfuehrer 'Sepp' Dietrich. Because the whole battle area was under constant attack from marauding enemy strafing planes, the journey was particularly hazardous due to the visible dust thrown up from the road.

Around 16.00hrs, Field Marshal Rommel departed SS-Obergruppenfuehrer Dietrich's field HQ and started on the journey back to Army Group. Since midday, enemy air activity had become more intense. Burning vehicles were to be seen frequently along the road; enemy fighter-bombers on nearby errands streaked to and fro. About 18.00hrs, the field marshal's car reached the neighbourhood of Livarot. Here we came upon more recently shot-up vehicles; clearly a powerful enemy ground attack squadron had been at work here. From this point a covered road descended from Livarot until it reached the highway some 4km (2.5 miles) outside Vimoutiers. As we approached, we saw about eight enemy fighter-bombers over Livarot which, it later turned out, had been observing and attacking traffic on the roads leading to Livarot. It was decided, since the enemy had not yet seen us, to continue on the straight stretch from Livarot to Vinoutiers.

Suddenly, the air observer, Lance-Corporal Holke, reported two aircraft closing in right above the road. The driver, Sergeant Daniel, drove at top speed towards a turning some 300m (990ft) ahead, trying to reach a track and take cover there. Just as he reached it, the enemy aircraft, going flat out, flew just metres above the road and at about 500m (1650ft) distance, the leading aircraft opened fire. Field Marshal Rommel at that moment glanced backwards. A burst of fire from the aircraft sent explosive shells ripping down the left side of the vehicle. Sergeant Daniel was hit in the left shoulder and arm. Field Marshal Rommel was injured in the face by glass splinters, and took a shrapnel hit in the left temple and cheekbone, causing a triple fracture of the skull which led to immediate unconsciousness. Major Neuhaus took an explosive shell on his pistol-holster; this caused a fracture of the pelvis.

His severe injuries caused driver Daniel to lose control of the vehicle; it ricocheted off a treestump on the right side of the road, and ended up embedded at a sharp angle on the far side of the road. Field Marshal Rommel, who had been in the right-hand jump-seat when the attack began, was thrown out of the vehicle by this movement and lay some 20m (66ft) behind the car on the right side of the road. Captain Lang and Corporal Holke jumped clear of the vehicle and ran for cover by the roadside. A second aircraft at this point flew back over the crash site firing at the wounded where they lay. Field Marshal Rommel lay bloodspattered and unconscious on the ground. He was bleeding profusely from his facial injuries, from the eyes and mouth in particular. He was apparently hit in the left temple. Field Marshal Rommel still was unconscious when recovered to safety.

BELOW: A nervous Goering picks his way through the wreckage of the bomb-blast that failed to dispose of Hitler, July 1944. Rommel, tenuously, was eventually linked to the plot.

attacked to defend themselves against them. When the airborne formations drop into territory occupied by us, they immediately organise themselves for defence and can be ejected only with difficulty by German infantry units with artillery support. Further enemy reinforcements are anticipated, especially in areas not occupied by our forces. Our own air force has unfortunately not been able to attack any of these formations, as was originally contemplated.

I request that the Fuehrer be informed of this.
Rommel
High Command Army Group B

At a meeting of 17th June, Hitler promised more support for the front in Normandy. This support was not – could not – be forthcoming. But the German troops still held the line in Normandy, aided by a three-day storm that played havoc with Allied logistics. The pressure increased on Caen all the time, however, and

Our position is becoming very difficult, since the enemy, as has been shown in the last few days, can cripple our mobile formations throughout the day but himself operates with quickly moving formations and troops landing from the air.

The troops of all branches of the Wehrmacht are fighting with the greatest doggedness and the utmost readiness for battle in spite of the enemy's immense display of material.

the German commanders again had disagreements as to how to deal with it. Von Schweppenberg wished to move armoured formations back, to construct a more elastic and stronger defence: for this he was sacked, early in July, together with von Rundstedt. The latter was replaced as supreme commander in the West by Field Marshal von Kluge – who had commanded Fourth Army in 1940, and in whose successful advance Rommel's 7th Panzer Division had played such a notable part.

By mid-July, pressure was building not only in the eastern sector, around Caen, but also further west, where American forces were moving on St Lô. It was a measure of the excellence of the German Army and the SS divisions, even at this late stage of the war, that the line was still being held; but these formations would soon be unable to go on, as von Kluge, initially sceptical of Rommel's pessimism, himself soon realised. On 16th July, Rommel signed a document, with which Kluge was in agreement, and which the two field marshals agreed gave an accurate representation of the situation. Rommel was persuaded by two of his staff, Speidel and Tempelhof, to take out a key word – 'political' – from the key phrase in the final paragraph: 'It is in my opinion necessary to draw the appropriate [political] conclusions from this situation.' The removal of this loaded word, which implied an intervention in the political sphere and a direct plea for peace, did not make much difference to Rommel's prospects, however. On the 17th July, his car was attacked by an Allied fighter-bomber; on 20th July, the assassination attempt on Hitler failed; and soon after, Rommel's report, backed up by Kluge but which the Commander-in-Chief in the West had delayed sending, reached Hitler's headquarters.

Report of Rommel sent by Kluge to Hitler:
My Fuehrer!
I present to you herewith a report of Generalfeldmarschall [Field Marshal] Rommel which he handed over to me before his accident and which he has discussed with me.

I have now been here about a fortnight and after long discussions with the responsible commanders of the fronts here, especially those of the SS, have been convinced that the views of the Feldmarschall are unfortunately right. My discussion yesterday with the commanders of individual formations provided regrettable evidence that in our present position – including the materiel situation – there is no way by which, in the face of the enemy air force's complete supremacy, we can find a strategy which will counterbalance its devastating effect without giving up the field of battle. Whole armoured formations allotted to counter-attacks have been caught in bombing attacks of the greatest intensity – the only way the tanks could be got out of the churned-up ground afterwards was to drag them out with armoured recovery vehicles. These delays ruined the counter-attacks. The

Below left: Urbane Field Marshal von Rundstedt, a reluctant Fuehrer's representative, finds himself called on to extol the supposed Nazi virtues he personally detested of a German hero secretly liquidated on account of his suspected involvement in the plot to kill Hitler. Rommel's state funeral was a masterpiece of political cynicism, and the antithesis of all that he stood for.

psychological effect of such a mass of bombs coming down with all the power of elemental nature on the fighting force, especially the infantry, is a factor which has to be given specially serious consideration. It is immaterial whether such a carpet of bombs catches good troops or bad. They are more or less annihilated and, above all, their materiel is shattered beyond repair. If that occurs frequently then the power of endurance of the whole army is put to the highest test. Consequently, the soldiers see themselves against an irresistible power which cannot be overcome by force of arms and lose heart. This must make itself evident to an ever-increasing degree.

ABOVE: Between his mother and his paternal aunt, Manfred Rommel – now in uniform with an anti-aircraft battery defending his fatherland against the relentless Allied air attacks – at his own father's funeral, 18th October 1944. He alone knew the full story.

I came here with the fixed determination of making effective your order to stand fast at any price. But when one has to see with one's own eyes that such a strategy will result in the slow but sure annihilation of the force...I am thinking here of the Hitler Jugend [Hitler Youth] Division which is earning the highest praise...when one sees that the materiel supplies coming up in almost all areas are at times completely insufficient (personnel also) and that fighting materiel, especially artillery and anti-tank weapons and their ammunition, are largely insufficient for the demands of the command, with the result that the brunt of the defence falls on the goodwill of the brave troops, anxiety about the immediate future of this front is only too well justified.

Rommel's observations on the situation:
The position on the front in Normandy is becoming more difficult daily and is approaching a serious crisis.

Owing to the intensity of the fighting, the exceptionally strong supplies of material of our foe, especially in artillery and armoured vehicles, and the effect of their air force, which commands the battlefield unchecked, our own losses are so high that the fighting strength of the divisions is sinking very rapidly. Reinforcements from home arrive only very scantily and, with the difficult transport situation, only reach the front after weeks. We have lost about 97,000 men (of whom 2360 are officers) – that is to say a daily average of 2500 to 3000 men – as against 10,000 men in reserve (of whom about 6000 have arrived). The materiel losses of the troops engaged are also exceptionally high, and have been replaced so far only to a very small extent. For example, of 225 panzers destroyed only 17 have been replaced.

The supply situation is so difficult, owing to the disruption of the railway network and the great danger on the major and minor roads up to 150km (90 miles) behind the front because of the enemy air forces. Only what is most essential can be brought up. Above all, artillery and Werfer [mortar] ammunition must be conserved if at all possible. These conditions are unlikely to improve in future, as the supply area is perpetually being decreased by enemy action, and enemy air activity is likely to become still more effective by reason of their occupation of the many airfields around the landing beaches.

No forces worth mentioning can be brought to the Normandy front without weakening the front of the Fifteenth Army on the Channel or the Mediterranean front in southern France. But the front of the Seventh Army is in urgent need of two fresh divisions, as the forces which are there have been fought to a standstill.

On the enemy's side new forces and masses of war materiel are flowing to the front daily. I may invite attention to the attached reports from the Seventh Army and from the II Fallsch Jg Korps [Parachute Corps]. Apart from local reserves of the Panzergroup West – who are immediately tied down by the fighting on the the Panzergroup's front and, owing to enemy command of the air, can march only by night – no mobile reserves to defend against Alled breakthroughs are at the disposal of the Seventh Army. The support of our own air force is, as before, of little weight.

The force is fighting heroically everywhere, but the unequal combat is nearing its end. It is in my opinion necessary to draw the appropriate conclusions from this situation. I feel it my duty as Oberbefehlshaber [Commander-in-Chief] of the Army Group to express this clearly.

Sgd Rommel
Generalfeldmarschall

The firmness of Rommel's statements in this report did not mean that he was failing to perform his duties. Having decided to hold fast around Caen, his defensive preparations proved extremely effective when the expected British attack took place on 18th July. Although he was then in hospital, Rommel would have been pleased at the outcome: a multi-layered defence absorbed intense pressure, and was able to prevent a breakthrough, although over 700 tanks had been assembled for the assault. This was Rommel's last victory, won when he was in hospital, and when his military career was over.

Rommel made an astonishingly good recovery from the serious wounds he sustained on 17th July and, after a number of operations, he was pronounced well enough to move from military hospital to his house at Herrlingen, near Ulm, in August, where he continued to make progress. He was, however, effectively isolated. Both he and Kluge were regarded with suspicion, and Kluge's suicide when summoned to Berlin in mid-August confirmed his guilt in the eyes of the Nazi hierarchy. Rommel had no contact with the army group he still technically commanded, and in September he realised that he was being watched. Early in October, he was asked to go to Berlin: he refused, on medical grounds, telling his friend Admiral Ruge: 'I know they would kill me on the way.'

At noon on 14th October, two officers, General Burgdorf and General Maise, came to visit. They told Rommel that his name had been found on a conspirator's list as successor to Hitler, and that he was strongly suspected as being party to the plot. He was given a stark choice: either he took poison and his family would be unharmed, or he would be stripped of his military status and put before a Nazi People's Court – with all the consequences that this certainly would have for his family.

Rommel chose the first course of action – estimating that Hitler would keep his part of the bargain, and that a great soldier's status as a national hero would still be worth much to the Nazis, and would keep his family safe. Rommel told his family of his decision and drove off in a staff car with the two generals. Less than a mile from the house, the car pulled up and the field marshal took poison. Afterwards the body was driven to Ulm, where he was pronounced to have died of a brain haemorrhage.

BELOW: Perpetuating the myth, 1946. Yet another American war correspondent visits the field marshal's sombre grave after the war, ensuring that the German commander would join the community of the righteous in death and defeat.

Conclusion

Rommel's death in 1944 robbed the Germans of one of their most adventurous and impressive commanders. Whether or not he could have defeated the Allies in the West if he had survived is a moot point – the general feeling is that he would not have been able to counter the superior numbers and growing skill of the Allied armies and would, at best, have done no more than impose delays on their campaign. But the effect on the German nation of his demise must have been profound.

The 'Desert Fox' was a genuine hero, revered not just for his personal bravery in battle but also for his apparent ability to out-fight a succession of enemy generals, many of whom enjoyed numerical and even technological superiority. He did have the disadvantage of never having fought the Soviets – his impact on the Eastern Front if he had been transferred in 1943, as Hitler seems to have intended, can only be the subject of speculation – but his record against the Western Allies, who did after all constitute a very real threat to the future of Germany, undoubtedly raised him to the status of a potential saviour of the Fatherland. In addition, to those in Germany who clung to the hope that a separate peace might be made with the West, Rommel was one of the few generals with sufficient credibility to lead any delegation that might negotiate such an arrangement.

This appears to have contributed to his downfall, for many members of the July 1944 Bomb Plot clearly regarded Rommel as a possible leader of post-Nazi Germany, with special emphasis on negotiations with the West. His direct involvement in the Bomb Plot is difficult to prove. Although by 1944 he had lost faith in the Nazi leadership, blaming Hitler's entourage for a series of strategic miscalculations in North Africa and Italy, there is little evidence that he was aware of the intention to assassinate the Fuehrer and would almost certainly have disassociated himself from the attempt. But the mere mention of his name in the interrogation of key prisoners was enough to seal his fate. By then Hitler was convinced that he had lost the loyalty of the German officer class and was prepared to believe any rumour of association with the plotters that emerged.

Even so, Rommel's part in these events, however tenuous, does raise the obvious queries about his political affiliations and loyalties. Like many of his contemporaries in Germany, he was prepared to wear the swastika and to fight for National Socialism, in full awareness of what that meant to conquered peoples. He may not have seen (perhaps he chose to ignore) any evidence of the true nature of Nazi rule – manifested in anti-Semitism and the death camps – but he can never be exonerated from a degree of guilt through association with such policies. Any attempt to regard him as no more that a highly professional soldier who was perfectly justified in accepting the views of his political masters because he was subordinate to them does not convince. All soldiers have the right, even the duty, to query immoral orders – not to do so relegates them to the status of unthinking mercenaries.

But what were Rommel's political views? His writings, which have formed the basis of this book, do not provide a great deal of evidence, so we have to turn to his actions in an attempt to answer the question. Although he appears to have distanced himself from the tortuous politics of Germany in the aftermath of World War I, he must have been affected by the impact of defeat in that conflict.

However much he threw himself into his military career, concentrating on tactical rather than strategic lessons of 1914-18, his sense of frustration, having fought a successful war at his own level, must have been profound. Indeed, he would have been a unique officer if he had not laid the blame to a certain extent at the feet of the politicians who had directed the war. This probably undermined his confidence in the political process and reinforced his decision to remain aloof from it – there is no evidence he voted in the various elections of the 1920s and 1930s, for example – but it must have also made him susceptible to the promises put forward by the Nazi Party when it gained power in 1933.

Hitler's emphasis on his own World War I experience and his belief that Germany had been 'stabbed in the back' by corrupt politicians in 1918 struck a chord with many army officers, attracting them to a philosophy that promised to restore Germany's 'greatness'. Rommel's willing acceptance of the new oath of loyalty in 1934, by which the armed forces swore allegiance to Hitler personally, implies that he regarded the Fuehrer as a political leader he could support.

The 1944 Bomb Plot is evidence that Nazi failures in the war and the mass murders that were taking place in the death camps had resulted in some officers relinquishing their oaths. Rommel was regarded as potentially one of their number. That he was dissatisfied with some of the strategic decisions that had been taken was well known, but was this enough to turn him against a leader under whom he had enjoyed military favours (some would argue that his promotion to command the 7th Panzer Division, and even the Afrika Korps, was a direct result of his association with Hitler)? We shall never know for sure.

What we do know is that Hitler liked Rommel, recognising those qualities of bravery and leadership within him that, to a front-line soldier of World War I, must have been impressive. Rommel, for his part, was flattered by such attention. The result was that Rommel embraced all that Hitler stood for, and fought for the Nazi cause with vigour, at least in the early years of the war.

This, of course, ignores that fact that Rommel was also fighting for his country, though a country that was led by a man bent on naked aggression. In the end Rommel must bear some responsibility for promoting the Nazi cause, exposing a flaw in his record that has been disguised by the circumstances of his death. He was undoubtedly an impressive military commander who richly deserves his reputation as a leading exponent of mobile war, but he did fight for an immoral cause and any doubts he expressed about the Nazi leadership were based on strategic rather than political issues. It is all too easy to regard him as a 'Desert Fox', fighting a 'clean' war in the wastes of North Africa; as his writings show, he was far more complex than that, reflecting the realities of his social and political environment. To concentrate on one aspect of his character and to ignore the complexities is to do a disservice to his memory.

BELOW: *Rommel as he is remembered, with his Afrika Korps in his desert.*

Bibliography

The following sources have been used as reference or in translation in the production of this book.

Printed Primary Sources

Rommel, General Field Marshal Erwin, *Infantry Attacks*, Greenhill Books (1990)

Imperial War Museum, London

Papers relating to Field Marshal Erwin Rommel and miscellaneous German units:
AL 451: Personal papers pertaining to Rommel
AL 510: Rommel on the defence of the West
AL 561: Papers relating to the situation in Normandy, 1944
AL 596: Reports concerning the 7th Panzer Division in France, 1940
AL 994: A report on the war in the Western Desert
AL 1249: Official reports to OKH and OKW
AL 1322: Reports and orders after El Alamein
AL 1349: Letters to his wife
AL 13491-16: Correspondence and reports to the High Command
AL 1520: Papers relating to the Totenkopf Division
AL 1531: Rommel's reports on the Atlantic Wall defences
AL1551: Papers relating to the 12th SS Panzer Division Hitler Jugend in Normandy
AL 1625: Papers relating to the Atlantic Wall defences
AL 1697: Reports and views on the situation in North Africa
AL 2596: Transcripts of Rommel's letters
AL 2729: Papers relating to the 2nd Panzer Division in Normandy

US National Archives, Washington

EAP 21-x-14/64: Combat report signed by Rommel concerning the 7th Panzer Division in France, 1940
EAP 21-x-14/67: A narrative of the 7th Panzer Division's actions in France, 1940
EAP 21-x-14/76: Rommel's critique of the advance of the 7th Panzer Division in France, 1940
EAP 21-x-14/6-7: The Rommel Collection
Letters and correspondence contained in Rolls 273 and 274

Recommended Further Reading

Douglas-Home, Charles, *Rommel*, Weidenfeld and Nicolson (1973)
Forty, George, *The First Victory: General O'Connor's Desert Triumph, Dec 1940-Feb 1941*, The Nutshell Pubishing Company (1990)
Forty, George and Duncan, John, *The Fall of France*, The Nutshell Publishing Company (1990)
Fraser, David, *Knight's Cross: The Life of Field Marshal Erwin Rommel*, HarperCollins (1993)
Heckmann, Wolf, *Rommel's War in Africa*, Granada (1981)
Irving, David, *The Trail of the Fox: The Life of Field-Marshal Erwin Rommel*, Weidenfeld and Nicolson (1977)
Liddell Hart, Basil (ed.), *The Rommel Papers*, Collins (1953)
Macksey, Kenneth, *Guderian, Panzer General*, Greenhill Books (1992)
Young, Desmond, *Rommel*, Collins (1950)

Index